# Interactive FRENCH GRAMMAR Made Easy

### Rosi McNab

New York   Chicago   San Francisco   Lisbon   London   Madrid   Mexico City
Milan   New Delhi   San Juan   Seoul   Singapore   Sydney   Toronto

**The McGraw·Hill Companies**

Visit us at: www.books.mcgraw-hill.com

First published in Great Britain in 2005 by
Hodder Education, a member of the Hodder Headline Group,
338 Euston Road, London NW1 3BH
North American Edition published by The McGraw-Hill Companies.

The advice and information in this book are believed to be true and
accurate at the date of going to press, but neither the authors nor the publisher
can accept any legal responsibility or liability for any errors or omissions.

*McGraw-Hill books are available at special quantity discounts to use as premiums
and sales promotions, or for use in corporate training programs. For more
information, please write to the Director of Special Sales, Professional Publishing,
McGraw-Hill Trade, Two Penn Plaza, New York, NY 10121-2298. Or contact
your local bookstore.*

*British Library Cataloguing in Publication Data:* A catalogue record for this book is
available from the British Library

Library of Congress Catalog Card Number: on file.

ISBN 0-07-146089-6

All illustrations drawn by Chris Blythe/Daedalus Studio

1 2 3 4 5 6 7 8 9 10

Typeset in 10.5/12pt New Baskerville by Servis Filmsetting Ltd, Manchester
Printed and bound in Malta

# CONTENTS

Introduction 1
A simple guide to the parts of speech 2

## 1 Verbs

**1.1** Verbs: talking about doing things 4
**1.1.1** What is the infinitive? 5
**1.1.2** Groups of verbs 6
**1.1.3** Irregular verbs 7
**1.1.4** The 'persons' of the verb 9
**1.1.5** Fast track: Verbs 11

**1.2** The present tense 11
**1.2.1** Talking about yourself ('I'): *je* 12
**1.2.2** Talking to a child or someone you know well ('you'): *tu* 22
**1.2.3** Talking about someone or something else ('he/she/it'): *il/elle* 25
**1.2.4** Talking about yourself and someone else ('we'): *nous* 28
**1.2.5** Talking to someone else ('you'): *vous* 32
**1.2.6** Talking about other people or things ('they'): *ils/elles* 36
**1.2.7** Fast track: Present tense 39

**1.3** Negatives, interrogatives and imperatives 43
**1.3.1** Negatives: how to say what doesn't happen 43
**1.3.2** Interrogatives: asking questions 44
**1.3.3** Imperatives: giving orders, directions or instructions 46
**1.3.4** Fast track: Negatives, interrogatives and imperatives 49

**1.4** The past tenses 50
**1.4.1** The perfect tense 51
**1.4.2** How to form the past participle 53
**1.4.3** Verbs which go with *être* 57
**1.4.4** Verbs with *être*: past participle agreement 59

| | | |
|---|---|---|
| 1.4.5 | Reflexive verbs in the perfect tense | 60 |
| 1.4.6 | The imperfect tense | 62 |
| 1.4.7 | How to form the imperfect tense | 63 |
| 1.4.8 | Perfect or imperfect? | 65 |
| 1.4.9 | Fast track: The past tenses | 66 |
| **1.5** | The future tenses and conditional tense | 67 |
| 1.5.1 | The near future: 'I am going to ...' | 68 |
| 1.5.2 | The future tense: 'I will ...' | 69 |
| 1.5.3 | The conditional: 'I would ...' | 72 |
| 1.5.4 | Fast track: Future and conditional | 75 |
| **1.6** | The subjunctive | 76 |
| 1.6.1 | How to form the subjunctive | 77 |
| 1.6.2 | Expressions which take the subjunctive | 78 |
| 1.6.3 | Recognising the subjunctive | 79 |
| 1.6.4 | Fast track: The subjunctive | 79 |
| **1.7** | Fast track: Verbs | 81 |
| **1.8** | Useful expressions using verbs | 83 |
| 1.8.1 | Special uses of *avoir* | 83 |
| 1.8.2 | There is/there are: *il y a* | 86 |
| 1.8.3 | To know: *connaître* or *savoir?* | 86 |
| 1.8.4 | To take and to bring | 87 |
| 1.8.5 | To remember: *se souvenir de* | 88 |
| 1.8.6 | More negative expressions | 88 |
| 1.8.7 | Question words and word order: *Comment?* | 90 |
| 1.8.8 | Since (*depuis*); to have just (*venir de*) | 91 |
| 1.8.9 | Fast track: Useful expressions with verbs | 92 |
| **2** | **Nouns and Determiners** | |
| **2.1** | Nouns and gender | 95 |
| **2.2** | Nouns and the word for 'the': *le* and *la* | 96 |
| **2.3** | Nouns and the word for 'the' in the plural: *les* | 97 |
| 2.3.1 | Common irregular plurals | 98 |

**2.4**   Nouns and the word for 'a': *un* and *une*   99

**2.5**   How to tell if a noun is masculine or feminine   101

**2.6**   How to say: my, your, his, her, etc.   102
**2.6.1**   My (*mon, ma, mes*)   103
**2.6.2**   Your (*ton, ta, tes*)   104
**2.6.3**   His, her and its (*son, sa, ses*)   104
**2.6.4**   Our (*notre/nos*)   105
**2.6.5**   Your (*votre/vos*)   105
**2.6.6**   Their (*leur/leurs*)   106
**2.6.7**   Fast track: Nouns and determiners   106

**2.7**   More determiners   107
**2.7.1**   This, that, these: *ce, cet, cette* and *ces*   108
**2.7.2**   Which? *Quel, quelle, quels and quelles*   108
**2.7.3**   Some, other, certain, every etc.   109

**3   Pronouns**

**3.1**   *Je, tu, il/elle*, etc.: Subject pronouns   111
**3.1.1**   *Je* – I *The first person singular*   111
**3.1.2**   *tu* – you *The second person singular*   112
**3.1.3**   *il/elle* – he/she/it *The third person singular*   112
**3.1.4**   *nous* – we *The first person plural*   112
**3.1.5**   *vous* – you *The second person plural*   113
**3.1.6**   *ils/elles* – they *The third person plural*   113
**3.1.7**   Fast track: Subject pronouns   114

**3.2**   *Le, la, les*, etc.: Direct object pronouns   115
**3.2.1**   *Le, la* and *les*: Him, her, it, them   116
**3.2.2**   *Me, te, nous* and *vous*: Me, you, us   117
**3.2.3**   Past participle agreement with object pronouns   117
**3.2.4**   Fast track: Direct object pronouns   118

**3.3**   *Me, lui, leur*, etc.: Indirect object pronouns   119
**3.3.1**   Word order when using the indirect object   120
**3.3.2**   Word order of pronouns: Direct and indirect   121
**3.3.3**   Fast track: Indirect object pronouns   122

**3.4**   *Y*: there                                                          122

**3.5**   *En*: of it/of them                                                 123

**3.6**   More about word order                                               125
**3.6.1**   Pronouns with *devoir, pouvoir, savoir, vouloir* and *falloir*    126

**3.7**   *Moi!* etc.: Emphatic pronouns                                      127
**3.7.1**   Using pronouns for emphasis                                       127
**3.7.2**   Emphatic pronouns and prepositions                               128

**3.8**   Pronouns and the imperative                                         129
**3.8.1**   Pronouns with reflexive verbs                                     129
**3.8.2**   Order of pronouns in the imperative                               129

**3.9**   *Qui? Que?* Interrogative pronouns                                  130
**3.9.1**   *Qui* or *que*?                                                   131

**3.10**   *Le mien, la mienne*: Possessive pronouns                          131

**3.11**   *Qui, que, dont*: Relative pronouns                                133
**3.11.1**   *Qui, que, dont*: Who, which, whose                              133

**3.12**   *Lequel?* Which one?                                               135

**3.13**   *Celui, celle*: The one which/whose/etc.                           135
**3.13.1**   *Celui-ci, celui-là*: This one, that one                         136

**3.14**   Fast track: Pronouns                                               136

**4**   **Adjectives**
**4.1**   Adjectival agreement: *grand(e) et petit(e)*                        140
**4.1.1**   Regular adjectives                                                141
**4.1.2**   Irregular adjectives                                              142
**4.1.3**   Colours                                                           146
**4.1.4**   Colours that don't change                                        147

**4.2** The position of adjectives 148

**4.3** Fast track: Adjectives 148

**4.4** Adjectives with two meanings 150

**4.5** Big, bigger, biggest: The comparative and
superlative 150
**4.5.1** Comparing two people or things 151
**4.5.2** The superlative: 'the most . . .' and 'the least . . .' 152
**4.5.3** Saying 'as (big) as' 152
**4.5.4** Good, better, best: Irregular comparisons 153
**4.5.5** *Meilleur* and *mieux* 154

**4.6** Fast track: Comparative and superlative 154

**5  Adverbs**
**5.1** Formation of adverbs 156
**5.1.1** Regular adverbs 156
**5.1.2** Adjectives ending in *-ent* and *-ant* 156
**5.1.3** Irregular adverbs 157

**5.2** Adjectives used as adverbs 157

**5.3** Other useful adverbs 158

**5.4** Fast track: Adverbs 158

**6  Prepositions**
**6.1** The preposition *à* 159
**6.1.1** *à* and the definite article 160
**6.1.2** Where? *Où?* 160
**6.1.3** What kind of? *Quel genre de?* 161
**6.1.4** When? *Quand?* 162
**6.1.5** Whose? *C'est à qui?* 162
**6.1.6** What's wrong? *Qu'est-ce qu'il y a?* 162
**6.1.7** Fast track: *à* 163

**6.2**   The preposition *de*                                    164
**6.2.1**  *de* and the definite article                        164
**6.2.2**  *de* meaning some or any                             165
**6.2.3**  *de* and how to say 'not any'                        165
**6.2.4**  Other expressions with *de*                          166
**6.2.5**  *de* in expressions of quantity                      167

**6.3**   Prepositions of position                             167

**6.4**   The prepositions *en* and *chez*                     169

**6.5**   Useful prepositional phrases                         169

**6.6**   Expressions of time                                  170

# 7 Conjunctions and other useful words

**7.1**   Conjunctions                                        171

**7.2**   Useful phrases                                       171

**7.3**   Help with understanding spelling and numbers         172

Verb tables                                                    173
Answers                                                        182

# INTRODUCTION

**French Grammar Made Easy** is a French grammar workbook aimed at adult non-linguists, that is adults with some rudimentary knowledge of French, who do not necessarily know anything about grammar, but need to learn about it so they can progress beyond phrasebook French.

In the past, grammar has been seen as a barrier to language learning. It has put more people off learning a language than it has helped. Because of the way grammar has been portrayed, students were often made to feel that only those who could master 'conjugations' and 'declensions' could learn a language. In fact, you can drive a car without mastering the principles of the internal combustion engine – but if you do learn where to put the oil and how to check the tyres and fill up the windscreen wash, it does help!

Grammar is about recognising word patterns which give you a framework to a language; if you know the framework, you can 'build' new language of your own instead of having to learn everything by heart.

For those who already know some French grammar, short cuts are marked with ▶▶ to enable you to go straight to the information you need. If you feel you would like to have more in-depth knowledge about a particular grammar point, please refer to *French Grammar and Usage*, R. Hawkins and R. Towell, 1996/2001, 2nd edn.

An interactive CD-ROM accompanies this book for use with a PC. The CD-ROM contains most of the exercises from the book as well as some additional material. Most exercises are recorded so that you can listen to a native speaker saying the sentences and there is a 'click on' facility to allow you to read the English translation. There is also some additional listening material which provides a useful resource and brings the language to life.

# A simple guide to the parts of speech

▶▶ **If you know what verbs, nouns, pronouns, adverbs, etc. are, go on to 1.1.**

The most useful categories of words to recognise are:

## 1 Verbs – 'doing' words

Verbs tell you what someone or something is doing.

> I *am going* to France. My friend *booked* the flight. I *am going* to a meeting.

You also use them to ask questions . . .

> *Have* you *seen* the film? *Are* you all right?

. . . and to give instructions.

> *Fetch* it! *Slow* down! *Help* me! *Wait!*

Verbs usually present the most problems, so the section dealing with them is the longest one and comes first in the book.

## 2 Nouns – 'naming' words

Nouns are the words which tell you:

- what something is:
  a *timetable*, a *train*, a *station*, a *town*, a *secret*
- who someone is:
  a *steward*, a *bank clerk*, a *baker*, a *student*

## 3 Pronouns

Pronouns are words which 'stand in' for a noun.

> M. Bleriot is French. M. Bleriot lives in Paris.

Instead of repeating *M. Bleriot*, you can say *he*.

> M. Bleriot is French. *He* lives in Paris.

In the same way, you can say *she* instead of repeating *Florence* in the following sentence.

> Florence works in Strasbourg. *She* works at the European Parliament.

These are also pronouns: *I, you, it, one, we, they, me, us, them.*

## 4 Adjectives

Adjectives are 'describing' words. They are used to describe something or someone.

the *new* house, the *red* car, a *tiny* flat, a *wet* day, a *busy* secretary

## 5 Adverbs

Adverbs are words which usually describe a verb, e.g. they describe how something is done. They often answer the question *How?* and in English they often end in *-ly*.

He runs *fast*. She eats *slowly*. It comes *naturally*!

## 6 Prepositions

Prepositions are words which usually tell you where something is, e.g. *in, under, on*. Words such as *to, for, with,* and *without* are also prepositions.

# 1 VERBS

## 1.1 Talking about doing things

▶ ▶ **If you know what a verb is, go on to 1.1.1.**

You use a verb to talk about what someone or something does, is doing, has done or intends to do. A verb is often called a *doing* word.

 To find out if a word is a verb, ask yourself if it is about *doing* something.

**I**  Which of these words are things you can do?

| | |
|---|---|
| **a** run | **f** eat |
| **b** jeans | **g** under |
| **c** sleep | **h** blue |
| **d** make | **i** think |
| **e** easy | **j** after |

Some words can be used as verbs, nouns or adjectives, e.g. *play* can be a play at the theatre or part of the verb *to play*.

 Ask: Are they 'doing' it? If they are, it is a verb.

**II**  Which of the highlighted words are being used as verbs?

**a** Jason and Lily **run** a homework club in the church hall.
**b** They go for a **run** every morning.
**c** They both **work** at the local school.
**d** After **work** they go straight to the hall.
**e** Tonight they are having a **meeting** to discuss funding.
**f** They are **meeting** in the church hall.
**g** They need more **chairs** for the children.
**h** Jason usually **chairs** the meetings.
**i** Lily **records** the proceedings and types them up.
**j** The **records** show that they have met three times this year.

▶▶ **If you know what the infinitive is, go on to 1.1.2.**

When you look up a verb in a dictionary, you will find the infinitive. This is the 'name' of the verb.

In English, the infinitive consists of *to* + verb, e.g. *to read, to buy, to travel.*

**III** Here are some French infinitives. You probably know some of them already or can guess what they mean. See how many you can match up with their English counterparts.

Try to look for similarities between the French and the English. Some are obvious: for example, **organiser** means *to organise*. Others are less obvious, such as **laver** meaning *to wash* (a lavatory was the place where people used to wash) and **porter** meaning *to carry* (a porter was someone who carried something).

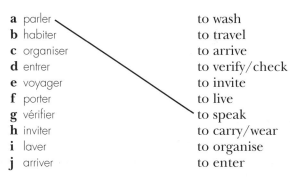

**a** parler — to wash
**b** habiter — to travel
**c** organiser — to arrive
**d** entrer — to verify/check
**e** voyager — to invite
**f** porter — to live
**g** vérifier — to speak
**h** inviter — to carry/wear
**i** laver — to organise
**j** arriver — to enter

**IV** The verbs in **III** are usually referred to as '-**er**' verbs (pronounced *E.R.*) because they end in -**er**. Here are some more -**er** verbs. How many of them do you know already? They all have to do with food and eating.

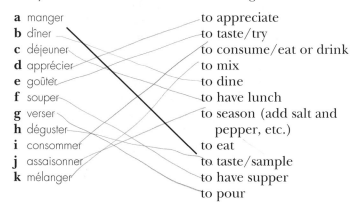

**a** manger — to appreciate
**b** dîner — to taste/try
**c** déjeuner — to consume/eat or drink
**d** apprécier — to mix
**e** goûter — to dine
**f** souper — to have lunch
**g** verser — to season (add salt and pepper, etc.)
**h** déguster — to eat
**i** consommer — to taste/sample
**j** assaisonner — to have supper
**k** mélanger — to pour

If you find it difficult to learn new words, try to find a 'hook' to hang them on: e.g. **manger**, a manger where you put the food for an animal. And if you have travelled in France, you will almost certainly have seen signs at places selling wine, saying **Dégustation**, which means they are inviting you to sample their wines.

More than 50% of English words derive from French words or have the same stem. If you don't know a verb, try saying the English word with a French accent – you have a 50% chance of being understood!

New words made into verbs are usually **-er** verbs: e.g. **faxer** = to fax; **surfer** = to surf; **monopoliser** = to monopolise, etc.

**V**  What do you think the French for these verbs would be? Cover up the French and see if you can work it out.

| | | |
|---|---|---|
| **a** | to decide | décider |
| **b** | to prefer | préférer |
| **c** | to separate | séparer |
| **d** | to turn | tourner |
| **e** | to return | retourner |
| **f** | to develop | développer |
| **g** | to insist | insister |
| **h** | to change | changer |
| **i** | to continue | continuer |
| **j** | to accept | accepter |

## 1.1.2  Groups of verbs

 **If you know how to find the 'stem' or 'root' of a verb, go on to 1.1.3.**

In English, we just have regular and irregular verbs. A verb such as *to dance* is regular:

*dance, dances, danced, has danced*

... and a verb such as *to fly* is irregular:

*fly, flies, flew, has flown.*

As you have probably already noticed, French verbs are more complicated! French schoolchildren have to spend years learning all about French verbs, but we can find some shortcuts. French also has regular and irregular verbs, but we usually divide French regular verbs into three main groups to make them easier to learn, depending on whether the infinitive ends in **-er**, **-ir** or **-re**.

| group 1: *-er* verbs | group 2: *-ir* verbs | group 3: *-re* verbs |
|---|---|---|
| jouer | finir | répondre |
| regarder | dormir | descendre |

The stem, or root, of the verb is that part which is left after you take off the ending. It is used in creating the other forms of the verb.

**VI**   Which group do these belong to and what is the stem of these verbs? (Remember: take off the **-er**, **-ir**, or **-re** to find the stem.)

| | | | |
|---|---|---|---|
| **a** | vendre | to sell | (3/vend) |
| **b** | montrer | to show | . . . . . . |
| **c** | chanter | to sing | . . . . . . |
| **d** | sortir | to go out | . . . . . . |
| **e** | laver | to wash | . . . . . . |
| **f** | finir | to finish/end | . . . . . . |
| **g** | écouter | to listen | . . . . . . |
| **h** | fermer | to close/shut | . . . . . . |
| **i** | partir | to leave | . . . . . . |
| **j** | prendre | to take | . . . . . . |
| **k** | choisir | to choose | . . . . . . |
| **l** | porter | to wear/carry | . . . . . . |
| **m** | rentrer | to return | . . . . . . |
| **n** | venir | to come | . . . . . . |
| **o** | dormir | to sleep | . . . . . . |

Fortunately, over 80% of French verbs belong to group 1 (**-er** verbs) and they are mostly regular. When we say they are regular, we mean they follow the same pattern, so if you learn one, you can work out the endings you need for all the others.

## 1.1.3   Irregular verbs

Some verbs are awkward and don't really fit into any pattern. They are called *irregular* verbs. This means that you have to learn them separately, and, in fact, they are the verbs you are likely to want to use most. Fortunately, you probably know quite a lot of them already, although you might not be aware of it: for example, you probably know that *I know* is **je sais** or *I don't know* is **je ne sais pas** but you may not know that the infinitive is **savoir**.

These are the infinitives of the most important irregular verbs to learn, because they are the most used:

être – to be        avoir – to have        aller – to go

**je** form: je suis – I am, j'ai – I have, je vais – I am going

Most verbs which end in **-oir** and **-ire** are irregular, but they are also very useful.

| *-oir* **verbs** | *-ire* **verbs** |
|---|---|
| devoir – to have to | boire – to drink |
| pouvoir – to be able to | dire – to say |
| recevoir – to receive | écrire – to write |
| savoir – to know (something)/ | lire – to read |
| know how to do (something) | faire – to do/make |
| voir – to see | rire – to laugh |
| vouloir – to want | |

It is the same for all verbs made up of these verbs, for example:

écrire – to write → décrire – to describe
dire – to say → interdire – to forbid
rire – to laugh → sourire – to smile
faire – to do → refaire – to do again

 Always look for patterns which will help you to remember new words, e.g. **rire** – laugh → **sourire** – smile.

**VII**  Match the infinitives.

**a** to know (something)          pouvoir
**b** to see                       aller
**c** to have                      être
**d** to go                        savoir
**e** to be able to                devoir
**f** to have to                   faire
**g** to want to                   voir
**h** to take                      avoir
**i** to be                        prendre
**j** to do                        vouloir

▶▶ **If you know about the 'persons' of the verb, go to 1.1.5.**

- When we talk about ourselves, we are using the 'first person'.
- When we talk about (or to) 'you', we are using the 'second person'.
- When we talk about someone else we are using the 'third person'.

In English, we only change the ending when we are talking about *he/she* or *it*:

|  | singular | plural |
|---|---|---|
| **first person** | I talk | we talk |
| **second person** | you talk | you talk |
| **third person** | he/she/it talks | they talk |

In many languages, including French, the verb-ending changes according to who is doing the action and you have to learn the pattern of the verb.

 Fortunately in French, although the endings are often spelt differently, they mostly *sound* the same.

In French, the ending changes according to the person or thing doing the action.

|  | singular | plural |
|---|---|---|
| **first person** | je parle | nous parlons |
| **second person** | tu parles | vous parlez |
| **third person** | il/elle parle | ils/elles parlent |

| I | je | we | nous |
|---|---|---|---|
| you | tu | you | vous |
| he | il | they | ils |
| she | elle | they | elles (if all female) |

**Je, tu, il, elle**, etc. are called pronouns because they represent a person or thing (a noun). Mr Smith – *he*; Mr and Mrs Smith – *they*; Jim Smith and I – *we*, etc.

**Tu** is only used when talking to a child, a relation or very good friend. It implies a certain degree of intimacy and should not be used to address an adult unless he or she invites you to use it (see page 22).

**Il/elle** – *he/she.* There is no word for *it* as everything in French is either masculine or feminine: even a table and chair are feminine words.

Although **vous** is always followed by a plural verb, it is the word you use for *you* in formal and professional conversation, even when addressing only one person. It is also used to address a stranger.

**Ils** is used for a group of male people (or masculine words) or a group if it includes one or more males (or masculine words), even if there are more females than males present.

**Elles** is only used for a group of all female people or all feminine words.

▶▶ **For more information on pronouns, go to page 111.**

**VIII**  Which pronoun would you use?

**a** You are talking about yourself: I am            tu/je/il
speaking.

**b** You are talking about a girlfriend.            je/vous/elle

**c** You are talking about a male friend.            nous/il/elle

**d** You are talking about yourself and a            il/elle/nous
friend.

**e** You are talking to a child.            tu/vous/il

**f** You are talking to a stranger.            tu/vous/il

**g** You are talking about a group of            ils/elle/elles
women.

**h** You are talking about a mixed group or            ils/vous/il
a group of men.

**IX**  And which pronoun would you use when you are talking about these?

**a** your friend Paul            nous/il/elle

**b** your friend Martine            elles/elle/tu

**c** Monsieur Leblanc            vous/nous/il

**d** Monsieur et Madame Lavoine            ils/elles/vous

**e** Mesdames Leblanc et Bouvoir            elles/ils/nous

**f** Sylvie et Charlotte            ils/elles/vous

**g** yourself            tu/vous/je

**h** Paul, Guillaume et Martine            ils/vous/elles

**i** Messieurs Meugeot, Briand et Duclos            nous/vous/ils

**j** yourself and your friend            nous/vous/je

**Verbs are 'doing' words: you use them to say what you (or someone/something else) are doing and to ask someone what he/she is doing.**

In English, when we look up a verb in the dictionary it is preceded by the word *to*: *to go*; *to drive*; *to eat* etc. This is called the infinitive.

In French, the infinitive is not preceded by *to*; it is the **end** of the verb which is important. French infinitives end in **-er**, **-ir** or **-re**.

In English, we just have two main sorts of verbs: regular and irregular.

In French, there are:

**-er** verbs which are regular and **-er** verbs which are irregular

**-ir** verbs which are regular and **-ir** verbs which are irregular

**-re** verbs which are regular and **-re** verbs which are irregular

In English, regular and irregular verbs change the ending when talking about *he/she/it*:

> *I speak* → *he speaks*    *I go* → *she goes*    *I fly* → *it flies*

In French, the verb's ending changes for all the different people. The different persons are:

| singular | | plural | |
|---|---|---|---|
| I | je | we | nous |
| you | tu | you | vous |
| he/she/it | il/elle | they | ils/elles |

# 1.2 Talking about what is happening now: the present tense

▶▶ **If you know about the present tense and when to use it, go on to 1.2.7.**

The present tense is used

- to say what you are doing now: *I am reading.*
- to make a general statement about what happens: *It often rains in Scotland.*
- to say what usually happens: *We go out on Friday evenings.*

In English, we have two ways of talking about the present. We can either use *am, is* or *are* to say what we are doing now:

> *I am working.*
> *My friends are going out.*
> *It is raining.*

… or we can say what usually/generally happens, using the verb without the *am, is* or *are*:

> *I read magazines.*
> *They are vegetarian.*
> *It rains every day.*

In French, there is only one way of expressing the present tense. You just use the verb on its own without the *am, is* or *are*.

 In French you do **not** use *am, is* or *are* to talk about what you are doing now.

| | |
|---|---|
| Je lis le journal. | I read/I am reading the newspaper. |
| Ils travaillent à la Défense. | They work/They are working in the *Défense* business area. |
| M. Berriot prend le bus. | Mr Berriot is taking/takes the bus. |

**I**  Identify the verb in each of these sentences.

  **a** I am downloading my e-mails.
  **b** My friend is ringing me when she gets home.
  **c** She is accompanying her parents to the airport.
  **d** We are going to the cinema later.
  **e** She is fetching me.
  **f** She is borrowing her parents' car.
  **g** They are flying to New York.
  **h** They are visiting their other daughter.
  **i** She is studying in America.
  **j** After the cinema we are dining at Louis's.

télécharger – to download/upload

## **1.2.1** Talking about yourself ('I'): *je*
Remember that in French the verb-ending changes according to who is doing the action.

**▶▶** **If you know about the je form, go to the checklist on page 21.**

A   Regular **-er** verbs

These are verbs which end in **-er** in the infinitive.

The infinitive is the form you find in the dictionary when you look a verb up.

 Over 80% of French verbs end in **-er** and are regular.

In the **je** form (or first person) of the present tense, all **-er** verbs end in **-e**, but the **-e** is not pronounced. Try reading the 'first person' column below aloud.

| infinitive | meaning | first person | meaning |
|---|---|---|---|
| aimer | to like | j'aime | I like |
| décider | to decide | je décide | I decide/I am deciding |
| écouter | to listen | j'écoute | I listen/I am listening |
| habiter | to live | j'habite | I live/I am living |
| jouer | to play | je joue | I play/I am playing |
| manger | to eat | je mange | I eat/I am eating |
| parler | to speak | je parle | I speak/I am speaking |
| porter | to wear | je porte | I wear/I am wearing |
| regarder | to watch | je regarde | I watch/I am watching |
| travailler | to work | je travaille | I work/I am working |

 Remember not to translate the *am*.

**II**   How would you say these in French?

**a** I speak English.          Je ___ anglais.
**b** I eat cheese.             Je ___ du fromage.
**c** I am wearing jeans.       Je ___ un jean.
**d** I work in an office.      Je ___ dans un bureau.
**e** I am watching the news.   Je ___ le journal.
**f** I play tennis.            Je ___ au tennis.
**g** I like the town.          J'___ la ville.
**h** I am listening to a CD.   J'___ un CD.
**i** I live in England.        J'___ en Angleterre.
**j** I am deciding about the   Je ___ de la politique de
firm's policies.                l'entreprise.

Now cover up the French column and see if you can do them again. Say them aloud!

**III** These are all **-er** verbs. Fill in the gaps.

**a** Je ___ dans un bureau. (travailler)  I work in an office.
**b** J'___ à huit heures. (arriver)  I arrive at 8 o'clock.
**c** Je ___ ma voiture. (garer)  I park my car.
**d** J'___ dans l'immeuble. (entrer)  I enter the building.
**e** Je ___ le concierge. (saluer)  I greet the caretaker.
**f** Je ___ au huitième étage. (monter)  I go up to the eighth floor.
**g** Je ___ le code d'entrée.  I key in the door code.
   (composer)
**h** J'___ dans mon bureau. (entrer)  I go into my office.
**i** J'___ mon manteau derrière la  I hang my coat up behind
   porte. (accrocher)  the door.
**j** Je ___ à travailler. (commencer)  I begin to work.

Choose five of the verbs which you didn't know before (or had forgotten) and which you think would be useful for you to learn. Write down the meaning and the first letter of the verb. See how many you can remember.

B  *Je* and **-er** verbs which change their spelling

Some **-er** verbs take an accent, change the accent or modify the spelling in the first person. This is to make the verb easier to pronounce. They all still end in **-e** and sound more or less as you would expect.

The most important irregular **-er** verb to learn is **aller** (*to go*). The *je* form is **je vais** (*I go/I am going*).

The **-s** of *vais* is only sounded if the next word begins with a vowel.

**IV** Read the following verbs aloud. Remember that **j** sounds like the *s* in *treasure*, **é** sounds like *ay* and **è** sounds like *eh*.

**a** acheter – to buy → ash-e-tay  j'achète → jash-ett
**b** espérer – to hope →  j'espère → jes-pear
   ay-spay-ray
**c** lever – to lift → luv-vay  je lève → je lev
**d** préférer – to prefer →  je préfère → je pray-fair
   pray-fay-ray

Verbs with a **y** in them usually change the **y** to **i** (as in some English verbs: *dry* → *dries*).

**e** essayer – to try → es-say-ay  j'essaie → jes-say
**f** payer – to pay (for) →  je paie → je pay
   pay-ay

**g** envoyer – to send →      j'envoie → jahn-v-wuh
ahn-v-why-ay

Some verbs double the **t** or **l**.

**h** appeler – to call → apple-ay    j'appelle → jappel
**i** jeter – to throw (away) →     je jette → je jet
jut-ay

**V**   How would you say ...?

**a** I am going to town.      Je ___ en ville. (aller) *vais*
**b** I am buying a new car.    J'___ une nouvelle voiture. *J'achète*
(acheter)
**c** I am calling my office.    J'___ mon bureau. (appeler) *J'appelle*
**d** I prefer beer.      Je ___ la bière. (préférer) *préfère*
**e** I'm paying.      Je ___. (payer) *paie*
**f** I am sending a letter.    J'___ une lettre. (envoyer) *envoie*
**g** I hope it'll be fine.    J'___ qu'il va faire beau. (espérer) *espère*
**h** I am trying to answer the   J'___ de répondre à la question.
question.      (essayer) *essaie*
**i** I am throwing out the    Je ___ les vieux journaux. (jeter)
old newspapers.        *jette*
**j** I raise my glass to your   Je ___ mon verre à votre santé.
good health.      (lever) *lève*

 Highlight any verbs which you might want to use.

 Most **-er** verbs are regular. All **-er** verbs except *aller* end in **-e** in
the first person.

**VI**   Complete these sentences with the right form of the verb in
brackets and read them aloud.

**a** Je ___ anglais. (parler) *parle*
**b** J'___ à Londres. (habiter) *habite*
**c** Je ___ à Paris. (aller) *vais*
**d** J'___ un taxi. (appeler) *J'appelle*
**e** J'___ à la gare. (arriver) *arrive*
**f** J'___ dans le terminal international. (entrer) *entre*
**g** Je ___ dans le train. (monter) *montre*
**h** Je ___ dans la voiture-bar. (déjeuner) *déjeune*
**i** J'___ un fax. (envoyer) *envoie*
**j** Je ___ une question. (poser) *pose*
**k** Je ___ aux échecs avec ma compagne de voyage. (jouer) *joue*
**l** Je ___ cent euros. (gagner) *gagne*
**m** Je ___ à mon meilleur ami. (téléphoner) *téléphone*
**n** Je ___ la campagne qui défile à 360 km/h. (regarder) *regarde*

## C  *Je* and regular **-ir** verbs

▶▶  **If you already know about regular -ir verbs, go on to the irregular verbs in section D.**

 Remember that most verbs are **-er** verbs, so there aren't so many of the other types.

| infinitive | meaning | first person | meaning |
|---|---|---|---|
| choisir | to choose | je choisis | I choose/I am choosing |
| finir | to finish | je finis | I finish/I am finishing |
| grossir | to put on weight | je grossis | I am putting on weight |
| maigrir | to lose weight | je maigris | I am losing weight |
| remplir | to fill in/to fill up | je remplis | I am filling in/up |
| vieillir | to grow old | je vieillis | I am growing old |
| applaudir | to applaud | j'applaudis | I applaud |
| réfléchir | to reflect/think | je réfléchis | I am reflecting/thinking |
| ralentir | to slow down | je ralentis | I am slowing down |
| rougir | to blush | je rougis | I am blushing |

 Remember that in French you don't sound the final **-s**.

**VII**  Which verb would you use?

   **a** You have to fill in this form.
   **b** He has to finish the test.
   **c** She has to put on more weight.
   **d** He has to lose weight.
   **e** You have to choose a prize.
   **f** We have to think about it.
   **g** You must slow down at the bend.
   **h** You have to clap when they have finished.
   **i** You have to try to grow old gracefully.
   **j** Don't blush!

**VIII**  Match the English and the French.

| | |
|---|---|
| ✓ **a** I am filling in | j'applaudis  h |
| ✓ **b** I am finishing | je maigris  d |
| ✓ **c** I am putting on weight | je choisis  e |
| ✓ **d** I am losing weight | je vieillis  i |
| ✓ **e** I am choosing | je rougis  j |
| ✓ **f** I am thinking/reflecting | je ralentis  g |
| ✓ **g** I am slowing down | je remplis  a |
| ✓ **h** I am clapping | je grossis  c |

i I am growing old      je finis *b*
j I am blushing      je réfléchis *F*

D *Je* and irregular **-ir** verbs

In the singular (*je, tu, il/elle*), some **-ir** verbs drop the final consonant of the stem and then add **-s**, which is not sounded, to make them easier to pronounce: e.g. the **m** of **dormir** is dropped from the stem **dorm**.

| infinitive | meaning | first person | meaning |
|---|---|---|---|
| dormir | to sleep | je dors | I sleep/I am sleeping |
| partir | to leave | je pars | I leave/I am leaving |
| sentir | to smell | je sens | I smell (something) |
| sortir | to go out | je sors | I go out/I am going out |

**IX** Practise saying them aloud, it will help you to remember them. Here the **s** is in brackets just to remind you not to pronounce it!

| je choisi(s) | je fini(s) | je grossi(s) | je maigri(s) |
|---|---|---|---|
| je par(s) | je sen(s) | je sor(s) | je dor(s) |

**X** How would you say the following?

a I am going out.    Je ___. (sortir) *sors*
b I am finishing the dishes.    Je ___ la vaisselle. (finir) *finis*
c I am choosing a wine.    Je ___ un vin. (choisir) *choisis*
d I am leaving tomorrow.    Je ___ demain. (partir) *pars*
e I am putting on weight.    Je ___. (grossir) *grossis*
f I sleep in a big bed.    Je ___ dans un grand lit. (dormir) *dors*
g I slow down at the bends.    Je ___ dans les virages. (ralentir) *ralentis*
h I am thinking about it.    J'y ___. (réfléchir) *réfléchis*
i I am filling in this form.    Je ___ ce formulaire. (remplir) *remplis*
j I am getting old!    Je ___! (vieillir) *vieillis*

Now cover up the French column and see if you can still do them.

The following verbs add an **i** in the middle, but they still end in **-s** (which is not sounded).

| infinitive | meaning | first person | meaning |
|---|---|---|---|
| tenir | to hold | je tiens | I hold/I am holding |
| venir | to come | je viens | I come/I am coming |

And there are some **-ir** verbs which behave as though they ended in **-er**.

| infinitive | meaning | first person | meaning |
|---|---|---|---|
| ouvrir | to open | j'ouvre | I open/I am opening |
| couvrir | to cover | je couvre | I cover/I am covering |
| découvrir | to discover | je découvre | I discover/I am discovering |
| offrir | to offer | j'offre | I offer/I am offering |

**XI** How would you say the following?

     *Je viens*

   **a** I am coming from the office.    \_\_\_ du bureau. (venir)

   **b** I am offering some flowers.    \_\_\_ des fleurs. (offrir) *J'offre*

   **c** I discover the truth. *Je découvre*    \_\_\_ la vérité. (découvrir)

   **d** I am holding the door. *Je tiens*    \_\_\_ la porte. (tenir)

   **e** I am covering the baby. *Je couvre*    \_\_\_ le bébé. (couvrir)

   **f** I am opening the window. *J'ouvre*    \_\_\_ la fenêtre. (ouvrir)

> Say them aloud to get used to the sound of the words. Which ones sound a little like the English?

E *Je* and verbs which end in **-oir**

These verbs look as if they end in **-ir**, but they actually end in **-oir**, so they are a bit different. Unfortunately, they are verbs that you will probably need a lot, so you should make sure you know any you might need. Look for patterns to help you remember them.

| infinitive | meaning | first person | meaning |
|---|---|---|---|
| avoir | to have | j'ai | I have |
| savoir | to know (how to) | je sais | I know (how to) |
| devoir | to have to | je dois | I must/I have to |
| voir | to see | je vois | I see |
| recevoir | to receive | je reçois | I receive/I am receiving |
| apercevoir | to notice | j'aperçois | I notice |
| pouvoir | to be able | je peux | I can/I am able |
| vouloir | to want | je veux | I want |

**XII** How would you say the following? Use the verbs in brackets.

   **a** I have a brother.    \_\_\_ un frère. (avoir) *J'ai*

   **b** I have to go.    \_\_\_ partir. (devoir) *Je dois*

   **c** I know!    \_\_\_! (savoir) *Je sais*

   **d** I can come.    \_\_\_ venir. (pouvoir) *Je peux*

**e** I must arrive punctually.    *Je dois* ___ arriver à l'heure. (devoir)

**f** I want to go there.    ___ y aller. (vouloir) *Je veux*

**g** I see the house.    ___ la maison. (voir) *Je vois*

**h** I can speak Spanish.    ___ parler espagnol. (savoir) *Je sais*

**i** I have a new car.    ___ une nouvelle voiture. (avoir)

Cover up the French. Can you still do them? *J'ai*

## F   *Je* and verbs which end in **-re**

► ►   **If you already know about regular -re verbs, go on to section G.**

| infinitive | meaning | first person | meaning |
|---|---|---|---|
| attendre | to wait (for) | j'attends | I wait/I am waiting (for) |
| descendre | to go down | je descends | I go down/I am going down |
| entendre | to hear | j'entends | I hear |
| répondre | to reply | je réponds | I reply/I am replying |
| vendre | to sell | je vends | I sell/I am selling |

 Cover up the meanings and see how many you know or can work out. Try to find a 'related' English word, e.g. *vendre* → vendor. Look for ways of remembering the ones that you think are important for you.

These verbs all end in **-s** when you are talking about yourself (in the first person singular), but remember you do not sound the **-s** at the end of a word. Practise saying them aloud, as it will help you to remember them.

**XIII**   How would you say the following?

**a** I am selling my car.    *Je vends* ___ ma voiture. (vendre)

**b** I am replying to the question.    *Je réponds* ___ à la question. (répondre)

**c** I am going down the road.    *Je descends* ___ la rue. (descendre)

**d** I am waiting for the bus.    ___ le bus. (attendre) *Je attends*

**e** I hear voices.    ___ des voix. (entendre) *Je entends*

**f** I understand.    ___. (comprendre) *Je comprends*

Cover up the French and see if you can still do them.

## G   *Je* and irregular **-re** verbs

These verbs end in **-re** but in some cases they change their stem. The changes have usually been made to make them easier to pronounce. These are the ones you are likely to need most. Say them aloud and look for patterns.

| infinitive | meaning | first person | meaning |
|---|---|---|---|
| être | to be | je suis | I am |
| boire | to drink | je bois | I drink/I am drinking |
| croire | to believe | je crois | I believe |
| dire | to say | je dis | I say/I am saying |
| écrire | to write | j'écris | I write/I am writing |
| faire | to do/make | je fais | I do/I am doing |
| lire | to read | je lis | I read/I am reading |
| connaître | to know | je connais | I know (a person or thing) |
| mettre | to put | je mets | I put/I am putting |
| prendre | to take | je prends | I take/I am taking |

Cover up the English and see if you can remember what they all mean, then cover up the French and see how many you can remember. Which first-person forms look really different from what you would expect?

**XIV** How would you say the following? Remember that it is helpful to say the sentences aloud.

*Je bois*

**a** I am drinking red wine. ___ du vin rouge. (boire)

**b** I am writing a letter. *J'écris* ___ une lettre. (écrire)

**c** I do sport. *Je fais* ___ du sport. (faire)

**d** I read the newspaper. *Je lis* ___ le journal. (lire)

**e** I lay the table. *Je mets* ___ la table. (mettre)

**f** I am English-speaking. *Je suis* ___ anglophone. (être)

**g** I am saying 'hello'. *Je dis* ___ «Bonjour». (dire) *Je décris*

**h** I am describing M. Bonnard. ___ M. Bonnard. (décrire)

**i** I believe in God. ___ en Dieu. (croire) *Je crois*

**j** I am taking the train. ___ le train. (prendre)

*Je prends*

H *Je* and reflexive verbs

 **If you know about reflexive verbs, go on to the checklist on page 21.**

We don't have an equivalent form in English but you probably already know the reflexive verb **s'appeler**, *to be called*. **Je m'appelle** means *I am called* or literally *I call myself*.

When you are talking about yourself, you use **me** (or **m'** if the verb begins with a vowel) and the first person of the verb just as normal.

| infinitive | meaning | first person | meaning |
|---|---|---|---|
| s'asseoir | to sit down | je m'assieds | I sit down/I am sitting down |
| s'endormir | to fall asleep | je m'endors | I fall asleep/I am falling asleep |
| s'ennuyer | to get bored | je m'ennuie | I get bored/I am getting bored |
| s'habiller | to dress yourself/ to get dressed | je m'habille | I get dressed/I am getting dressed |
| se coucher | to go to bed | je me couche | I go to bed/I am going to bed |
| se demander | to wonder | *je me demande* | I wonder/I am wondering |
| se disputer | to quarrel | je me dispute | I quarrel/I am quarrelling |
| se doucher | to shower yourself/ to have a shower | je me douche | I have a shower/I am having a shower |
| se laver | to wash yourself/ to get washed | je me lave | I wash (myself)/I am washing (myself) |
| se lever | to get up | je me lève | I get up/I am getting up |
| se réveiller | to wake up | je me réveille | I wake up/I am waking up |

**XV**   How would you say the following?

a  I wake up at seven o'clock.   ___ à sept heures.
b  I get up straight away.   ___ toute de suite.
c  I am washing my hair.   ___ les cheveux.
d  I am having a shower.   ___.
e  I get dressed.   ___.
f  I sit down.   ___.
g  I wonder whether the taxi has arrived already.   ___ si le taxi est déjà là.
h  I am getting bored.   ___.
i  I quarrel with my friend.   ___ avec mon ami
j  I am going to bed.   ___.

## Checklist: the *je* form

- When talking about yourself in the present tense, you use *je* and the right part of the verb.
- To find the right part of the verb, you take off the **-er/-ir/-re** ending.
- If it is an **-er** verb, you put the **-e** back, but you do not sound it.
- Most other verbs add an **-s**, but you do not sound the **s** either.
- The most important irregular verbs to remember are:
  avoir – to have → j'ai
  être  – to be   → je suis
  aller – to go   → je vais
  faire – to do   → je fais

Check you know these other useful irregular verbs:

devoir – to have to → je dois – I have to/I must
savoir – to know → je sais – I know (how to do something)
pouvoir – to be able to → je peux – I am able to/I can
vouloir – to want → je veux – I want to
venir – to come → je viens – I come/I am coming
tenir – to hold → je tiens – I hold/I am holding

## 1.2.2 Talking to a child or someone you know well ('you'): *tu*

This is the *you* form, or the 'second person' of the verb.

There are two forms of *you* in French: the **tu** form and the **vous** form. You use the **tu** form if you are talking to someone you know really well – a friend, a child or an animal. You do **not** use it to a stranger, a business acquaintance or an older person (except within the family). You only use it to someone you know well if they invite you to.

There is a special verb which means *to call someone **tu*** – **se tutoyer**. If someone asks: **On se tutoie?**, it means 'Let's use the **tu** form.' (**Se vouvoyer** means *to use the **vous** form*.)

 The **tu** form is easy as, in most verbs, it sounds exactly the same as the **je** form.

▶▶ **If you are not going to need the tu form, go to 1.2.3.**

A *Tu* and regular verbs

**-er verbs**

The **tu** form ends in **-es** but the **-s** is not sounded, so it sounds just like the **je** form:

je mange, tu manges

**-ir and -re verbs**

The **tu** form is the same as the **je** form:

je finis, tu finis; je prends, tu prends

**Exceptions**

**aller**: je vais, tu vas
**avoir**: j'ai, tu as
**être**: je suis, tu es

**I**    What is the **tu** form of these verbs?

| | |
|---|---|
| **a** dance | **f** eat |
| **b** like | **g** listen |
| **c** live | **h** play |
| **d** speak | **i** wash |
| **e** watch | **j** work |

**II**    Use the right form of the verbs in brackets to tell someone what they are like.

| | |
|---|---|
| **a** You are talkative. | Tu ___ bavard(e). (être) |
| **b** You have got a spot on your nose. | Tu ___ un bouton sur le nez. (avoir) |
| **c** You like swimming. | Tu ___ bien nager. (aimer) |
| **d** You eat pizzas. | Tu ___ des pizzas. (manger) |
| **e** You watch soaps. | Tu ___ des feuilletons. (regarder) |
| **f** You live in Paris. | Tu ___ à Paris. (habiter) |
| **g** You speak English. | Tu ___ anglais. (parler) |
| **h** You wear jeans. | Tu ___ un jean. (porter) |
| **i** You do sport. | Tu ___ du sport. (faire) |
| **j** You play tennis. | Tu ___ au tennis. (jouer) |

B    *Tu* and reflexive verbs

These are formed in the same way as in the **je** form but the reflexive pronoun is **te** instead of **me**:

| infinitive | meaning | Second person |
|---|---|---|
| s'appeler | to be called | tu t'appelles |
| se coucher | to go to bed | tu te couches |
| s'habiller | to get dressed | tu t'habilles |
| se lever | to get up | tu te lèves |

**III**    Match the questions. How would you ask a child ...

| | | |
|---|---|---|
| **a** his or her name? | **i** | Tu ne t'intéresses pas à l'actualité? |
| **b** what time he/she gets up? | **ii** | Comment tu t'appelles? |
| **c** when he/she goes to bed? | **iii** | Tu te disputes avec ton frère? |
| **d** if he/she argues with his/her brother? | **iv** | Tu te lèves à quelle heure? |
| **e** if he/she is not interested in current affairs? | **v** | Tu te couches à quelle heure? |

## C  *Tu* and asking questions

To make a question in French, you can change the
intonation by making the voice rise towards the end of the
phrase, as in English:

| | |
|---|---|
| Tu es fatigué(e)? | You are tired? |
| Tu te reposes? | You are having a rest? |
| Tu t'intéresses au football? | You're interested in football? |
| Tu te souviens du jour où …? | Do you remember the day when …? |

You can also make a question by changing the order and
putting the verb first.

(This is one of those times when French is actually easier
than English. In English, there are two different ways of
forming a question, one for each of the two forms of the
present tense.)

| | |
|---|---|
| Habites-tu à Paris? | Do you live/Are you living in Paris? |
| Joues-tu au tennis? | Do you play/Are you playing tennis? |
| Aimes-tu aller au cinéma? | Do you like going to the cinema? |
| Écoutes-tu les informations? | Do you listen/Are you listening to the news? |
| Entends-tu bien? | Do/Can you hear well? |
| Manges-tu des pissenlits? | Do you eat/Are you eating dandelions? |
| Parles-tu bien l'allemand? | Do you speak German well? |
| Prends-tu le bus? | Do you take the bus?/Are you going by bus? |

Practise saying questions to get used to the sound. Remember to
make your voice rise towards the end. You will probably feel silly
at first, but don't worry, practice eventually makes perfect!

**IV**  Practise asking your friend what he/she is going to do. Just
add the **tu** form of the verb in brackets.

**a** Have you got a meeting in
London next Tuesday?  ___ un rendez-vous à Londres
mardi prochain? (avoir)

**b** Are you leaving very early?  ___ très tôt? (partir)

**c** Are you taking the Eurostar? ___ l'Eurostar? (prendre)

**d** Do you get in to Waterloo?  ___ à Waterloo? (arriver)

**e** Will you eat with us?  ___ avec nous? (dîner)

**f** Are you going back the
same evening?  ___ le soir même? (rentrer)

**V**   Chatting up – imagine you have already got to the **tu** stage!
Match the phrases, then cover the right-hand side of the
page and see if you can remember the French translations.

| | | | |
|---|---|---|---|
| **a** | Would you like a drink? | **i** | Tu veux une cigarette? |
| **b** | Would you prefer red or white wine? | **ii** | Tu es fatigué(e)? |
| **c** | Do you smoke? | **iii** | Tu veux boire quelque chose? |
| **d** | Do you mind if I smoke? | **iv** | Tu veux aller dîner quelque part? |
| **e** | Do you want a cigarette? | **v** | Tu fumes? |
| **f** | Are you hungry? | **vi** | Tu préfères du vin rouge ou du vin blanc? |
| **g** | Would you like to go out to dinner? | **vii** | Ça te dérange si je fume? |
| **h** | Are you tired? | **viii** | Tu as quelqu'un dans ta vie? |
| **i** | Do you like sci-fi films? | **ix** | As-tu faim? |
| **j** | Have you got someone special? | **x** | Tu aimes les films de science-fiction? |

Checklist: the *tu* form

You only use the **tu** form when speaking to younger
children, pets and people you know very well, or people
who have invited you to use it.

You do NOT use it to people you don't know.

The **tu** form sounds the same as the **je** form.

• The **tu** form of **-er** verbs is the same as the **je** form, but
with an **-s** on the end.
• The **tu** form of **-ir** and **-re** verbs is the same as the **je** form.
• Questions are formed by changing the intonation or
inverting the verb and the pronoun.
• Negatives are formed by putting **ne** … **pas** around the
verb.

**1.2.3**   Talking about someone or something
else ('he/she/it'): *il/elle*

▶▶   **If you know how to use the il/elle form, go on to
the checklist on page 27.**

This form is called the 'third person'. In English it is the *he,
she, it* form of the verb.

 In French, there is no word for *it*. Everything is masculine or
feminine. **Une maison** (*a house*) is feminine, so you say *'she' is
old*; **un livre** (*a book*) is masculine, so you say *'he' is new*.

It is easy to learn, as it sounds just the same as the **je** form except for **aller**, **avoir** and **être**.

> **aller**: je vais, il/elle va
> **avoir**: j'ai, il/elle a
> **être**: je suis, il/elle est

## A Il/elle and regular verbs

- **-er** verbs end in **-e** (just as in the first person, the **je** form).
  il/elle mange; parle; habite
- **-ir** verbs change the **-s** of the **je** form to **-t** (but sound the same).
  il/elle finit; choisit
- **-re** verbs don't usually have an ending, but they sound the same as the **je** form because the **-s** wasn't pronounced anyway!
  il/elle répond

**I** Give the right part of the verb.

**a** Thierry Henry ___ au football. (jouer)
**b** Céline Dion ___ des chansons en français et en anglais. (chanter)
**c** Mon fils ___ sur l'Internet. (surfer)
**d** Sa petite copine ___ bien les histoires de Stephen King. (aimer)
**e** M. Berriot ___ des appartements. (louer)
**f** M. Patte ___ sa maison. (vendre)
**g** Mme Peugeot ___ acheter une maison. (désirer)
**h** La banque ___ de l'argent à ses clients. (prêter)
**i** Le notaire ___ les documents relatifs au contrat de vente. (préparer)
**j** Mme Peugeot ___ l'acte de vente devant le notaire. (signer)

## B Il/elle and irregular verbs

The most common, and most useful, verbs are irregular – but remember most of them sound like the **je** form.

| infinitive | meaning | third person | meaning |
|---|---|---|---|
| avoir | to have | il/elle a | he/she has/is having |
| être | to be | il/elle est | he/she is |
| aller | to go | il/elle va | he/she goes/is going |
| faire | to do/make | il/elle fait | he/she does/is doing |
| mettre | to put | il/elle met | he/she puts/is putting |

**II** What happens to Mr Patte?

**a** M. Patte ___ parisien. (être)
**b** Il ___ à Paris. (habiter)
**c** Il ___ à Nice. (aller)
**d** Il ___ le train. (prendre)

**e** Il ___ la nuit dans le train. (passer)

**f** Le lendemain matin, il ___ à Nice. (arriver)

**g** Il ___ deux grandes valises à roulettes. (avoir)

**h** Il ___ ses valises sur un chariot. (mettre)

**i** Il ___ signe à un taxi. (faire)

**j** Quand il se ___ , ses valises ont disparu. (retourner)

C  *Il/elle* and reflexive verbs

The reflexive pronoun for the **il/elle** form is **se**. The **se** becomes **s'** (it 'elides') before a vowel.

| infinitive | meaning | third person | meaning |
|---|---|---|---|
| s'appeler | to be called | il/elle s'appelle | he/she is called |
| se brosser les dents | to brush your teeth | il/elle se brosse les dents | he/she brushes his/her teeth |
| se chausser | to put on your shoes | il/elle se chausse | he/she puts on his/her shoes |
| se coucher | to go to bed | il/elle se couche | he/she goes/is going to bed |
| se doucher | to shower | il/elle se douche | he/she showers/is showering |
| s'ennuyer | to get bored | il/elle s'ennuie | he/she gets/is getting bored |
| s'essuyer | to get dry | il/elle s'essuie | he/she gets dried/is getting dried |
| s'étirer | to stretch | il/elle s'étire | he/she stretches/is stretching |
| s'étonner | to be surprised | il/elle s'étonne | he/she is surprised |
| se faire un shampooing | to wash your hair | il/elle se fait un shampooing | he/she washes his/her hair |
| s'habiller | to get dressed | il/elle s'habille | he/she gets/is getting dressed |
| se laver | to get washed | il/elle se lave | he/she gets/is getting washed |
| se lever | to get up | il/elle se lève | he/she gets/is getting up |
| se réveiller | to wake up | il/elle se réveille | he/she wakes/is waking up |

**III**  How does Hugo start his day?

**a** Il ___. (se réveiller)

**b** Il ___ en baîllant. (s'étirer)

**c** Il ___. (se lever)

**d** Il ___ longuement. (se doucher)

**e** Il ___ un shampooing. (se faire)

**f** Il ___ les dents. (se brosser)

**g** Il ___. (se raser)

**h** Il ___ avec un drap de bain. (s'essuyer)

**i** Il ___. (s'habiller)

**j** Il ___. (se chausser)

**k** Il ___ son petit déjeuner. (prendre)

**l** Il ___ de chez lui. (sortir)

Checklist: the *il/elle* form

You use the **il/elle** form when you are talking about someone or something.

The **il/elle** form usually sounds just like the **je** form.

- The **il/elle** form of regular **-er** verbs is made by adding **-e** to the stem, just like the **je** form: **il arrive**.
- The **il/elle** form of regular **-ir** verbs is made by adding **-it** to the stem, but it sounds just like the **je** form: **il dit**.
- The **il/elle** form of regular **-re** verbs is the same as the stem and sounds just like the **je** form: **il répond**.
- The most common irregular verbs are **aller** (**va**), **avoir** (**a**), **être** (**est**) and **faire** (**fait**).

The reflexive pronoun for the **il/elle** form is **se**, which becomes **s'** (elides) before a vowel: **Il s'appelle Lionel**.

## **1.2.4** Talking about yourself and someone else ('we'): *nous*

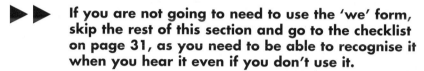

**If you are not going to need to use the 'we' form, skip the rest of this section and go to the checklist on page 31, as you need to be able to recognise it when you hear it even if you don't use it.**

You use the **nous** form (the first person plural) where you use *we* in English, i.e. when talking about yourself and someone else: *we, my husband and I, my colleagues and I, my friend and I, Mrs Brown and I*, etc.

### A Verbs that are regular in the *nous* form

The **nous** form is regular in most verbs. It is made by adding **-ons** to the stem. (Remember: the stem is made by taking the **-er/-ir/-re** off the infinitive. See page 7.)

| infinitive | first person pl. | meaning |
|---|---|---|
| arriver | nous arrivons | we arrive/we are arriving |
| aller | nous allons | we go/we are going |
| sortir | nous sortons | we leave/we are leaving |
| répondre | nous répondons | we answer/we are answering |
| parler | nous parlons | we talk/we are talking |
| jouer | nous jouons | we play/we are playing |

**I** How would you say the following? Use the verb given in brackets.

**a** We are working today.     ___ aujourd'hui. (travailler)
**b** We are playing volleyball tonight.     ___ au volley ce soir. (jouer)
**c** We are going out at 6 p.m.     ___ à 18h00. (sortir)
**d** We are dining in a restaurant.     ___ au restaurant. (dîner)
**e** We are going back home at 10 p.m.     ___ à 22h00. (rentrer)

**f** We are going to Paris tomorrow.  ___ à Paris demain. (aller)

**g** We are leaving at 8 a.m.  ___ à 8h00. (partir)

**h** We arrive at 11.15 a.m.  ___ à 11h15. (arriver)

**i** We buy our tickets at the station.  ___ nos billets à la gare. (acheter)

**j** We have lots of luggage.  ___ beaucoup de bagages. (avoir)

B Verbs that are irregular in the *nous* form

The **nous** form of all verbs except **être** (**nous sommes**) ends in **-ons**. Most irregular verbs change their spelling slightly to make the **nous** form easier to pronounce. Look for patterns to help you to remember them.

| infinitive | meaning | first person plural | meaning |
|---|---|---|---|
| faire | to do/make | nous faisons | we do/we are doing |
| lire | to read | nous lisons | we read/we are reading |
| dire | to say | nous disons | we say/we are saying |
| écrire | to write | nous écrivons | we write/we are writing |
| boire | to drink | nous buvons | we drink/we are drinking |
| prendre | to take | nous prenons | we take/we are taking |
| comprendre | to understand | nous comprenons | we understand |
| avoir | to have | nous avons | we have/we are having |
| devoir | to have to | nous devons | we have to/we must |
| pouvoir | to be able to | nous pouvons | we are able to/we can |
| vouloir | to want to | nous voulons | we want to |
| voir | to see | nous voyons | we see |
| croire | to believe | nous croyons | we believe |
| être | to be | nous sommes | we are |

Verbs ending in **-ger** (**manger**, **diriger**, **changer**, **nager**, etc.) add an **e** to keep the **g** soft, so they are pronounced as you would expect.

| infinitive | meaning | first person plural | meaning |
|---|---|---|---|
| manger | to eat | nous mangeons | we eat/we are eating |
| diriger | to direct/manage | nous dirigeons | we direct/we are directing |
| changer | to change | nous changeons | we change/we are changing |
| nager | to swim | nous nageons | we swim/we are swimming |
| loger | to stay/lodge | nous logeons | we stay/are staying |

Some **-ir** verbs take **ss**.

| infinitive | meaning | first person plural | meaning |
|---|---|---|---|
| finir | to finish | nous finissons | we finish/we are finishing |
| choisir | to choose | nous choisissons | we choose/we are choosing |

**II**  How would you say the following in French?

**a** We are English.  Nous ___ anglais.

**b** We speak French.  Nous ___ français.

**c** We are going to France.  Nous ___ en France.

**d** We are choosing the day.  Nous ___ le jour.

**e** We are taking the train.  Nous ___ le train.

**f** We change trains in Paris.  Nous ___ de train à Paris.

**g** We understand the instructions.  Nous ___ les instructions.

**h** We stay in a hotel.  Nous ___ à l'hôtel.

**i** We eat in a restaurant.  Nous ___ au restaurant.

**j** We are working late this evening.  Nous ___ tard ce soir.

**k** We finish at 6 p.m.  Nous ___ à 18h00.

**l** We are playing tennis later.  Nous ___ au tennis tout à l'heure.

C  *Nous* with reflexive verbs

The reflexive form is made by adding an extra **nous**.

Nous nous appelons Neil et Ruth. **We are called Neil and Ruth.**

| infinitive | meaning | first person plural | meaning |
|---|---|---|---|
| se dépêcher | to hurry | nous nous dépêchons | we hurry up/ we are hurrying up |
| se lever | to get up | nous nous levons | we get up/ we are getting up |
| se coucher | to go to bed | nous nous couchons | we go to bed/ we are going to bed |
| se promener | to go for a walk | nous nous promenons | we go for a walk/ we are going for a walk |
| se reposer | to rest | nous nous reposons | we have a rest/ we are having a rest |
| se séparer | to separate, part | nous nous séparons | we separate/ we are separating |

**III**  How would you say the following?

**a** We wake up at seven o'clock.  ___ à sept heures. (se réveiller)

**b** We get up at eight o'clock.  ___ à huit heures. (se lever)

**c** We go to bed at 11 p.m.  ___ à 23h00. (se coucher)

**d** We are having a shower.  ___. (se doucher)

**e** We are having a rest.     \_\_\_. (se reposer)
**f** We are hurrying.     \_\_\_. (se dépêcher)
**g** We are getting dressed.     \_\_\_. (s'habiller)
**h** We are getting washed.     \_\_\_. (se laver)
**i** We go for a walk every morning.     \_\_\_ chaque matin. (se promener)
**j** We are separating.     \_\_\_. (se séparer)

### Checklist: the *nous* form

- To talk about yourself and someone else (*we*), use *nous* in French.
- Most verbs end in **-ons** except **être – nous sommes**.
- Some verbs have minor spelling changes to make them easier to pronounce.

**IV** Match these English verbs with their French counterparts.

| | | |
|---|---|---|
| **a** | we have | ✓nous voulons |
| **b** | we are | ✓nous lisons |
| **c** | we are staying | ✓nous venons |
| **d** | we are eating | ✓ nous ne comprenons pas |
| **e** | we can | ✓ nous sommes |
| **f** | we are not coming | ✓ nous pouvons |
| **g** | we do not understand | ✓nous arrivons |
| **h** | we want | ✓nous logeons |
| **i** | we are going | ✓nous avons |
| **j** | we are seeing | ✓ nous faisons |
| **k** | we are leaving | ✓ nous ne venons pas |
| **l** | we are arriving | ✓nous allons |
| **m** | we are coming | ✓ nous mangeons |
| **n** | we are doing | ✓ nous partons |
| **o** | we are reading | ✓ nous voyons |

Now cover up the French and see if you can do them without help!

There is also another way to talk about *we* in French. You can use **on** (*one*) and the **il/elle** form of the verb.

| | |
|---|---|
| On va en ville cet après-midi | We are going to town this afternoon (lit: one is going to town...) |
| Qu'est-ce qu'on fait ce soir? | What shall we do this evening? |
| On va au cinéma? | Shall we go to the cinema? |

This way is commonly used in conversation.

### 1.2.5 Talking to someone else ('you'): *vous*

  **If you know about the vous form, go to the checklist on page 35.**

This is more important than the **tu** form as it is the form you will use most. It is sometimes also called the 'polite' form. Just like *you* in English, it can be used when addressing one person or more than one person, but it is always followed by the **vous** form of the verb.

 You probably already know lots of expressions that use *vous*:

Parlez-vous anglais? Allez! Avez-vous..?

The **vous** form usually ends in the sound **ay**.

A *Vous* and regular verbs

The **vous** form is usually made by adding **-ez** to the stem. It is easy to learn, and there are fewer exceptions than usual.

The ending sounds like **ay** as in **Parlez-vous …?** You probably know a lot of words already.

| | |
|---|---|
| Parlez-vous anglais? | Do you speak English? |
| Habitez-vous en France? | Do you live in France? |
| Avez-vous une voiture? | Have you got a car? |

**I** What do these mean? Match each instruction to a sign.

a) Enter your PIN.

b) Pull.

c) Wait for the tone.

d) Speak into the microphone.

e) Sign here.

f) Date-stamp your (bus/train) ticket.

g) Push.

h) Please hold the line.

i) Wait.

j) Press the button.

APPUYEZ SUR LE BOUTON

*Parlez dans le micro*

COMPOSTEZ VOTRE BILLET

COMPOSEZ VOTRE CODE:

*Signez ici*

Attendez le bip sonore

Ne quittez pas

PATIENTEZ

TIREZ

POUSSEZ

## B Verbs that are irregular in the *vous* form

In most irregular verbs, the **vous** form is made from the same stem as the **nous** form. Look at these irregular verbs and try to find patterns which will help you to remember them. They are often like the infinitive, but not always!

| | | | | | | |
|---|---|---|---|---|---|---|
| aller | vais | vas | va | allons | **allez** | vont |
| avoir | ai | as | a | avons | **avez** | ont |
| boire | bois | bois | boit | buvons | **buvez** | boivent |
| connaître | connais | connais | connaît | connaissons | **connaissez** | connaissent |
| devoir | dois | dois | doit | devons | **devez** | doivent |
| dire | dis | dis | dit | disons | **dites** | disent |
| dormir | dors | dors | dort | dormons | **dormez** | dorment |
| être | suis | es | est | sommes | **êtes** | sont |
| faire | fais | fais | fait | faisons | **faites** | font |
| lire | lis | lis | lit | lisons | **lisez** | lisent |
| pouvoir | peux | peux | peut | pouvons | **pouvez** | peuvent |
| prendre | prends | prends | prend | prenons | **prenez** | prennent |
| savoir | sais | sais | sait | savons | **savez** | savent |
| voir | vois | vois | voit | voyons | **voyez** | voient |
| vouloir | veux | veux | veut | voulons | **voulez** | veulent |

**Comprendre** is like **prendre**.

**II** Tick the **vous** forms you know already. Highlight any which are different from what you would have expected and choose three new ones to try to remember.

**III** Your employee is slacking. Tell him/her what he/she is doing.

**a** You read the paper every morning.
Vous ___ le journal tous les matins. (lire)

**b** You go to the toilet eight times a day.
Vous ___ aux toilettes huit fois par jour. (aller)

**c** You take two hours for your lunch break.
Vous ___ deux heures pour déjeuner. (prendre)

**d** You sleep a good part of the afternoon.
Vous ___ une bonne partie de l'après-midi. (dormir)

**e** You do the crossword every afternoon.
Vous ___ les mots croisés tous les après-midis. (faire)

**f** You drink a double Scotch at tea break.
Vous ___ un double whisky à la pause. (boire)

**g** You have to do something about it.
Vous ___ faire quelque chose. (devoir)

**h** Do you have anything to say in your defence?
Qu'___-vous à dire pour votre défense? (avoir)

## C  *Vous* and the imperative

The **vous** form is also used to tell someone what to do. In this case you can drop the **vous**. This is called the 'imperative'.

**IV**  Your assistant is not well. Give him/her some advice.

| | |
|---|---|
| **a** You look ill. | Vous ___ l'air malade. (avoir) |
| **b** Go to see the doctor. | ___ voir le médecin. (aller) |
| **c** Drink more water. | ___ plus d'eau. (boire) |
| **d** Eat more fruit. | ___ plus de fruits. (manger) |
| **e** Walk more. | ___ davantage. (marcher) |
| **f** Smoke less. | ___ moins. (fumer) |
| **g** Go jogging. | ___ du jogging. (faire) |
| **h** Get more fresh air. | ___ à l'air frais. (aller) |
| **i** Go to bed earlier. | ___ -vous plus tôt. (se coucher) |
| **j** Sleep well. | ___ bien. (dormir) |

## D  *Vous* and asking questions

▶▶ **If you know all about asking questions, go straight to 1.2.6.**

Questions are formed in the same way as in the **tu** form: either by changing the intonation or by inverting the verb and pronoun.

**V**  Cover up the French and see if you can ask these questions.

| | |
|---|---|
| **a** Are you going to the meeting? | Allez-vous à la réunion? |
| **b** Have you got an appointment? | Avez-vous rendez-vous? |
| **c** Do you know the MD? | Connaissez-vous le P.D.G.? |
| **d** Do you know how to operate the video link-up? | Savez-vous faire marcher le branchement vidéo? |
| **e** Can you contact your boss? | Pouvez-vous contacter votre chef? |
| **f** Do you have to go back to the hotel? | Devez-vous retourner à l'hôtel? |
| **g** Do you want to use the OHP? | Voulez-vous utiliser le rétroprojecteur? |
| **h** Can you see the screen? | Voyez-vous l'écran? |
| **i** Do you take notes? | Prenez-vous des notes? |
| **j** Are you making a recording? | Faites-vous un enregistrement? |
| **k** Are you ready? | Êtes-vous prêt(e)? |
| **l** Do you understand? | Comprenez-vous? |

E  *Vous* and reflexive verbs

The reflexive pronoun for the **vous** form is **vous**.

| | |
|---|---|
| Vous vous reposez tous les après-midis. | You have a rest every afternoon. |
| Vous vous en sortez? | Can you manage alright? |
| Vous vous occupez de l'enfant? | Are you looking after the child? |
| Vous vous levez à quelle heure? | What time do you get up? |
| À quelle heure vous couchez-vous? | What time do you go to bed? |

**VI**  Match the following English and French phrases, then cover up the right-hand side and see if you can remember the French.

| | |
|---|---|
| **a** Can you manage? | Vous vous moquez de moi? |
| **b** Are you interested in the firm? | Vous vous occupez des achats? |
| **c** Are you responsible for buying? | Vous vous rappelez M. Pantin? |
| **d** Are you making fun of me? | Vous vous levez tôt? |
| **e** Do you get up early? | Vous vous intéressez à la société? |
| **f** Do you remember M. Pantin? | Vous vous en sortez? |

Checklist: the *vous* form

The **vous** form is used when talking to someone else or telling someone what to do.

- You are most likely to use the **vous** form to ask questions:

| | |
|---|---|
| Pouvez-vous m'indiquer … | Can you tell me the way … |
| Savez-vous …? | Do you know (how to do something)? |
| Connaissez-vous M. Vernon? | Do you know Mr Vernon? |
| Où habitez-vous? | Where do you live? |

- The **vous** form of regular verbs is made by adding **-ez** to the stem. Most verbs are regular.
- The **vous** form of most irregular verbs is made from the same stem as the **nous** form (**buvons/buvez**).

- Questions are formed by intonation or inverting the verb and the pronoun:
  Avez-vous une voiture?
- Reflexive verbs add the pronoun **vous**.
  Vous vous levez de bonne heure!    You get up early!
  Vous vous en sortez bien!              You are managing well!
- For giving orders and instructions use the **vous** form without the **vous**.
  Attendez! – Wait! Écoutez! – Listen!
  (See page 46 for more on the imperative.)

## 1.2.6 Talking about other people or things ('they'): *ils/elles*

This is easy, as most verbs sound just the same as for the **il/elle** forms in 1.2.3.

▶▶ **If you know all about the ils/elles form, go to the checklist on page 39.**

 Remember, you only use **elles** if ALL the people (or things) are feminine. If there is one male in a group, however big the number of females, you still have to use **ils**. See 3.1 for more details.

A  *Ils/elles* and regular **-er** verbs
   The **ils/elles** form is the same as the **il/elle** form, but with -nt added (but not pronounced).

   elle joue – she is playing → elles jouent – they are playing
   il mange – he is eating → ils mangent – they are eating

   However, if the verb begins with a vowel, you pronounce the **s** of **ils/elles** before the beginning of the verb.

   il aime → ils aiment
   elle adore → elles adorent

B  *Ils/elles* and regular and semi-irregular **-ir** verbs
   The **ils/elles** form is made by adding -ent to the stem, but the -ent is not pronounced:

   il cour(t) – he is running → ils cour(ent) – they are running
   il dor(t) – he is asleep → ils dorm(ent) – they are asleep
   elle sor(t) – she is going out → *elles sort(ent) – they are going out
   elle par(t) – she is leaving → *elles part(ent) – they are leaving

   *The **t** will now be pronounced as it is no longer the last letter of the word.

Some **-ir** verbs add **-issent**.

il finit – he is finishing → ils finissent – they are finishing
il choisit – he is choosing → ils choisissent – they are choosing

C *Ils/elles* and regular **-re** verbs
The **ils/elles** form is made by adding **-ent** to the stem. The **-ent** is not pronounced, but we do hear the end of the stem.

il attend – he is waiting → ils attendent – they are waiting
elle répond – she answers → elles répondent – they answer
il vend – he is selling → ils vendent – they are selling

## Important irregular verbs
These are verbs to watch because they change unexpectedly. Look for patterns to help you remember them.

| infinitive | third person singular | third person plural | meaning |
|---|---|---|---|
| aller | il/elle va | ils/elles vont | they go |
| avoir | il/elle a | ils/elles ont | they have |
| faire | il/elle fait | ils/elles font | they make/do |
| être | il/elle est | ils/elles sont | they are |

D *Ils/elles* and some more irregular (and useful!) verbs
Remember that you don't pronounce the **t** or **nt** at the end of a word.

| infinitive | third person singular | third person plural | meaning |
|---|---|---|---|
| boire | il/elle boit | ils/elles boivent | they drink |
| dire | il/elle dit | ils/elles disent | they say |
| lire | il/elle lit | ils/elles lisent | they read |
| vouloir | il/elle veut | ils/elles veulent | they want |
| voir | il/elle voit | ils/elles voient | they see |
| pouvoir | il/elle peut | ils/elles peuvent | they can |
| devoir | il/elle doit | ils/elles doivent | they have to |

 Choose the verbs you think you may find useful and look for ways to remember them.

**I** Use the verbs in brackets to tell this tale.

**a** M. et Mme Périgord ___ faire des courses. (devoir)
**b** Ils ___ une nouvelle voiture. (avoir)
**c** Ils ___ à l'hypermarché. (aller)
**d** Ils ___ la voiture sur le parking. (garer)
**e** Ils ___ leurs courses. (faire)
**f** Ils ___ de l'hypermarché. (sortir)
**g** Ils ne ___ plus leur voiture. (trouver)
**h** Ils la ___ partout. (chercher)
**i** Ils ne la ___ pas. (trouver)
**j** Ils ___ la police. (appeler)

E *Ils/elles* and reflexive verbs

The reflexive pronoun for the **ils/elles** form is **se** (the same as the **il/elle** form). You will find that the singular (**il/elle** form) and the plural (**ils/elles** form) usually sound the same, as most reflexive verbs are **-er** verbs. Remember to elide the **se** if the next word begins with a vowel.

**II** Fill in the missing plurals.

| infinitive | meaning | third person singular | third person plural |
|---|---|---|---|
| s'appeler | to be called | il/elle s'appelle | ils/elles s'appellent |
| se coucher | to go to bed | il/elle se couche | **a** ___ |
| se doucher | to have a shower | il/elle se douche | **b** ___ |
| s'ennuyer | to get bored | il/elle s'ennuie | ils/elles s'ennuient |
| s'étonner | to be surprised | il/elle s'étonne | **c** ___ |
| s'habiller | to get dressed | il/elle s'habille | **d** ___ |
| s'intéresser à | to be interested in | il/elle s'intéresse à | **e** ___ |
| se laver | to get washed | il/elle se lave | **f** ___ |
| se lever | to get up | il/elle se lève | **g** ___ |
| se réveiller | to wake up | il/elle se réveille | **h** ___ |
| s'asseoir | to sit down | il/elle s'assied | ils/elles s'asseyent |
| s'en aller | to go away | il/elle s'en va | ils/elles s'en vont |

**III** Tell the story of Florence and Véronique's night out.

**a** Elles ___. (se reposer)
**b** Elles ___. (se réveiller)
**c** Elles ___. (se lever)
**d** Elles ___. (se doucher)
**e** Elles ___. (se préparer)
**f** Elles ___. (sortir)
**g** Elles ___ dans un bar à vins. (aller)
**h** Leurs copains n'___ pas. (arriver)
**i** Elles ___. (s'ennuyer)
**j** Elles ___. (s'en aller)

Checklist: the *ils/elles* form

- The **ils/elles** form of regular **-er**, **-ir** and **-re** verbs is made by adding **-ent** to the stem, and they mostly sound the same as the **il/elle** form.
- Some **-ir** verbs add **-issent** *(finir – ils finissent; choisir – choisissent).*
- The four most useful irregular verbs are **aller (vont)**, **avoir (ont)**, **être (sont)** and **faire (font)**.
- Verbs ending in **-ire** or **-oir** are often irregular and need to be learned:

  boire – boivent; écrire – écrivent

  vouloir – veulent; devoir – doivent; pouvoir – peuvent
- The reflexive pronoun for the **ils/elles** form is **se**.

  ils se reposent; elle se disputent; ils s'appellent

## 1.2.7 ▶**Fast track:** Present tense

French verbs change the spelling of their endings according to the person who is doing the action. Fortunately, most of them still sound the same except for the *we* (**nous**) form, which ends in **-ons**, and the *you* (**vous**) form, which ends in **-ez**.

Unfortunately, some of the most common verbs are irregular. But you probably know a lot of them already: **je suis**, **j'ai**, **je sais**, etc.

A **-er** verbs

- Most French verbs are **-er** verbs.
- The regular endings for **-er** verbs are **-e**; **-es**; **-e**; **-ons**; **-ez**; **-ent**.
- All new verbs are **-er** verbs, e.g. **faxer**, **surfer**.
- Most **-er** verbs are regular, i.e. they follow the same pattern.
- Most endings sound the same, but the two marked * in the table sound different.

| **habiter** *to live* present tense | |
|---|---|
| j'habite | nous habitons* |
| tu habites | vous habitez* |
| il/elle habite | ils/elles habitent |

B **-ir** verbs

- There are not many **-ir** verbs.
- In the singular, the endings are **-s**, **-s**, **-t**, but you don't pronounce any of them, so they all sound the same!

- **-ir** verbs split into two different sorts: those which take **ss** in the plural (such as **finir** and **choisir**) and those which don't (such as **sortir** and **partir**).

Highlight a phrase that you might use, which includes a word that you are trying to remember, e.g. **Nous finissons à cinq heures**.

| finir | choisir | sortir | partir |
|---|---|---|---|
| je finis | je choisis | je sors | je pars |
| tu finis | tu choisis | tu sors | tu pars |
| il/elle finit | il/elle choisit | il/elle sort | il/elle part |
| nous finissons | nous choisissons | nous sortons | nous partons |
| vous finissez | vous choisissez | vous sortez | vous partez |
| ils/elles finissent | ils/elles choisissent | ils/elles sortent | ils/elles partent |

C   Irregular **-ir** verbs

**Venir** (*to come*) and **tenir** (*to hold*) are irregular, as are verbs made up of these, e.g. **revenir**, **retenir**.

| venir | tenir |
|---|---|
| je viens | je tiens |
| tu viens | tu tiens |
| il/elle vient | il/elle tient |
| nous venons | nous tenons |
| vous venez | vous tenez |
| ils/elles viennent | ils/elles tiennent |

D   **-oir** verbs

These verbs are not classed as **-ir** verbs, because they have a pattern of their own; they are, however, very useful verbs. Cover them up and see if you can remember their pattern.

| devoir | savoir | voir | pouvoir | vouloir |
|---|---|---|---|---|
| je dois | je sais | je vois | je peux | je veux |
| tu dois | tu sais | tu vois | tu peux | tu veux |
| il/elle doit | il/elles sait | il/elle voit | il/elle peut | il/elle veut |
| nous devons | nous savons | nous voyons | nous pouvons | nous voulons |
| vous devez | vous savez | vous voyez | vous pouvez | vous voulez |
| ils/elles doivent | ils/elles savent | ils/elles voient | ils/elles peuvent | ils/elles veulent |

## E  -re verbs

There are not so many -re verbs and most of them end with
-dre and follow the same pattern.

| répondre | descendre |
| --- | --- |
| je réponds | je descends |
| tu réponds | tu descends |
| il/elle répond | il/elle descend |
| nous répondons | nous descendons |
| vous répondez | vous descendez |
| ils/elles répondent | ils/elles descendent |

## F  More irregular verbs

The following verbs are irregular, but they are also the most
used verbs:

| avoir | être | aller | faire |
| --- | --- | --- | --- |
| j'ai | je suis | je vais | je fais |
| tu as | tu es | tu vas | tu fais |
| il/elle a | il/elle est | il/elle va | il/elle fait |
| nous avons | nous sommes | nous allons | nous faisons |
| vous avez | vous êtes | vous allez | vous faites |
| ils/elles ont | ils/elles sont | ils/elles vont | ils/elles font |

**I**  You are talking about yourself. Use the verbs in brackets.

**a** J'___ rendez-vous avec l'un de mes collègues. (avoir)
**b** Je ___ prêt(e). (être)
**c** Je ___ en ville. (aller)
**d** Je ___ le métro. (prendre)
**e** Je ___ à la station Opéra. (descendre)
**f** Je ___ du métro. (sortir)
**g** Je ___ la place. (traverser)
**h** J'___ mon collègue sur les marches de l'Opéra. (attendre)
**i** Je n'___ pas attendre. (aimer)
**j** Au bout d'une demi-heure, je ___ à l'hôtel. (rentrer)

**II**  Still using the same sentences, ask someone you know really
well the same things. Use the **tu** form. For example:

*As-tu* rendez-vous avec quelqu'un?

**a** ___ **-tu** rendez-vous avec l'un de tes collègues?
**b** ___ **-tu** prêt(e)?
**c** ___ **-tu** en ville?
**d** ___ **-tu** le métro?

**e** ___ **-tu** à la station Opéra?
**f** ___ **-tu** du métro?
**g** ___ **-tu** la place?
**h** ___ **-tu** ton collègue sur les marches de l'Opéra?
**i** ___ **-tu** attendre?
**j** Au bout d'une demi-heure, ___ **-tu** à l'hôtel?

**III** Now report back in the third person, saying he/she does the same things. This time, choose the one correct verb from the three in brackets. For example:

Il/elle a rendez-vous en ville avec l'un de ses collègues.

**a** Il/elle ___ rendez-vous en ville avec l'un de ses collègues. (a va fait)
**b** Il/elle ___ prêt(e). (a fait est)
**c** Il/elle ___ en ville. (sort va arrive)
**d** Il/elle ___ le métro. (descend monte prend)
**e** Il/elle ___ à la station Opéra. (va est descend)
**f** Il/elle ___ du métro. (sort monte attend)
**g** Il/elle ___ la place. (court va traverse)
**h** Il/elle ___ son collègue sur les marches de l'Opéra. (attend voit regarde)
**i** Il/elle n'___ pas attendre. (préfère aime arrive)
**j** Au bout d'une demi-heure, il/elle ___ à l'hôtel. (sort rentre trouve)

**IV** Now you are talking about yourself and a partner: say we do (or don't do) the same things. For example:

Nous *avons* rendez-vous avec l'un de nos collègues.

**a** Nous ___ rendez-vous avec l'un des nos collègues.
**b** Nous ___ prêt(e)s.
**c** Nous ___ en ville.
**d** Nous ___ le métro.
**e** Nous ___ à la station Opéra.
**f** Nous ___ du métro.
**g** Nous ___ la place.
**h** Nous ___ notre collègue sur les marches de l'Opéra.
**i** Nous n'___ pas attendre.
**j** Au bout d'une demi-heure, nous ___ à l'hôtel.

**V** Using the same sentences, ask someone else the same things, using the **vous** form. For example:

*Avez*-vous rendez- avec quelqu'un ?

**a** ___ -vous rendez-vous avec l'un de vos collègues?
**b** ___ -vous prêt(e)?
**c** ___ -vous en ville?
**d** ___ -vous le métro?

**e** ___ -vous à la station Opéra?
**f** ___ -vous du métro?
**g** ___ -vous la place?
**h** ___ -vous votre collègue sur les marches de l'Opéra?
**i** ___ -vous attendre?
**j** Au bout d'une demi-heure, ___ -vous à l'hôtel?

**VI** Finally, say it in the plural: they do it. Choose the correct verb. For example:

Ils/elles *ont* rendez-vous en ville avec l'un de leurs collègues.

**a** Ils/elles ___ rendez-vous en ville avec l'un de leurs collègues. (ont font vont)
**b** Ils/elles ___ prêt(e)s. (sont vont font)
**c** Ils/elles ___ en ville. (descendent vont sortent)
**d** Ils/elles ___ le métro. (prennent changent travaillent)
**e** Ils/elles ___ à la station Opéra. (courent sont descendent)
**f** Ils/elles ___ du métro. (descendent sortent préfèrent)
**g** Ils/elles ___ la place. (arrivent sortent traversent)
**h** Ils/elles ___ leur collègue sur les marches de l'Opéra. (attendent voient regardent)
**i** Ils/elles n' ___ pas attendre. (préfèrent aiment dînent)
**j** Au bout d'une demi-heure, ils/elles ___ à l'hôtel. (sortent rentrent trouvent)

# 1.3 Negatives, interrogatives and imperatives

- The **negative** is used to say *no* you *don't* do something, you *haven't* got something, or to tell someone *not* to do something. A negative sentence is a sentence with a *no*, *not* or *don't* in it.
- The **interrogative** is used to ask questions.
- The **imperative** is used to give orders, directions or instructions: to tell someone what to do or what not to do!

## 1.3.1 Negatives: how to say what doesn't happen

▶▶ **If you know how to use ne ... pas, go on to 1.3.2.**

To say you don't do something, you put **ne** in front of the verb and **pas** after it.

Je ne sais pas.                    I don't know.

The **ne** becomes **n'** before a vowel: **Je n'ai pas de ...**

**I** Say you/they don't do these things by putting **ne** in front of the verb and **pas** after it. Say the sentences aloud to get used to the sound.

**a** They don't drink wine.     Ils ___ de vin. (boire)
**b** I don't often write letters.   Je ___ souvent de lettres. (écrire)
**c** She doesn't read her      Elle ___ ses méls. (lire)
   e-mails.
**d** We don't buy magazines.    Nous ___ de revues. (acheter)
**e** I don't know!                Je ___! (savoir)
**f** He can't find the         Il ___ l'entrée. (trouver)
   entrance.
**g** They are not coming     Ils ___ ce soir. (venir)
   tonight.
**h** I don't want to go.        Je ___ y aller. (vouloir)
**i** We don't like going there.  Nous ___ y aller. (aimer)
**j** You don't eat snails!      Vous ___ d'escargots! (manger)

## 1.3.2 Interrogatives: asking questions.

**If you know how to ask questions, go on to 1.3.3.**

There are five main ways of asking a question. You can:

- make a statement and change the intonation;
- invert the subject and the verb;
- use **Est-ce que ...** (*Is it that* ...?) and keep the word order;
- use a question word, and then invert the subject and the verb;
- use a question word and **est-ce que** ...

In the following sections, read the examples and then cover up the English and see if you understand the meanings; then cover up the French and see if you can put them back into French.

A Changing the intonation

This is probably the easiest way to ask a question, but it is colloquial and not used in formal speech. Remember you have to use a rising tone towards the end of the question. Practise saying them aloud. If you are not happy with your intonation go on to method B!

| | |
|---|---|
| Vous comprenez? | You understand? |
| Vous parlez anglais? | You speak English? |
| Vous connaissez l'hôtel Superbe? | You know the Hotel Superbe? |
| Ce train va à Rouen? | This train is going to Rouen? |

## B Inverting the subject and the verb

This is the normal way of asking a question.

| | |
|---|---|
| Comprenez-vous? | Do you understand? |
| Parlez-vous anglais? | Do you speak English? |
| Connaissez-vous l'hôtel Superbe? | Do you know the Hotel Superbe? |
| Ce train va-t-il à Rouen? | Is this train going to Rouen? |
| Joue-t-elle au tennis? | Does she play tennis? |
| A-t-il une nouvelle voiture? | Has he got a new car? |

 When you invert with *il/elle*, you usually have to add **-t-** to make it easier to pronounce, as French does not like the sound of two vowels together.

## C Using *Est-ce que...?*

| | |
|---|---|
| Est-ce que vous comprenez? | Do you understand? |
| Est-ce que vous parlez anglais? | Do you speak English? |
| Est-ce que vous connaissez l'hôtel Superbe? | Do you know the Hotel Superbe? |
| Est-ce que ce train va à Rouen? | Is this train going to Rouen? |

## D Using a question word and inverting the subject and verb

| | |
|---|---|
| Où allez-vous? | Where are you going? |
| Comment va-t-il à Paris? | How is he going to Paris? |
| Pourquoi est-elle à Paris? | Why is she in Paris? |
| Quand partez-vous? | When are you leaving? |
| Que faites-vous? | What are you doing? |
| Qui connaissez-vous? | Who do you know? |
| Combien de chambres avez-vous? | How many bedrooms do you have? |

## E Using a question word and *est-ce que* ...

With this method, you don't need to invert the subject and verb.

| | |
|---|---|
| Où est-ce que vous allez? | Where are you going? |
| Comment est-ce qu'il va à Paris? | How is he going to Paris? |
| Pourquoi est-ce que vous allez à Paris? | Why are you going to Paris? |
| Quand est-ce que je dois partir? | When do I have to leave? |
| Qu'est-ce qu'il fait? | What is he doing? |
| Qui est-ce que vous connaissez déjà? | Who do you know already? |
| Combien de chambres est-ce qu'il y a? | How many rooms are there? |

**I** Use method B to turn these statements into questions.

**a** M. et Mme Leblanc habitent en banlieue parisienne.
**b** Ils partent en vacances.
**c** Ils prennent le train.
**d** Ils vont sur la côte d'Azur.
**e** Ils ont une résidence secondaire.
**f** Ils louent une voiture.
**g** Ils jouent au golf.
**h** Ils font du ski nautique.
**i** Ils ont des amis qui habitent à St-Tropez.
**j** Le soir ils dînent au restaurant.

**II** Use method D with these question words.

| | |
|---|---|
| **a** Where are they going? | Où ___? (aller) |
| **b** When are they leaving? | Quand ___ ? (partir) |
| **c** How are they travelling? | Comment ___ à Paris? (aller) |
| **d** Why are they in Paris? | Pourquoi ___ à Paris? (être) |
| **e** What are they doing? | Que ___? (faire) |
| **f** Who are they meeting? | Avec qui ___ rendez-vous? (avoir) |
| **g** How long are they staying at the hotel? | Combien de temps ___ à l'hôtel? (loger) |

**III** Now do them again using method E. For example:

Où est-ce qu'ils vont? Quand est-ce qu'ils partent? etc.

## **1.3.3** Imperatives: giving orders, directions or instructions

▶▶ **If you know how to give orders and instructions, go on to 1.3.4.**

The imperative is the part of the verb you use when you are telling someone to do something, or giving instructions or an order: *Watch out! Stop! Turn left!* etc.

When you use the imperative you usually use the **vous** part of the verb. You use the **tu** form only when speaking to someone you know well or a child.

Look at these examples. You will probably have heard some of these before. Which ones do you know already?

| | |
|---|---|
| Come on! | Venez!/Allez! |
| Cross the road! | Traversez la rue! |
| Turn left. | Tournez à gauche. |
| Listen! | Écoutez! |
| Wait! | Attendez! |
| Hold the line! | Ne quittez pas! |
| Hurry up! | Dépêchez-vous! |

A Using the *vous* form

To make the imperative, you use the **vous** form of the verb without the **vous**: **Prenez ce livre**.

For a reflexive verb (e.g. *vous vous asseyez*), drop one *vous* and invert the rest: **Asseyez-vous!**

B Using the *tu* form

You use the **tu** form of the verb, but **-er** verbs lose the final **-s** (as it isn't pronounced, it sounds the same): **Regarde!**

For a reflexive verb (e.g. *tu te couches*), use this pattern: **Couche-toi!**

**I**   How would you give these instructions? If you are likely to need to use the **tu** form (**Mange tes légumes! Va au lit!**) practise both forms; otherwise just do the **vous** form.

**a** ___ à gauche. (tourner)
**b** ___ les marches. (monter)
**c** ___ la première rue à gauche. (prendre)
**d** ___ tout droit. (continuer)
**e** ___ jusqu'aux prochains feux. (aller)
**f** ___ à droite et à gauche. (regarder)
**g** ___ la rue. (traverser)
**h** ___ le bus. (prendre)
**i** ___ devant le théâtre. (descendre)
**j** ___ -moi un texto quand vous arrivez. (envoyer)

**II**   These instructions are from a soufflé recipe. Put them in the **vous** form of the imperative.

**a** Pre-heat the oven.          ___ le four. (préchauffer)
**b** Slice the onions thinly.    ___ les oignons. (émincer)
**c** Beat the eggs.              ___ les œufs. (battre)
**d** Put the onions into a bowl. ___ les oignons dans un saladier. (mettre)
**e** Add the oil and the         ___ l'huile et les œufs battus. beaten eggs.        (ajouter)
**f** Mix well.                   ___ bien. (mélanger)
**g** Butter an oven-proof dish.  ___ un moule allant au four. (beurrer)
**h** Pour the mixture into       ___ le mélange dans le moule. the dish.           (verser)
**i** Put the dish into the oven. ___ le moule. (enfourner)
**j** Cook for ten minutes.       ___ cuire pendant dix minutes (faire)

**III** How would you tell someone to do these things? Use the **vous** form.

    **a** Watch less television.    \_\_\_ moins la télévision. (regarder)
    **b** Eat more vegetables.    \_\_\_ plus de légumes. (manger)
    **c** Drink more water.    \_\_\_ plus d'eau. (boire)
    **d** Go jogging.    \_\_\_ du jogging. (faire)
    **e** Close the door.    \_\_\_ la porte. (fermer)
    **f** Open the window.    \_\_\_ la fenêtre. (ouvrir)
    **g** Show your passport.    \_\_\_ votre passeport. (présenter)
    **h** Speak more slowly.    \_\_\_ plus lentement. (parler)
    **i** Come with me.    \_\_\_ avec moi. (venir)

**IV** Let's try a keep fit session. Give the **vous** form.

    **a** Come in!    \_\_\_! (entrer)
    **b** Get in a line.    \_\_\_ en rang. (se mettre)
    **c** Find a space.    \_\_\_ une place. (trouver)
    **d** Run on the spot.    \_\_\_ sur place. (courir)
    **e** Stand with your feet apart.    \_\_\_ les pieds. (écarter)
    **f** Stretch your arms.    \_\_\_ les bras. (tendre)
    **g** Pull your stomach in.    \_\_\_ le ventre. (rentrer)
    **h** Lower your shoulders.    \_\_\_ les épaules. (baisser)
    **i** Bend your knees.    \_\_\_ les genoux. (plier)
    **j** Don't move.    Ne \_\_\_ pas. (bouger)

**V** Tell some French visitors the way to the town hall.

    **a** Quand vous \_\_\_ d'ici, (sortir)
    **b** \_\_\_ à droite. (tourner)
    **c** \_\_\_ la deuxième rue à gauche. (prendre)
    **d** \_\_\_ tout droit. (continuer)
    **e** \_\_\_ la place. (traverser)
    **f** \_\_\_ la rue jusqu'au rond-point. (suivre)
    **g** \_\_\_ à droite: la mairie est en face de vous. (tourner)

## C Telling someone what not to do

As with other forms, you make an imperative negative by adding **ne...pas** around the verb.

Reflexives work like this: **Ne vous asseyez pas**.

**VI** First match the English and French, then cover up the French and see if you can remember it.

    **a** Don't smoke.    Ne vous penchez pas par la
    **b** Don't walk on the grass.    fenêtre.
    **c** Don't eat in the shop.    N'ouvrez pas la porte.
    **d** Don't leave your luggage    Ne mettez pas vos chaussures de
      here.    ski sur le comptoir.
    **e** Don't cross the road.    Ne buvez pas cette eau.

| | |
|---|---|
| **f** Don't lean out of the window. | Ne portez pas de noir. |
| **g** Don't drink this water. | Ne marchez pas sur l'herbe. |
| **h** Don't wait here. | N'attendez pas ici. |
| **i** Don't put ski boots on the counter. | Ne mangez pas dans le magasin. |
| **j** Don't wear black. | Ne fumez pas. |
| **k** Don't open the door. | Ne laissez pas vos bagages ici. |
| | Ne traversez pas la rue. |

Some common imperatives are irregular:

| | | |
|---|---|---|
| avoir | N'ayez pas peur. | Don't be afraid. |
| être | Soyez sages! | Be good! |
| vouloir | Veuillez trouver ci-joint ... | Please find enclosed ... |

# 1.3.4 ▶Fast track: Negatives, interrogatives and imperatives

A Negatives: saying something doesn't happen

You put **ne** in front of the verb and **pas** after it.

| | |
|---|---|
| Je ne sais pas. | I don't know. |
| Il ne vend pas sa voiture. | He isn't selling his car. |
| Je ne peux pas venir. | I can't come. |

B Interrogatives: asking questions

You can:

- make a statement and change the intonation: **Vous allez à Paris?**
- invert the subject and the verb: **Allez-vous à Paris?**
- use **Est-ce que ...** and keep the word order: **Est-ce que vous allez à Paris?**
- use a question word, and then invert the subject and the verb: **Où allez-vous?**
- use a question word and **est-ce que**: **Où est-ce que vous allez?**

Useful question words:

| | | | |
|---|---|---|---|
| Combien? | How much?/How many? | Quand? | When? |
| Comment? | How?/Pardon? | Que ...? | What ...? |
| Où? | Where? | Qui? | Who? |
| Pourquoi? | Why? | | |

C Imperatives: giving orders, directions and instructions

To make the imperative, you use the **vous** form of the verb without the **vous**:

Attendez! – Wait! Allez! – Go on! Venez vite! – Come quick!

When talking to children (and pets) you use the **tu** form without the **tu**:

Attends! Va! Viens vite!

# **1.4** The past tenses

You use the past tenses to say what has happened or what was happening.

▶▶ **If you know when to use the perfect and imperfect tenses, go on to 1.5.**

In French, just as in English, there are different ways of expressing the past. The tenses you will need to use most are the perfect tense and the imperfect tense.

The **perfect** tense is made up of two parts: *have* and the past participle (e.g. *eaten/arrived*). Most verbs use **avoir** for *have* but some use **être**.

| | |
|---|---|
| I have eaten | j'ai mangé |
| I have arrived | je suis arrivé(e) |

In French, you use the perfect tense when you are talking or asking about something which happened at a specific time in the past and which is over and done with. The perfect tense translates all these forms: *I played, I have played* and *I did play*, and the question forms *Have you played?* and *Did you play?*

 Ask yourself: Did it happen once in the past? Is it over? Is it finished? Then use the **perfect** tense.

The **imperfect** tense translates *I was playing when ...*, *Were you playing when ...?* and *I used to play (a long time ago)*.

You use the imperfect tense:

* to talk about what used to happen in general:
  J'allais à l'école en bus.　　　I used to go to school by bus.
* to describe things in the past:
  Il pleuvait tout le temps.　　　It was always raining.
* to say what was happening when something else happened (an interrupted action):
  Je me douchais quand il est arrivé.　　I was having a shower when he arrived.

 Ask yourself: Did it use to happen in the past? Or was it happening when something else happened? If you can use 'used to' or 'was/were' + ... ing in English, you use the **imperfect** in French.

**I** Which tense are you going to use?

**a** Yesterday I went to town.
**b** I bought a new pair of trainers.
**c** Then I went to the gym.
**d** I used to go three times a week.
**e** I met my girlfriend at the gym.
**f** She was on the rowing machine.
**g** I was doing weights.
**h** She was laughing at me.
**i** I asked her why.
**j** My shorts were inside out.

## 1.4.1 The perfect tense

**If you know how to form the perfect tense with avoir and être, go to 1.4.3.**

The perfect tense in French is made up of two parts, like the English perfect tense: part of the verb **avoir** (*to have*) or **être** (*to be*) and the past participle.

| to have | past participle | avoir | participe passé |
|---------|----------------|-------|-----------------|
| I have | played | j'ai | joué |
| he has | spoken | il a | parlé |
| we have | moved (house) | nous avons | déménagé |

Most verbs go with **avoir**, but some go with **être**, e.g. **arriver**. Instead of saying *I have arrived*, in French you say *I am arrived*. Verbs that use **être** are shown in sections 1.4.3 and 1.4.5.

To get used to the sound of the perfect tense, choose one of the phrases below, or make up one of your own and practise saying it until you are really fluent.

| | |
|---|---|
| Je suis allé(e) au marché et j'ai acheté des tomates. | I went to the market and I bought some tomatoes. |
| Je suis allé(e) à la piscine et j'ai nagé pendant une heure. | I went to the swimming baths and I swam for an hour. |
| Je suis allé(e) en ville et j'ai fait des courses. | I went to town and I did some shopping. |
| Je suis allé(e) à la gare et j'ai pris le train de neuf heures. | I went to the station and I got the 9 o'clock train. |
| Je suis allé(e) dans un bar et j'ai commandé une bière. | I went to a bar and I ordered a beer. |

Here is a reminder of all the forms you need:

| **avoir** – to have | **être** – to be |
| --- | --- |
| j'ai | je suis |
| tu as | tu es |
| il/elle a | il/elle est |
| nous avons | nous sommes |
| vous avez | vous êtes |
| ils/elles ont | ils/elles sont |

Most verbs go with **avoir**.

I   Practise with **avoir**. How would you say ...?

| | |
| --- | --- |
| **a** I have eaten | J'___ mangé |
| **b** you have eaten | tu ___ mangé |
| **c** we have eaten | nous ___ mangé |
| **d** they have eaten | ils ___ mangé |
| **e** he has eaten | il ___ mangé |
| **f** she has eaten | elle ___ mangé |
| **g** you have eaten | vous ___ mangé |
| **h** John has eaten | John ___ mangé |
| **i** Have you eaten? | ___ -vous mangé? |
| **j** my wife and I have eaten | ma femme et moi, nous ___ mangé |

II   Who watched the 9 o'clock news? Complete these sentences by adding the right form of **avoir**.

**a** Nous ___ regardé le journal de 21h.
**b** J'___ regardé le journal de 21h.
**c** Il ___ regardé le journal de 21h.
**d** ___-tu regardé le journal de 21h?
**e** Ils ___ regardé le journal de 21h.
**f** Elle ___ regardé le journal de 21h.
**g** Elles n'___ pas regardé le journal de 21h.
**h** ___-vous regardé le journal de 21h?
**i** Julie ___ regardé le journal de 21h.
**j** Mes parents n'___ pas regardé le journal de 21h.

## Checklist: perfect tense

To make the perfect tense for most verbs you use the right person of **avoir** (*to have*) + the past participle:

avoir: j'ai; tu as; il/elle a; nous avons; vous avez; ils/elles ont ... mangé

▶▶ **If you know how to form the past participle, go to 1.4.3.**

A Regular verbs

In English, the past participle of regular verbs is formed by adding *-ed* to the infinitive:

play → played; watch → watched; dance → danced

In French, **-er**, **-ir** and **-re** verbs form their past participles in different ways. You take off the ending (**-er**, **-ir** or **-re**) and add the following:

| -er verbs | -ir verbs | -re verbs |
|---|---|---|
| -é | -i | -u |

parler → parlé; dormir → dormi; répondre → répondu

I Using these rules, what would the past participles of these verbs be?

a jouer      k laver
b manger      l demander
c finir      m fermer
d vendre      n pousser
e écouter      o tirer
f perdre      p oublier
g choisir      q sortir
h attendre      r entrer
i organiser      s entendre
j inviter      t partir

II What did Marc do last night? Add the right form of the past participle of the verb in brackets.

a Après mon travail, j'ai ___ au squash avec Jacques. (jouer)    After work I played squash with Jacques.

b Puis j'ai ___ avec ma femme. (dîner)    Then I had dinner with my wife.

c Après le dîner, j'ai ___ à mon collègue Jules. (téléphoner)    After dinner, I rang my colleague Jules.

d Nous avons ___ du nouveau projet. (discuter)    We discussed the new plan/ project.

e Il m'a ___ de sa coopération. (assurer)    He assured me of his co-operation.

**f** Nous avons ___ d'une date pour la conférence de presse. (décider)

We decided on a date for the press conference.

**g** Il m'a ___ la nouvelle plaquette produit par e-mail. (envoyer)

He sent me the new brochure by e-mail.

**h** J'ai ___ une page. (changer)

I changed a page.

**i** J'ai ___ cette page. (imprimer)

I printed this page.

**j** Après ça, j'ai ___ un feuilleton à la télévision. (regarder)

After that I watched a soap on TV.

## B Irregular past participles

Many English past participles are irregular, but we are so used to them that we don't notice:

run, eaten, drunk, bought, been, sat, etc.

Some French verbs also have irregular past participles. Although there seem to be quite a lot, they are easy to learn, as they mostly follow the same patterns.

The following verbs all have past participles which end in **-u**.

| infinitive | past participle | example | meaning |
|---|---|---|---|
| avoir | eu | Il a eu une surprise. | He had a surprise. |
| boire | bu | Nous avons bu du vin. | We have drunk some wine. |
| croire | cru | J'ai cru le reconnaître. | I thought I recognised him. |
| devoir | dû | Il a dû y aller. | He has had to go there. |
| lire | lu | Il a lu le livre. | He has read the book. |
| pouvoir | pu | Vous avez pu manger? | You were able to eat? |
| recevoir | reçu | Elle a reçu une lettre. | She has received a letter. |
| savoir | su | Ils ont su la réponse. | They knew the answer. |
| voir | vu | Il a vu l'accident. | He saw the accident. |
| vouloir | voulu | Nous avons voulu partir. | We wanted to leave. |

The past participles of **prendre** and **mettre** (and other verbs made up of them) end in **-s**.

| infinitive | past participle | example | meaning |
|---|---|---|---|
| prendre | pris | Elle a pris son manteau. | She took her coat. |
| comprendre | compris | J'ai compris. | I've understood. |
| apprendre | appris | Elle a appris son nom. | She learned his name. |
| mettre | mis | Il a mis son imperméable. | He put on his raincoat. |

The past participles of **faire**, **dire** and **écrire** end in **-t**.

| infinitive | past participle | example | meaning |
|---|---|---|---|
| faire | fait | J'ai fait du sport. | I've done some sport. |
| dire | dit | Il m'a dit le nom de son amie. | He told me the name of his friend. |
| écrire | écrit | Elle a écrit une lettre. | She wrote a letter. |

Some verbs don't follow a pattern.

| infinitive | past participle | example | meaning |
|---|---|---|---|
| ouvrir | ouvert | Il a ouvert la fenêtre. | He opened the window. |
| être | été | J'ai été fatigué(e). | I have been tired. |
| suivre | suivi | Elle a suivi la voiture. | She followed the car. |

Choose the five participles which you think you will need most and learn them.

III    Complete these sentences by adding the past participle of the verb given in brackets.

a Notre client japonais a ___ la maquette du nouveau dépliant. (voir)
Our Japanese client has seen the proofs for the new brochure.

b Alain a ___ les photos. (faire)
Alain did the photos.

c Nous avons ___ le texte. (écrire)
We wrote the text.

d Mme Brandt l'a ___ dans l'ordinateur. (entrer)
Mrs Brandt put it on the computer.

e La société de M. Patte en a ___ deux versions en couleur. (imprimer)
Mr Patte's company printed two colour versions.

f Avez-vous ___ les dernières épreuves? (voir)
Have you seen the latest proofs?

g Nous avons ___ en faire imprimer 5000 exemplaires. (devoir)
We had to make 5,000 copies.

h Les délais ont ___ respectés. (être) The deadline has been met.

IV    Now tell the story of Marcel's car. Complete these sentences using the perfect tense of the verb given in brackets. Not all the past participles are irregular!

a Marcel ___ 100 000 euros au loto. (gagner)
Marcel won 100,000 euros in the lottery.

b Il ___ acheter une nouvelle voiture pour sa femme. (vouloir)
He wanted to buy a new car for his wife.

**c** Il ___ une pub pour une voiture électrique. (voir)

He saw an advert for an electric car.

**d** Il ___ la voiture. (acheter)

He bought the car.

**e** La voiture n'a pas plu à sa femme et elle ___ de la vendre. (décider)

His wife didn't like the car and she decided to sell it.

**f** Elle ___ une petite annonce sur le panneau d'affichage du supermarché. (mettre)

She put an advertisement on the notice board in the supermarket.

**g** Un ami de son mari ___ rendez-vous pour essayer la voiture. (prendre)

A friend of her husband made an appointment to try the car out.

**h** Marcel ___ sa femme avec son ami dans la voiture. (voir)

Marcel saw his wife in the car with his friend.

**i** Il ___ qu'ils avaient une liaison. (croire)

He thought they were having an affair.

**j** Il ___ la voiture. (suivre)

He followed the car.

**k** Il ___ des excès de vitesse. (faire)

He went too fast.

**l** Les gendarmes l'___. (arrêter)

The police stopped him.

**m** Il ___ payer une amende. (devoir)

He had to pay a fine.

**V** Now can you translate these?

**a** Stéphanie has read his latest novel (son dernier roman).
**b** Have you read the book?
**c** We haven't read the book.
**d** They have seen the film.
**e** Stéphanie saw the film yesterday.
**f** We haven't seen the film yet.
**g** Have you seen the film?

## Checklist: past participles

- Most past participles end in **-é**.

- Regular verbs:

  **-er** verbs end in **-é**,
  **-ir** verbs end in **-i**,
  **-re** verbs end in **-u**.

- Many of the most commonly used verbs have irregular past participles.

- Look for patterns to try to remember them:

  eu; bu; cru; dû; lu; pu; reçu; su; vu; voulu
  pris; compris; appris; mis
  fait; dit; écrit

- Some don't follow a pattern:

  ouvert; été; suivi

## 1.4.3 Verbs which go with *être*

►► **If you know which verbs go with être, go on to 1.4.4.**

The following verbs go with **être**. They are the 'going and coming' verbs, and fall naturally into six pairs. It is a good idea to learn them. Try making up a story, rhyme or picture using them.

| | |
|---|---|
| aller – to go | venir – to come |
| arriver – to arrive | partir – to leave |
| entrer – to come in | sortir – to go out |
| monter – to climb/go up | descendre – to descend/go down |
| rester – to stay | tomber – to fall |
| naître – to be born | mourir – to die |

All verbs made up of these verbs, e.g. **rentrer**, **redescendre**, etc., also form the perfect tense with **être**.

> All the past participles of verbs that go with **être** are regular except **naître** – to be born (**né**) (which you probably know already) and **mourir** – to die (**mort**) (which sounds like the beginning of mortuary).

**I** What does the past participle end in?

**a** aller: all   é / i / u / t
**b** venir: ven   é / i / u / t
**c** arriver: arriv   é / i / u / t
**d** partir: part   é / i / u / t
**e** sortir: sort   é / i / u / t
**f** monter: mont   é / i / u / t
**g** descendre: descend   é / i / u / t
**h** tomber: tomb   é / i / u / t
**i** rester: rest   é / i / u / t
**j** naître: n   é / i / u / t
**k** mourir: mor   é / i / u / t
**l** faire: fai   é / i / u / t

> You'll notice an extra **-e**, **-s**, or **-es** at the end of some past participles. These are explained in section 1.4.4.

**II** Who went to town? Complete these sentences by adding the right form of **être**. See the table on page 52.

**a** Je ___ allé en ville.
**b** Mon mari ___ resté à la maison.

**c** Mes aînés ___ allés au Parc des Sciences et de l'Industrie de la Villette avec leur grand-mère.

**d** Ma fille cadette ___ restée à la maison.

**e** ___ -tu allé en ville?

**f** M. Hibbert ___ allé au cinéma.

**g** Sa femme ___ restée à la maison.

**h** Leur fils ___ allé à un match de rugby.

**i** ___-vous restés à la maison?

**j** Nous ___ allés aux courses à Longchamp.

A   More practice with *être* and *aller*

**Remember, some verbs go with être. Aller is the one you use most:**

| | |
|---|---|
| je suis allé(e) | nous sommes allé(e)s |
| tu es allé(e) | vous êtes allé(e)(s) |
| il est allé/elle est allée | ils sont allés/elles sont allées |

III   **Which form of être would you use to complete these sentences?**

**a** Nous ___ allées en ville.

**b** Je ___ allée au cinéma.

**c** ___-vous allé au cinéma?

**d** Mes collègues ___ allés au théâtre.

**e** Mon ami ___ allé au concert.

**f** Où ___-tu allé?

**g** Ma fille ___ allée chez le dentiste.

**h** Mes stagiaires ___ sorties.

**i** Où ___-vous allés?

**j** Nous ___ rentrés tard.

> Reminder on how to form regular past participles:
> **-er** verbs: take off the **-er** and add **-é**
> **-ir** verbs: take off the **-ir** and add **-i**
> **-re** verbs: take off the **-re** and add **-u**

IV   **Complete these sentences by adding the past participle. What did Marcel do?**

**a** Marcel est ___ à l'hôpital voir son père. (aller)

**b** Il est ___ de chez lui à neuf heures vingt. (sortir)

**c** Le bus est ___ à neuf heures et demie. (partir)

**d** Il est ___ à dix heures. (arriver)

**e** Marcel est ___ du bus devant l'hôpital. (descendre)

**f** Il est ___ dans l'hôpital. (entrer)

**g** Il est ___ au service de cardiologie. (monter)

**h** Il est ___ dans l'escalier. (tomber)

**i** Il est ___ à l'hôpital. (rester)

**V**   This time add the correct form of **être**.

   **a** Céline ___ allée à Paris voir ses parents.

   **b** Elle ___ sortie de chez elle à neuf heures vingt.

   **c** Je ___ allée avec elle.

   **d** Le train ___ parti à neuf heures et demie.

   **e** Nous ___ arrivées à dix heures à la Gare du Nord.

   **f** Nous ___ descendues du train.

   **g** Son frère ___ venu la chercher à la gare.

   **h** Ils ___ partis déjeuner chez ses parents.

   **i** Pendant ce temps-là, je ___ allée au musée du Louvre.

   **j** On ___ rentré le lendemain.

 Remember you can use **on** instead of *we*. It is followed by the **il/elle** form of the verb: **on est allé** – *one/we went*.

## 1.4.4  Verbs with *être*: past participle agreement

You may have noticed that after verbs which go with **être**, the past participle 'agrees' with the subject. That is, if the person doing the action is female, you add an **-e**, if there is more than one person doing the action, you add an **-s**, and if there is more than one person and they are all female, you add **-es**. The same applies to feminine or masculine things that do an action, e.g. **la lettre est arrivée**.

 **These endings are not pronounced so if you are not going to write in French, go on to 1.4.5.**

The past participle agrees with the subject (the person who is doing the action) by taking the following endings:

| masculine | feminine | masculine plural | feminine plural |
|---|---|---|---|
| – | -e | -s | -es |

**I**   Add endings to the past participles which need them.

   **a** Ma grand-mère est *né* en 1930.

   **b** Mon grand-père est *mort* l'année dernière.

   **c** Ma grand-mère est *allé* chez mes parents.

   **d** Elle est *parti* de chez elle à onze heures.

   **e** Elle est *arrivé* à la gare à onze heures et demie.

   **f** Mes parents sont *allé* la chercher à la gare.

   **g** Le train est *arrivé* en retard.

   **h** Ma tante est *venu* la voir.

   **i** Elle est *monté* chercher de vieilles photos au grenier.

   **j** En redescendant, elle est *tombé* et s'est fait mal au genou.

**II** Now see if you can add the correct form: **allé, allée, allés, allées.**

**a** M. Dupin est ___ à Londres.
**b** Son amie Charlotte est ___ à Paris.
**c** Ses parents sont ___ sur la côte d'Azur.
**d** Nous sommes ___ en Bretagne. **(two women)**
**e** Ses collègues sont ___ en Espagne. **(a mixed group)**
**f** Vous êtes ___ en Autriche. **(one person)**
**g** Ses grands-parents sont ___ en Italie.
**h** Son meilleur ami est ___ en Suisse.
**i** Tu es ___ aux États-Unis. **(your brother)**
**j** Et moi? Je suis ___ chez moi. **(yourself)**

## **1.4.5** Reflexive verbs in the perfect tense

All reflexive verbs also go with **être**.

| present | perfect |
|---|---|
| je me lève | je me suis levé(e) |
| tu te lèves | tu t'es levé(e) |
| il se lève | il s'est levé |
| elle se lève | elle s'est levée |
| nous nous levons | nous nous sommes levé(e)s |
| vous vous levez | vous vous êtes levé(e)(s) |
| ils se lèvent | ils se sont levés |
| elles se lèvent | elles se sont levées |

At first you will probably only need to use reflexive verbs in the first person (**je**), so learn one phrase by heart and use it as a model to make other phrases later.

| | |
|---|---|
| Je me suis couché(e) tard. | I went to bed late. |
| Je me suis bien débrouillé(e). | I managed fine. |
| Je me suis trompé(e) de route. | I went the wrong way. |
| Je me suis arrêté(e) au bord de la route. | I stopped at the roadside. |

**I** For more practice with the other persons, see if you can give the right form of the perfect tense of **se lever** to complete these sentences: When did they get up?

**a** Ce matin, je ___ à six heures.
**b** Le boulanger ___ à quatre heures.
**c** Sa femme ___ à quatre heures et demie.
**d** Gilles ___ à sept heures et demie.
**e** Patrick et Monique ___ à sept heures moins le quart.
**f** Céline, à quelle heure tu ___?
**g** Nous ___ à six heures.

**h** M. et Mme Bériot ___ à neuf heures.

**i** Aurélie et Cécile ___ à neuf heures et demie.

**j** À quelle heure vous ___ ce matin?

Here are some more reflexive verbs. You probably know most of them already.

| infinitive | meaning | present tense | perfect tense |
|---|---|---|---|
| s'arrêter | to stop | je m'arrête | je me suis arrêté(e) |
| se coucher | to go to bed | je me couche | je me suis couché(e) |
| se débrouiller | to manage/cope | je me débrouille | je me suis débrouillé(e) |
| s'égarer | to get lost | je m'égare | je me suis égaré(e) |
| s'endormir | to fall asleep | je m'endors | je me suis endormi(e) |
| s'énerver | to get impatient | je m'énerve | je me suis énervé(e) |
| s'intéresser à | to be interested in | je m'intéresse à | je me suis intéressé(e) à |
| se laver | to get washed | je me lave | je me suis lavé(e) |
| se moquer de | to make fun of | je me moque de | je me suis moqué(e) de |
| se promener | to go for a walk | je me promène | je me suis promené(e) |
| se reposer | to rest | je me repose | je me suis reposé(e) |
| se réveiller | to wake up | je me réveille | je me suis réveillé(e) |
| se souvenir de | to remember | je me souviens de | je me suis souvenu(e) de |
| se tromper | to be mistaken | je me trompe | je me suis trompé(e) |

**II** Luc is recounting what happened yesterday. Add the right part of the verb given in brackets.

**a** Nous ___ à huit heures. (se réveiller)

**b** Nous ___ à neuf heures. (se lever)

**c** Nous ___ le long de la rivière. (se promener)

**d** Nous ___ de route. (se tromper)

**e** Nous ___. (s'égarer)

**f** Nous ___ dans un petit village. (s'arrêter)

**g** Nous ___ un peu. (se reposer)

**h** Mon amie ___. (s'énerver)

**i** Elle ___ d'un ami qui habite dans le coin. (se souvenir)

**j** Elle est partie et je ___ tout seul. (se débrouiller)

**III** **Avoir** or **être**? Put in the correct form of the right verb.

L'année dernière nous ..**a**.. allés en France. Nous ..**b**.. passé deux semaines au bord de la mer. Nous ..**c**.. loué un gîte à Hossegor. Mon copain ..**d**.. fait du surf et je ..**e**.. restée allongée sur la plage toute la journée.

Mon frère et sa copine ..**f**.. venus passer le week-end chez nous. Nous nous ..**g**.. bien amusés. Le soir on ..**h**.. allé dîner au restaurant et puis on ..**i**.. dansé jusqu'à minuit. Ils ..**j**.. fait de la planche à voile. Où ..**k**..-vous allés et qu'est-ce que vous ..**l**.. fait?

If you are going to be writing French you have to remember that as reflexive verbs go with **être** the past participle has to take **-e/-s/-es** if the person or thing doing the action is feminine, plural or feminine and plural.

## Checklist: perfect tense

You use the perfect tense to talk about something which has happened at a specific time in the past.

Most verbs form the perfect tense with **avoir** and the past participle of the verb: **j'ai mangé**.

**avoir:** j'ai; tu as; il/elle a; nous avons; vous avez; ils/elles ont

Some verbs (verbs of going and coming and reflexive verbs) form the perfect tense with **être: je suis allé(e)**.

**être:** je suis, tu es, il/elle est, nous sommes, vous êtes; ils/elles sont

In written French, the past participle of verbs with **être** has to agree with the subject (the person doing the action).

## **1.4.6** The imperfect tense

 **If you know when to use the imperfect tense, go to 1.4.7.**

You use the imperfect tense to:

* describe what something was like in the past:

| | |
|---|---|
| When I was small, we lived in Scotland. | Quand j'étais petit(e), nous habitions en Écosse. |
| The house was old. | La maison était vieille. |
| It rained every day. | Il pleuvait tous les jours. |

* say what someone or something used to do:

| | |
|---|---|
| I used to walk to school. | J'allais à l'école à pied. |
| We used to collect wood for the fire. | Nous ramassions du bois pour faire du feu. |
| My father used to go fishing. | Mon père allait à la pêche. |

* describe an interrupted action (say what someone/something was doing when something else happened):

| | |
|---|---|
| I was watching (*imperfect*) television when the phone rang (*perfect*). | Je regardais la télévision quand le téléphone a sonné. |

If you would use 'was/were' or 'used to' in English, you need to use the imperfect tense to say the same thing in French.

**If you know how to form the imperfect tense, go on to 1.4.8.**

To form the imperfect tense, you need to know the **nous** form of the present tense, e.g. **nous parlons**, **nous dormons**, **nous finissons**, **nous répondons**. Then take off the **-ons** and add the following endings. This is the same for all verbs except **être**.

| person | ending | example |
|---|---|---|
| je | -ais | je parlais |
| tu | -ais | tu parlais |
| il/elle | -ait | il/elle parlait |
| nous | -ions | nous parlions |
| vous | -iez | vous parliez |
| ils/elles | -aient | ils/elles parlaient |

**I**  What were they doing when the lights went out?

**a** Mon mari ___ devant la télévision. (dormir)
**b** Jean-Claude ___ la télévision. (regarder)
**c** Mélanie ___ une revue. (lire)
**d** Je ___ avec ma voisine. (discuter)
**e** Nous ___ du nouveau premier ministre. (parler)
**f** Sandrine ___ une douche. (prendre)
**g** François ___ à sa petite amie. (téléphoner)
**h** Laurence et son amie ___ leurs motos dans le garage. (réparer)
**i** Nicolas et Alexandre ___ au billard dans la salle de jeux. (jouer)

A  Verbs with regular *nous* form in the present tense

| infinitive | *nous* | imperfect |
|---|---|---|
| avoir | avons | j'avais |
| aller | allons | j'allais |
| habiter | habitons | j'habitais |
| dormir | dormons | je dormais |
| finir | finissons | je finissais |
| répondre | répondons | je répondais |
| se lever | levons | je me levais |

B  Verbs with irregular *nous* forms in the present tense
These verbs are irregular in the **nous** form of the present tense, but they work in just the same way.

| infinitive | *nous* | imperfect |
|---|---|---|
| boire | buvons | je buvais |
| croire | croyons | je croyais |
| écrire | écrivons | j'écrivais |
| finir | finissons | je finissais |
| manger | mangeons* | je mangeais |
| lire | lisons | je lisais |
| faire | faisons | je faisais |
| voir | voyons | je voyais |

**II**   Give the correct form of **avoir**.

**a** She was ten.                    Elle ___ dix ans.
**b** They were hungry.               Ils ___ faim.
**c** We were thirsty.                Nous ___ soif.
**d** You were late.                  Vous ___ du retard.
**e** I had a terrible headache.      J'___ un mal de tête affreux.

For expressions with **avoir** see 1.8.1.

C   *Être* – a special case
    **Être** is a special case: the imperfect is formed from the **vous**
    form: *êtes* → *étais* (note the change of accent).

**III**   Now do the same with **être**.

**a** He was young.                   Il ___ jeune.
**b** They were handsome.             Ils ___ beaux.
**c** You were magnificent.           Vous ___ magnifique!
**d** It was sad.                     C'___ triste.
**e** We were tired.                  Nous ___ fatigués.

**IV**   Give the correct form of the imperfect.

**a** J'___ à l'arrêt du bus. (attendre)
**b** Tu ___ Milène Farmer sur ton baladeur. (écouter)
**c** Nous ___ en ville. (aller)
**d** Patrice ___ le journal. (lire)
**e** Il ___ sa petite amie. (attendre)
**f** Martin ___ de chez lui. (sortir)
**g** Ses parents ___ à la campagne. (être)
**h** Sylvie ___ du jogging. (faire)
**i** Vous ___ la télévision. (regarder)
**j** Mon père ___ un apéritif. (boire)

**V**   Complete the sentences by adding the correct form of the
        imperfect.

**a** Il ___ beau. (faire)
**b** Il ___. (neiger)*

\*In written French when **g** is followed by **a** or
**o**, you need to add an **e** to keep the sound soft.

**d** Le vent ___. (souffler)

**e** Le soleil ___. (briller)

**f** Il ___. (pleuvoir)

**g** La brume ___. (se dissiper)

**h** Il ___. chaud. (faire)

**i** Il y ___ un orage. (avoir)

**j** La mer ___ agitée. (être)

**VI** In the old days ...

**a** Quand mon arrière-grand-père ___ petit, il ___ à la campagne. (être, habiter)

**b** Les maisons ___ construites en pierre. (être)

**c** Il y ___ moins de vingt habitants dans son village. (avoir)

**d** On ___ la vigne. (cultiver)

**e** Les enfants ___ dans les champs. (travailler)

**f** Ils ___ le raisin. (cueillir)

**g** Leurs parents ___ du vin. (faire)

**h** Il n'y ___ pas d'éléctricité. (avoir)

**i** Sa mère ___ au feu de bois. (cuisiner)

**j** Il ___ aller partout à pied. (devoir)

**k** Pour aller à l'école, il y ___ une heure de marche. (avait)

# 1.4.8 Perfect or imperfect?

Remember to use the imperfect tense for the action that was ongoing, and the perfect tense for the action that 'interrupted' it.

**I** You need to use both the imperfect and the perfect in these sentences. Think carefully!

**a** Ses parents ___ (habiter) à Nice quand Sophie ___ (naître).

**b** Quand elle ___ (être) petite, sa famille ___ (déménager) à Paris.

**c** Elle ___ (avoir) cinq ans quand son frère ___ (naître).

**d** Il ___ (avoir) un accident quand il ___ (avoir) dix ans.

**e** Il ___ (traverser) la rue quand une voiture ___ (griller) le feu rouge.

**f** Sophie ___ (voir) l'accident pendant qu'elle ___ (attendre) le bus.

**g** Elle ___ (avoir) dix-neuf ans quand elle ___ (passer) son bac.

**h** Elle ___ (faire) des études de biologie quand elle ___ (décider) de quitter l'université.

**i** Elle ___ (suivre) des cours de dactylo quand elle ___ (voir) l'annonce de Megasoc.

**j** Elle ___ (travailler) dans la société quand elle ___ (rencontrer) son futur mari.

**k** Elle ___ (être) chef du personnel quand il ___ (poser) sa candidature.

**l** Il ___ (faire) beau quand ils ___ (se marier).

## Checklist: imperfect

- The imperfect tense is easy, as it is always formed in the same way. Take the **nous** form of the verb in the present tense, remove the **-ons** and add the new endings.
- The endings are the same for all verbs, and only the **nous** and **vous** forms are pronounced differently: **-ais, -ais, -ait, -ions, -iez, -aient**.
- You are most likely to need the imperfect tense when talking about yourself or about the weather: **j'étais content(e)**, **il faisait beau**, **il y avait du soleil**, etc.

## 1.4.9 ▶**Fast track:** The past tenses

There are different ways of saying what has happened in the past.

### The perfect tense

This is the most used tense. It is used to describe an action in the past which has been completed.

 If you use a time phrase referring to the past: *yesterday, last month, this morning*, etc., you use the perfect tense.

The perfect tense is made up of an 'auxiliary' ('helper') verb and the past participle, as in the English:

J'ai mangé. – I have eaten.

In French most verbs go with **avoir**. But some verbs go with **être** and these can be remembered as the going and coming verbs: **aller/venir**; **arriver/partir**; **entrer/sortir**; **monter/descendre**; **rester/tomber** and **naître/mourir**.

The phrase you are likely to need most is:

Je suis allé(e). – I went (lit: I have gone).

**Past participle agreement**

You only need this in written French as the endings all sound the same.

If the subject of the verb is:

- female you add **-e** to the past participle: **elle est allée**
- plural you add **-s** to the past participle: **ils sont allés**
- plural and female you add **-es** to the past participle: **elles sont allées**.

## The imperfect tense

The imperfect is used to talk about an ongoing or habitual action in the past.

 If you can use *was/were* or *used to* in English you use the imperfect tense in French.

It is formed by adding the endings **-ais, -ais, -ait, -ions, -iez, -aient** to the **nous** form of the verb in the present tense. Most verbs are regular in the **nous** form.

Verbs to watch: **finissais**; **buvais**; **écrivais**; **faisais**; **lisais**; **voyais**; **prenais**; **croyais**; **voyais**.

**Être** is always different: **étais, étais, était, étions, étiez, étaient**.

Spelling note: verbs ending in **-ger** keep the **e** when followed by **a** to keep the **g** sound soft:

je nageais – I used to swim/I was swimming

# 1.5 The future tenses and conditional tense

You use the future tense to talk about something that is going to happen, something you want to do or something you are going to do in the future. In French, just as in English, there are two ways of saying what is going to happen.

### A The 'near future'

This is like the English *I am going to ...*, e.g. *I am going to go, He is going to play*, and is made up of **aller** (*to go*) and the main verb, just as it is in English.

Je vais sortir. I am going to go out.

This is the most useful future tense to learn as it is the one used most frequently in conversation, usually when you would use *going to* in English.

### B The future

This is the 'proper' future tense. It translates the English *will* and can imply intention as well as future action, e.g. *He will go – I will make sure he does!*

je jouerai — I will play
il ira — he will go
ils écouteront — they will listen

The future tense is the easier tense to use if you are going to list a lot of things that you are going to do or that will happen. This avoids having to repeat **aller** all the time.

C   The conditional

This is not strictly considered a future tense but it talks about the future: what you would do if ...

It translates *would/should/could* in English. *I would like to go: if* ..., talking about something you would like to do in the future.

> I would like to go to Paris. We really should/ought to go. Could we go tomorrow?

It is also used as a more polite way of stating or asking for something:

> I would like a glass of wine. Je voudrais un verre de vin.

# 1.5.1   The near future: 'I am going to ...'

 **If you know all about the near future, go on to 1.5.2.**

To make the near future, you need to know the present tense of the verb **aller** and the infinitive of the verb you want to use.

**aller**

| singular | meaning | plural | meaning |
|----------|---------|--------|---------|
| je vais | I am going | nous allons | we are going |
| tu vas | you are going | vous allez | you are going |
| il/elle va | he/she is going | ils/elles vont | they are going |

| | |
|---|---|
| Je vais dîner plus tard. | I am going to have dinner later. |
| Tu vas regarder l'émission. | You are going to watch the programme. |
| Il va arriver en retard. | He is going to arrive late. |
| Nous allons déjeuner. | We are going to have lunch. |
| Vous allez visiter le musée. | You are going to visit the museum. |
| Ils vont faire du ski. | They are going to go skiing. |

**I**   What are these people going to do? Complete the sentences by adding the correct form of the verb **aller**.

**a** Je ___ faire de la planche à voile.
**b** Tu ___ faire du parapente.
**c** Maurice ___ faire du rafting.
**d** Nous ___ faire du VTT.
**e** Vous ___ faire du ski de fond.
**f** Nathalie et Simon ___ faire du surf de neige.
**g** Vous ___ faire du canyoning?
**h** Patrice et Benjamin ___ faire de l'escalade.
**i** Ce soir, je ___ rester à la maison.
**j** Mes parents ___ aller au cinema.

**II**   What are they going to do for Bénédicte's birthday? Add the missing part of **aller**.

**a** Ses collègues ___ organiser une fête.
**b** Thomas ___ faire un gâteau.
**c** Sabine ___ envoyer les invitations.
**d** Isabelle et Sylvie ___ préparer le buffet.
**e** Olivier ___ aller acheter du champagne.
**f** Son chef ___ lui offrir un cadeau.
**g** Roland ___ décorer la pièce.
**h** Nous ___ aider Roland.
**i** Sylvain ___ aller chercher des verres.
**j** Vous ___ chanter «Bon anniversaire».

## 1.5.2   The future tense: 'I will …'

▶▶   **If you know about the future tense, go on to 1.5.3.**

This is the 'proper' future tense. It translates the English *will* and is used to talk about events which will take place in the future.

| | |
|---|---|
| je jouerai | I will play |
| il ira | he will go |
| ils écouteront | they will listen |

A   Regular verbs

Fortunately, most verbs are regular in the future tense!

The future is made by adding these endings to the infinitive: **-ai, -as, -a, -ons, -ez, -ont**. If the infinitive ends in -e, take the **-e** off first: **comprendre → je comprendrai.**

Notice the endings are the same as the verb **avoir** (but without the **av-** in the **nous** and **vous** forms).

This may help you to remember the future tense.

| -er verbs | -ir verbs | -re verbs |
|---|---|---|
| **je parlerai** | **je finirai** | **je répondrai** |
| tu parleras | tu finiras | tu répondras |
| il/elle parlera | il/elle finira | il/elle répondra |
| nous parlerons | nous finirons | nous répondrons |
| vous parlerez | vous finirez | vous répondrez |
| ils/elles parleront | ils/elles finiront | ils/elles répondront |

 If you have had enough of tenses, just learn the **je** form and go on to 1.15.3.

**I** Give the correct future tense of the verbs in brackets.

**a** nous ___ (regarder)
**b** tu ___ (préparer)
**c** vous ___ (mettre)
**d** ils ___ (manger)
**e** il ___ (prendre)
**f** vous ___ (sortir)
**g** elles ___ (arriver)
**h** nous ___ (entrer)
**i** je ___ (partir)
**j** elle ___ (porter)

**II** What are they going to wear for the Mardi Gras carnival? Use the correct form of **porter**.

**a** Je ___ le costume traditionnel du pays niçois.
**b** Juliette ___ une jupe fleurie et une blouse blanche.
**c** Mon ami ___ son costume noir et une écharpe blanche.
**d** Nicolas ___ son jean délavé et un vieux tee-shirt, comme d'habitude.
**e** Mes amies ___ leurs robes traditionnelles brodées.
**f** Mes amis ___ un pantalon noir et une chemise blanche.
**g** Nous ___ des chaussettes blanches et des chaussures noires.
**h** Et vous, que ___-vous?

B Irregular verbs

Some of the most common verbs are irregular in the future tense.

 Look for patterns to help you remember the irregular futures. Choose the four that you think you are most likely to need, and learn the **je** form of them.

| infinitive | future | meaning |
|---|---|---|
| être | je serai, tu seras, … | I will be |
| avoir | j'aurai, tu auras, … | I will have |
| aller | j'irai, tu iras, … | I will go |
| faire | je ferai, tu feras, … | I will do/make |
| devoir | je devrai, tu devras, … | I will have to |
| pouvoir | je pourrai, tu pourras, … | I will be able to |
| savoir | je saurai, tu sauras, … | I will know |
| voir | je verrai, tu verras, … | I will see |
| vouloir | je voudrai, tu voudras, … | I will want to |
| falloir | il faudra | it will be necessary to |
| venir | je viendrai, tu viendras, … | I will come |
| tenir | je tiendrai, tu tiendras, … | I will hold |
| envoyer | j'enverrai, tu enverras, … | I will send |
| acheter | j'achèterai, tu achèteras, … | I will buy |
| amener | j'amènerai, tu amèneras, … | I will bring |
| se lever | je me lèverai, tu te lèveras, … | I will get up |
| appeler | j'appellerai, tu appelleras, … | I will call |

**Useful expressions:**

| | |
|---|---|
| on verra | we will see |
| il faudra | it will be necessary to |
| il pleuvra | it will rain |

**III** For more practice give the correct future form of the verb in brackets.

**a** j'___ (aller)  **e** il ___ (être)  **i** vous ___ (savoir)
**b** vous ___ (venir)  **f** elle ___ (voir)  **j** elles ___ (tenir)
**c** tu ___ (faire)  **g** ils ___ (vouloir)  **k** il ___ (falloir)
**d** nous ___ (avoir)  **h** nous ___ (devoir)  **l** vous ___ (pouvoir)

**IV** Write in the correct future form of the verb in brackets.

**a** L'année prochaine, j' ___ vingt ans. (avoir)
**b** Actuellement, je fais mes études en France, mais l'année prochaine j'___ en Angleterre. (aller)
**c** Je ___ un stage de langue à Oxford. (faire)
**d** Je vous ___ ma nouvelle adresse. (envoyer)
**e** J'espère que vous ___ me voir à Oxford. (venir)
**f** Quand vous ___, on ___ à Londres ensemble. (venir, aller)
**g** Nous ___ également aller faire un tour en Écosse, mais il ___ apporter un imper parce qu'il ___ sûrement! (pouvoir, falloir, pleuvoir)
**h** Quand j'___ fini mon stage, je ___ pour mon père dans son bureau. (avoir, travailler)

**V** Before they leave they go over the travel arrangements with the travel agent. Add the correct future form of the verb in brackets.

**a** Quand ___ -nous? (partir)

**b** Vous ___ le vol Air Inter de 14h50. (prendre)

**c** Un bus vous ___ à l'arrivée et il vous ___ jusqu'au chalet. (attendre, emmener)

**d** Tout le monde ___ faire du ski. (pouvoir)

**e** À midi, vous ___ au chalet ou sur les pistes, comme vous ___. (déjeuner, vouloir)

**f** Le soir, vous ___ sortir. (pouvoir)

**g** Il ___ froid, vous ___ emporter des vêtements chauds. (faire, devoir)

# **1.5.3** The conditional: 'I would ...'

If you don't want to practise the conditional go to the fast track (page 75), as you might need to be able to recognise it when you hear it.

 You probably already know the expression **je voudrais** – *I would like.*

The conditional is used to translate *would, could, should*. It is called the conditional because you use it when you are making a condition: *I would go if you paid me!* But it is also used to be more polite: *I would like a box of chocolates.*

The conditional is easy to learn as it is very similar to the future tense: infinitive + endings.

The endings are the same as the imperfect endings: **-ais, -ais, -ait, -ions, -iez, -aient**.

## A Regular verbs

Just as with the future tense, you drop the final **-e** of an **-re** verb before adding the endings.

| -er verbs | -ir verbs | -re verbs |
|---|---|---|
| je jouerais | je finirais | je répondrais |
| tu jouerais | tu finirais | tu répondrais |
| il/elle jouerait | il/elle finirait | il/elle répondrait |
| nous jouerions | nous finirions | nous répondrions |
| vous joueriez | vous finiriez | vous répondriez |
| ils/elles joueraient | ils/elles finiraient | il/elles répondraient |

**I** How would you say the following?

I would …

**a** eat (manger)
**b** drink (boire)
**c** sleep (dormir)
**d** speak (parler)
**e** live (habiter)

**f** buy (acheter)
**g** ask (demander)
**h** listen (écouter)
**i** watch (regarder)

**II** Add the right conditional form of **jouer** to the following.

**a** Je ___ au tennis.
**b** Mon amie ___ aussi.
**c** Ses amies ___ aussi.
**d** Nous ne ___ pas.
**e** Vous ___ au volley.

I would play tennis.
My friend would play too.
Her friends would play too.
We wouldn't play.
You would play volleyball.

**III** Add the right conditional form of **préférer** to these sentences.

**a** Je ___ aller à la plage.

I would prefer to go to the beach.

**b** Mon petit ami ___ faire de la planche à voile.

My boyfriend would prefer to go windsurfing.

**c** Mes amies ___ aller en ville.

My girlfriends would prefer to go to town.

**d** Nous ___ manger au restaurant.

We would prefer to eat in a restaurant.

**e** Que ___-vous faire?

What would you prefer to do?

**IV** Now add the right conditional form of **aimer**.

**a** J'___ sortir.
**b** Gilles ___ rester à la maison.
**c** Patrice ___ aller au cinéma.

I would like to go out.
Gilles would like to stay in.
Patrice would like to go to the cinema.

**d** Mes parents ___ aller aux États-Unis.
**e** Qu'est-ce que vous ___ faire?

My parents would like to go to the United States.
What would you like to do?

B   Irregular verbs

These are just the same as in the future, but with the new endings.

| infinitive | conditional | meaning |
|---|---|---|
| être | je serais | I would be |
| avoir | j'aurais | I would have |
| aller | j'irais | I would go |
| faire | je ferais | I would do/make |
| devoir | je devrais | I ought to |
| pouvoir | je pourrais | I could |
| savoir | je saurais | I would know |
| voir | je verrais | I would see |
| vouloir | je voudrais | I would like |
| falloir | il faudrait | it would be necessary to |
| venir | je viendrais | I would come |
| tenir | je tiendrais | I would hold |
| envoyer | j'enverrais | I would send |
| acheter | j'achèterais | I would buy |
| amener | j'amènerais | I would bring |
| se lever | je me lèverais | I would get up |
| appeler | j'appellerais | I would call |

**V**   Talking about yourself: how would you say the following?

**a** Je ___ une baguette de campagne. (vouloir) — I would like a farmhouse baguette.
**b** J'___ en ville. (aller) — I would go to town.
**c** J'___ un ami. (avoir) — I would have a friend.
**d** Je ___ mes amis. (voir) — I would see my friends.
**e** J'___ en France. (aller) — I would go to France.
**f** Je ___ faire de la planche à voile. (pouvoir) — I could windsurf.
**g** Je ___ heureux/heureuse. (être) — I would be happy.
**h** Je ___ la réponse. (savoir) — I would know the answer.
**i** Je ___ sortir. (devoir) — I would have to go out.
**j** Je lui ___ la main. (tenir) — I would hold his hand.

**VI**   What could they do? Fill in the correct form of **pouvoir**.

**a** Nicole ___ rentrer chez elle. — Nicole could go home.
**b** Nous ___ aller au cinéma. — We could go to the cinema.
**c** Nous ___ aller au centre de loisirs. — We could go to the leisure centre.
**d** Je ___ faire du judo. — I could do judo.
**e** Vous ___ jouer au volley-ball. — You could play volleyball.
**f** Camille ___ faire du cheval. — Camille could go riding.

**g** Les enfants ___ aller à la piscine.  The children could go swimming.

**h** Nous ___ nous retrouver après.  We could meet afterwards.

**i** Vous ___ aller au McDo.  You could go to McDonald's.

**j** Ils ___ rentrer chez moi.  They could go back to my house.

## 1.5.4 ▶Fast track: Future and conditional

There are two ways of saying what you are going to do or what is going to happen.

- The **near future** is like the English. It is made up of the verb *to go* (**aller: je vais, tu vas, il/elle va, nous allons, vous allez, ils/elles vont**) + the infinitive.
- The **future tense** is made up of the infinitive and the endings: **-ai, -as, -a, -ons, -ez, -ont**.

 The pattern of the endings is like the present tense of **avoir**, without the **av-** in the **nous** and **vous** forms.

If you can't manage learning both ways at the moment concentrate on the **near future**, but you should be able to recognise the future when someone uses it. The two forms are often interchangeable.

The **near future** is used more than the future in conversation.

- If you would use *going to* in English use **aller** + infinitive in French.
- It is used for something that you really expect to happen or know is going to happen:

Elle va avoir un bébé.  She is going to have a baby (she is pregnant).

The **future** is sometimes used for something that you expect to happen.

- It is also used in lists where repeating **aller** would be clumsy to say.
- It can be used to talk about something that 'may' happen:

Elle aura un bébé.  She will have a baby (one day, eventually) ...

- These are the most commonly used future tenses. It is useful to be able to recognise which verb they come from:

| | | | | | |
|---|---|---|---|---|---|
| j'irai | aller | je ferai | faire | je viendrai | venir |
| j'aurai | avoir | je pourrai | pouvoir | je verrai | voir |
| je devrai | devoir | je prendrai | prendre | je voudrai | vouloir |
| je serai | être | je saurai | savoir | | |

The **conditional** translates *would*, e.g. *I would go, I would like.*

- You probably already know **je voudrais** (*I would like*), so you already know the ending.
- Remember that the endings for **je/tu/il/elle/on** and **ils/elles** all sound the same, so you just have to remember the **-ions** and **-iez** endings for **nous** and **vous**.
- The most useful conditionals are:

| | |
|---|---|
| je voudrais | I would like |
| j'aimerais | I would like |
| je préférerais | I would prefer |
| on pourrait | one/we could |
| on devrait | one/we should |
| il faudrait | it would be necessary to |

# 1.6 The subjunctive

▶▶ **If you are not ready for the subjunctive yet, go on to 1.7.**

The subjunctive is not used much in English any more (only in expressions such as *If I were you ...*), but it is still used in many expressions in French. You are not likely to need to use those expressions yourself but it is useful to be able to recognise them when you hear them and you may need to know which verb is being used. Choose one or two of the expressions to learn by heart and then use them as a model.

If you want to know more about the subjunctive go to *French Grammar and Usage*, R. Hawkins and R. Towell, 1996/2001, 2nd edn.

The subjunctive is nearly always preceded by the word **que**, but this does not mean that **que** is always followed by the subjunctive!

In French, the subjunctive is used after verbs expressing a wish or desire:

| | |
|---|---|
| I would like him to go. | J'aimerais qu'il parte. |
| I wish that he would come. | Je voudrais qu'il vienne. |

... or a requirement (after **il faut que** – *it is necessary that*):

| | |
|---|---|
| He must be able to drive. | Il faut qu'il sache conduire. |

... or a doubt or uncertainty:

| | |
|---|---|
| Je ne crois pas qu'il ait de l'argent. | I don't think (that) he has any money |
| Il est possible que les enfants soient fatigués. | It is possible that the children are tired. |

... and after certain fixed expressions:

| | |
|---|---|
| afin que | in order that |
| afin qu'il arrive à l'heure | in order that he arrives on time |
| bien que | although |
| bien qu'il parte à 6h00 | although he is leaving at 6 o'clock |
| avant que | before |
| avant qu'il achète son billet | before he buys his ticket |
| jusqu'à ce que | until |
| jusqu'à ce qu'il arrive à la gare | until he arrives at the station |

Remember: Most **-er** verbs sound the same in the normal present tense and the subjunctive.

## 1.6.1  How to form the subjunctive

The subjunctive is formed by taking the **ils** form of the present tense, removing the **-ent** and then adding these endings: **-e**, **-es**, **-e**, **-ions**, **-iez**, **-ent**.

Fortunately, in regular **-er** verbs (and therefore most verbs), in most persons it sounds just like the present, so you can't tell whether someone is using it or not.

Unfortunately, the verbs you use most are irregular. Even if you do not want to learn them, you should be able to recognise them.

### A  Regular verbs

| porter | finir | dormir | répondre |
|---|---|---|---|
| je porte | je finisse | je dorme | je réponde |
| tu portes | tu finisses | tu dormes | tu répondes |
| il/elle porte | il/elle finisse | il/elle dorme | il/elle réponde |
| nous portions | nous finissions | nous dormions | nous répondions |
| vous portiez | vous finissiez | vous dormiez | vous répondiez |
| ils/elles portent | ils/elles finissent | ils/elles dorment | ils/elles répondent |

B Irregular verbs

The most useful irregular verbs are:

| aller | avoir | être | faire |
|---|---|---|---|
| j'aille | j'aie | je sois | je fasse |
| tu ailles | tu aies | tu sois | tu fasses |
| il/elle aille | il/elle ait | il/elle soit | il/elle fasse |
| nous allions | nous ayons | nous soyons | nous fassions |
| vous alliez | vous ayez | vous soyez | vous fassiez |
| ils/elles aillent | ils/elles aient | ils/elles soient | ils/elles fassent |

| pouvoir | savoir | vouloir |
|---|---|---|
| je puisse | je sache | je veuille |
| tu puisses | tu saches | tu veuilles |
| il/elle puisse | il/elle sache | il/elle veuille |
| nous puissions | nous sachions | nous voulions |
| vous puissiez | vous sachiez | vous vouliez |
| ils/elles puissent | ils/elles sachent | ils/elles veuillent |

## 1.6.2 Expressions which take the subjunctive

These expressions are always followed by the subjunctive.
Choose two to memorise to use as a pattern.

### Expressions of necessity

Il faut que je parte. — I have to go.
Il faut qu'elle sache. — She has to know.

### Wishes or preferences

Je veux qu'il soit à l'heure. — I want him to be on time.
Il préfère que j'y aille. — He prefers me to go (there).

### Possibility

Il est possible qu'il puisse venir. — It is possible that he can come.
Il est impossible qu'il soit en retard. — It is not possible for him to be late.

### Doubt and disbelief

Je ne crois pas qu'il soit malade. — I don't believe that he is ill.
Je doute qu'elle vienne. — I don't think she will come.

### Regret

Je regrette qu'il ait été blessé. — I'm sorry that he has been hurt.
Il est dommage que vous ne puissiez pas venir. — It's a pity that you can't come.

*Bien que* – **although**

| | |
|---|---|
| Bien que vous soyez malade, vous devez vous présenter au tribunal. | Although you are ill, you have to go to court. |

## 1.6.3 Recognising the subjunctive

Even if you do not feel ready to use the subjunctive yet, it is useful to be able to recognise it when you hear it.

**I** Which verb is being used? Read the sentence and work out the infinitive of the word in italics.

| | | |
|---|---|---|
| **a** | Il faut qu'il *vienne*. | He must come. |
| **b** | Je ne crois pas qu'il *prenne* le bus. | I don't believe he'll come by bus. |
| **c** | Je regrette qu'il ne *fasse* pas beau aujourd'hui. | I'm sorry that the weather is not fine today. |
| **d** | *Soyez* le bienvenu! | Welcome! |
| **e** | Il est possible qu'ils *soient* malades. | It's possible that they are ill. |
| **f** | Bien qu'elle *ait* une voiture, elle préfère prendre le métro. | Although she has a car, she prefers to take the tube. |
| **g** | Il faut qu'elle *sache*. | She will have to know. |
| **h** | Il est impossible que le chantier *puisse* être terminé dans les temps. | It's impossible for the work to be completed in time. |
| **i** | Je doute qu'ils *aient* une nouvelle voiture. | I don't think (I doubt) that they have a new car. |
| **j** | Je regrette que vous *vouliez* partir. | I am sorry that you want to go. |

## 1.6.4 ▶**Fast track:** The subjunctive

The subjunctive is used after certain verbs and expressions. It usually conveys a feeling of negativity, uncertainty, doubt or indecision: *I don't want (that) ..., I am not sure that ..., it is possible that ...* etc.

- It is usually preceded by another verb and **que** – *that. I hope/wish/doubt that ...*
- This means it is usually the second verb in the sentence.
- The subjunctive of most verbs is made from the **ils** form of the present tense. Remove the **-ent** and then add these endings: **-e, -es, -e, -ions, -iez, -ent**.
- In most **-er** verbs the subjunctive is just like the present tense:

| | |
|---|---|
| I'm glad that he arrives soon. | Je suis contente qu'il arrive bientôt. |

- In most verbs it *sounds* just like the present tense:

  I don't think he'll talk – Je ne pense pas qu'il parle

- Unfortunately the most-used verbs are irregular. You don't need to learn them but it is useful to be able to recognise which verb they come from:

  | aller | j'aille |
  | avoir | j'aie |
  | être | je sois |
  | faire | je fasse |
  | pouvoir | je puisse |
  | prendre | je prenne |
  | venir | je vienne |
  | savoir | je sache |
  | vouloir | je veuille |

You can try to avoid using the subjunctive by:

- being positive and avoiding making negative statements!
- using: **selon moi** or **à mon avis** to express an opinion;
- using the infinitive instead of **que** + subjunctive where possible:
  Il faut qu'on boive 2 litres d'eau par jour (*We have to drink 2 litres of water a day*) becomes: Il faut boire 2 litres d'eau par jour.
- using the verb **devoir** instead of the expression **il faut que**:
  Il faut que je parte becomes Je dois partir.
- thinking of an easier way of saying it in English. Don't use two verbs joined by *that* in one sentence. Split it up and make two sentences:
  *I am sorry that he is ill.* Je regrette qu'il soit malade becomes:
  Il est malade? Oh, je suis désolé!
- choose two or three examples to memorise and use them as a pattern.

Just when you think you have learned all the tenses, you pick up a book or a newspaper and find that there are even more. Fortunately, you don't have to learn to use them to speak good French. If you want to know more about these other tenses go to *French Grammar and Usage*, R. Hawkins and R. Towell, 1996/2001, 2nd edn.

# 1.7 ▶Fast track: Verbs

▶▶ **If you know how to use different verbs, go on to 1.8.**

A Present tense

You use the present tense to talk about what is happening now ...

| Je lis | I am reading |

... and to express generalisations:

| Je ne regarde pas la télé réalité. | I don't watch reality TV. |

These are the question forms:

| Lisez-vous le journal? | Do you read a daily paper? |
| Regardez-vous ...? | Do you watch ...? |

B Interrogative

The interrogative is used to ask questions.

| Avez-vous un ...? | Have you got a ...? |
| Avez-vous vu ...? | Did you see ...? |

C Imperative

The imperative is used to give orders or instructions.

| Va me chercher mes pantoufles! | Fetch me my slippers! (to the dog, hence the **tu** form) |
| Fermez la porte! | Shut the door! |

D Perfect tense

You use the perfect tense to talk about what has happened in the past.

| J'ai joué au tennis. | I played tennis. |
| J'ai essayé. | I have tried. |

These are the question forms:

| Avez-vous joué? | Have you played? |
| Avez-vous essayé? | Did you try? |

E Imperfect tense

You use the imperfect tense to talk about what has happened in the past if:

- it was a habitual action:

Je jouais quand j'étais petit(e).     I used to play when I was young.

- it was an ongoing and interrupted action:

Je regardais la télévision quand     I was watching television
j'ai entendu les voisins se disputer.   when I heard the neighbours arguing.

These are the question forms:

Jouiez-vous …?               Did you use to play …?
Regardiez-vous la télévision     Were you watching
quand …?                   television when …?

F Near future

You use the near future to translate what you are going to do.

Je vais venir.            I am going to come.
Il va partir.             He is going to leave.

These are the question forms.

Allez-vous venir?        Are you going to come?
Va-t-il partir?          Is he going to leave?

G Future

The future tense is used to express intention of what you will do in the future.

Je rangerai mon bureau la semaine   I will tidy my office next
prochaine.                week.
Quand nous irons en France,     When we (will) go to France,
j'irai voir …            I will go and see …

These are the question forms.

Que ferez-vous?        What will you do?
Quand partirez-vous?     When will you leave?

H Conditional

The conditional is used to put things more politely …

Je voudrais …           I would like …
Pourriez-vous m'aider?     Could you help me?

… or to express conditions.

Je vous achèterais un cadeau    I would buy you a present if
si j'avais assez d'argent.      I had enough money.

| Subjunctive

The subjunctive is used after certain verbs and expressions. It is usually preceded by another verb and **que** meaning *that*. You can avoid having to use it yourself by keeping sentences simple.

Most verbs sound the same as in the present tense but some irregular verbs sound quite different and it is useful to be able to recognise which verb they come from:

soit – être
aie – avoir
aille – aller
fasse – faire
puisse – pouvoir
sache – savoir

**Recognising a verb**

■ If a word that you don't know comes after a noun (e.g. **la ville**), the name of a person, or a pronoun (**je, tu, il/elle, nous, vous, ils/elles**), it is probably a verb.

■ If it ends in **-e**, **-es**, **-ons**, **-ez**, **-ent**, **-s**, **-t**, or **-ont**, it is probably a verb in the present tense.

■ If it comes after a part of **avoir** or **être** and ends with **é(e/s)**, **u(e/s)** or **i(e/s)**, it is probably the past participle of a verb.

■ If it ends in **-ais**, **-ait**, **-ions**, **-iez** or **-aient**, it is probably the imperfect tense of a verb.

■ If it ends in **-rai**, **-ras**, **-ra**, **-rons**, **-rez** or **-ront**, it is probably a verb in the future.

■ If it ends in **-rais**, **-rait**, **-rions**, **-riez** or **-raient**, it is probably the conditional of a verb.

# 1.8 Useful expressions using verbs

▶▶ **If you know all these, go on to 1.9.**

## 1.8.1 Special uses of *avoir*

**avoir**

| | |
|---|---|
| j'ai | nous avons |
| tu as | vous avez |
| il/elle a | ils/elles ont |

**Avoir** is used in some expressions where *have* is not used in English. Here are some examples.

## A When talking about one's age

You use **avoir** to say how old you are.

| | |
|---|---|
| J'ai trente ans. | I am 30. (lit: I have 30 years.) |
| Quel âge as-tu? | How old are you? |
| Il a dix ans. | He is ten. |
| Nous avons 29 et 30 ans. | We are 29 and 30 years old. |
| Vous avez quel âge? | How old are you? |
| Ils ont 50 ans. | They are 50. |

Now say how old you are: **J'ai ___ ans.**

## B Saying what you need

**avoir besoin de** – *to need*

| | |
|---|---|
| J'ai besoin d'un marteau. | I need a hammer. |
| As-tu besoin d'aide? | Do you need help? |
| Il a besoin de dormir. | He needs to sleep. |
| Nous avons besoin d'argent. | We need some money. |
| Avez-vous besoin de nous? | Do you need us? |
| Ils ont besoin d'une maison plus grande. | They need a bigger house. |

## C Expressing *fear*

**avoir peur de** – *to be afraid of*

| | |
|---|---|
| J'ai peur de l'altitude. | I am afraid of heights. |
| As-tu le vertige? | Do you suffer from vertigo? |
| Elle a peur des araignées. | She is afraid of spiders. |
| Nous avons peur de l'orage. | We are afraid of thunderstorms. |
| Avez-vous peur des fantômes? | Are you afraid of ghosts? |
| Ils n'ont pas peur de voyous. | They are not afraid of hooligans. |

## D Expressing *cold and heat*

**avoir froid/chaud** – *to be cold/hot*

| | |
|---|---|
| J'ai froid. | I am cold. |
| As-tu froid? | Are you cold? |
| Il n'a pas froid. | He is not cold. |
| Nous avons chaud. | We are hot. |
| Avez-vous trop chaud? | Are you too hot? |
| Ils ont chaud. | They are hot. |

## E Expressing *hunger and thirst*

**avoir faim/soif** – *to be hungry/thirsty*

| | |
|---|---|
| J'ai faim. | I am hungry. |
| N'as-tu pas faim? | Aren't you hungry? |
| Il a soif. | He is thirsty. |
| Nous avons soif. | We are thirsty. |
| Avez-vous faim? | Are you hungry? |
| Ils ont faim. | They are hungry. |

## F Being *right or wrong*

**avoir raison/tort** – *to be right/wrong*

| | |
|---|---|
| J'ai raison. | I am right. |
| Tu as raison! | You are right! |
| Il a tort. | He is wrong. |
| Nous avons raison. | We are right. |
| Vous avez tort! | You are wrong! |
| Ils ont tort. | They are wrong. |

## Checklist

These expressions take **avoir** in French:

| | |
|---|---|
| avoir … ans | to be … years old |
| avoir besoin de | to need |
| avoir peur de | to be afraid of |
| avoir froid/chaud | to be cold/hot |
| avoir faim/soif | to be hungry/thirsty |
| avoir raison/tort | to be right/wrong |

**I** How would you say the following?

**a** We are right.
**b** You are wrong.
**c** I am hot.
**d** He is thirsty.
**e** They are hungry.

**f** We are cold.
**g** I am thirsty.
**h** I need a beer.
**i** We need a new car.
**j** I am right.

And some more:

**k** They are wrong.
**l** I am very cold.
**m** They are hot.
**n** We are thirsty.
**o** I am afraid of spiders.
**p** Are you thirsty?
**q** Are you cold?
**r** Are you hot?

**s** Are you hungry?
**t** Are you right?
**u** You are wrong!
**v** Are you afraid?
**w** I am not afraid.
**x** He is not afraid.
**y** We are not afraid.
**z** He is always right.

## 1.8.2 There is/there are: *il y a*

*There is* and *there are* are both translated by **il y a** in French.
To say *there isn't* or *there aren't* add **ne … pas – il n'y a pas de**

*There was* and *there were* are both **il y avait**.
*There wasn't/there weren't* – **Il n'y avait pas de** …

| | |
|---|---|
| Il y a une déchetterie au coin, mais elle est toujours pleine. | There is a waste collection point on the corner but it's always full. |
| Il n'y a jamais de place. | There's never any space. |
| Il y avait un bar, mais comme il n'y avait pas assez de clients, il a fermé. | There was a bar but as there weren't enough customers it shut. |

**I**   Now you try it.

**a** Il ____ de banque mais il ____ un distributeur automatique de billets.   There isn't a bank but there is a cash machine.

**b** Il ____ beaucoup de caisses au supermarché, mais il ____ assez de caissiers.   There are lots of checkouts at the supermarket but there aren't enough cashiers.

**c** Heureusement, aujourd'hui, il ____ de queue.   Luckily today there wasn't a queue.

**d** Il ____ un car de ramassage scolaire mais aujourd'hui, il ____ assez d'enfants.   There used to be a school bus, but now there aren't enough children.

## 1.8.3 To know: *connaître* or *savoir?*

There are two verbs meaning *to know* in French – to know a person or thing (**connaître**) and to know a fact (**savoir**).

**Connaître** is to know a person, thing or place (to recognise by seeing, hearing, tasting or touching):

je connais; tu connais; il/elle connaît; nous connaissons; vous connaissez; ils connaissent

| | |
|---|---|
| Je le connais. | I know it/him. |
| Je l'ai connu. | I knew it/him/her. |

**Savoir** is to know something or how to do something (as a result of learning how to do it).

je sais; tu sais; il/elle sait; nous savons; vous savez; ils savent

| | |
|---|---|
| Je le sais. | I know. |
| Je sais conduire. | I can/I know how to drive a car. |
| Je savais cuisiner. | I used to know how to cook. |

**I**  Which part of which verb are you going to use? Use the present tense.

**a** Je ___ M. Peugeot depuis longtemps.
**b** Son fils ___ mon fils.
**c** Nos enfants ___ envoyer des méls.
**d** Nous ___ la famille.
**e** Ma femme ___ sa femme.
**f** Mes parents ___ ses parents.
**g** Ils ___ bien la région où ils habitent.
**h** Ma femme et moi, nous ne ___ pas envoyer des méls.
**i** Mes parents ne ___ même pas utiliser un portable.
**j** Ma fille ___ envoyer des photos par portable.
**k** Je ne ___ même pas envoyer des photos par mél.

## 1.8.4  To take and to bring

These English verbs can be translated in various ways.

- **prendre** – *to take transport*
  Je prends le bus.                I am taking the bus.
- **emporter** – *to take away* (something you can carry)
  une pizza à emporter           a take-away pizza
- **emmener** – *to take* (someone somewhere)
  J'ai emmené ma tante à          I took my aunt to the
  l'aéroport.                     airport.
- **apporter** – *to bring* (something you can carry)
  Je vous ai apporté un gâteau.   I have brought you a cake.
- **amener** – *to bring* (someone somewhere)
  Amenez un ami à la fête ce      Bring a guest to the party
  soir, si vous voulez.           tonight, if you like.

This phrase will help you remember *to take away*:

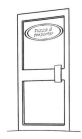

**Pizza à emporter**

## **1.8.5** To remember: *se souvenir de*

**se souvenir de** – *to remember* (lit: to remind yourself of something/someone)

| | |
|---|---|
| Je me souviens de Marc. | I remember Marc. |
| Il ne se souvient pas de moi. | He doesn't remember me. |
| Nous nous souvenons du jour où il est arrivé. | We remember the day when he arrived. |
| Je me souviendrai toujours du moment où j'ai eu mon accident. | I'll always remember the moment when I had the accident. |
| Je m'en souviens. | I remember it. |
| Mes parents ne s'en souviennent pas. | My parents don't remember it. |

**I**   How would you say the following?

**a** I remember John.
**b** He remembers me.
**c** He remembers my house.
**d** We remember the holidays.
**e** I remember his wife.
**f** I remember her smile.
**g** My children remember her.

 If you are not comfortable using **se souvenir de**, use **oublier** – *to forget*, and say *you haven't forgotten*.

On n'oublie pas Lionel. – One doesn't forget Lionel.
Je n'oublie pas les vacances. – I don't forget the holidays.

## **1.8.6** More negative expressions

Negative statements include saying what you don't do (*not*), and expressions with *no longer, nothing, never, nobody,* etc.

**ne … pas** – *not*

You already know to put **ne** in front of the verb and **pas** after the verb, for the simple negative *not*.

| | |
|---|---|
| Je ne sais pas. | I don't know. |
| Je ne parle pas français. | I don't speak French. |
| Je ne mange pas de viande. | I don't eat meat. |
| Il ne boit pas de vin. | He doesn't drink wine. |
| Ils n'habitent pas à Paris. | They don't live in Paris. |
| Vous n'êtes pas marié(e)? | You aren't married? |

There are other negative expressions where **pas** is replaced by a different word.

**ne ... plus** – *no longer/no more*

| | |
|---|---|
| Nous n'allons plus en ville. | We no longer go into town./We don't go to town any more. |

**ne ... que** – *only*

| | |
|---|---|
| Il ne boit que du coca. | He only drinks coca cola. |

**ne ... jamais** – *never*

| | |
|---|---|
| Elle n'est jamais allée à Paris. | She has never been to Paris. |

**ne ... rien** – *nothing/not anything*

| | |
|---|---|
| Je n'ai rien fait. | I didn't do anything. |

**ne ... personne** – *nobody/no one*

| | |
|---|---|
| Il n'a vu personne. | He didn't see anyone. |

> Remember to use **de** to replace **du/de la/des** after all negative expressions except **ne ... que**:
> Il ne boit pas de vin.
> Il ne boit que du vin.

**I** How would you say the following?

**a** I have never been to France.　Je ___ suis ___ allé(e) en France.

**b** They didn't hurt anyone.　Ils ___ ont fait de mal à ___.

**c** I don't see Aline any more.　Je ___ vois ___ Aline.

**d** They only have a small house.　Ils ___ ont ___ une petite maison.

**e** You have never learned to swim?　Vous ___ avez ___ appris à nager?

**f** I don't see anybody.　Je ___ vois ___.

**g** She doesn't ride a bike any more.　Elle ___ fait ___ de vélo.

**h** I have only ten euros left.　Il ___ me reste ___ dix euros.

**i** We only have a black and white printer.　Nous ___ avons ___ une imprimante noir et blanc.

**j** They never do anything.　Ils ___ font ___ rien.

**k** I didn't see anybody.　Je ___ ai vu ___.

**l** He has never seen Frédéric.　Il ___ a ___ vu Frédéric.

**m** Jean-Luc did nothing.　Jean-Luc ___ a ___ fait.

**n** Nobody saw Jean-Luc.    ＿＿ a vu Jean-Luc.
**o** We have never eaten in    Nous ＿＿ avons ＿＿ dîné
that restaurant.    dans ce restaurant.
**p** They don't live in Paris    Ils ＿＿ habitent ＿＿ à Paris.
any longer.
**q** There is only one    Il ＿＿ y a ＿＿ une chambre.
bedroom.
**r** I don't have anything.    Je ＿＿ ai ＿＿.
**s** He doesn't listen to his    Il ＿＿ écoute ＿＿ sa femme.
wife any more.
**t** You never do anything!    Vous ＿＿ faites ＿＿ rien.

Check your answers. If possible, then say the sentences aloud so that you can get used to the sound of them. Then cover up the English, read them again and think about the meaning. Finally cover up the French and translate the whole sentence.

**II** Match up these sentences.

**a** We haven't anything to    Je n'ai pas eu le temps d'aller en
eat.    ville.
**b** Nobody has been    Il n'y a que du pain et du
shopping.    fromage.
**c** I didn't have time to go    Je n'ai plus d'argent.
to town.    Nous n'avons rien à manger.
**d** There is only some bread    Vous n'allez jamais au
and cheese.    supermarché.
**e** You never go to the    Personne n'a fait les courses.
supermarket.
**f** I haven't any more money.

## 1.8.7 Question words and word order: *Comment...?*

| Comment? | How? |
| Où? | Where? |
| Quand? | When? |
| Pourquoi? | Why? |
| Combien? | How much/many? |
| Combien de temps? | How long? |
| Que ...? | What ...? |
| Qui? | Who? |

After these question words you invert the order of the subject and the verb. (See pages 24 and 45.)

| Où allez-vous? | Where are you going? |
| Comment va-t-il à Paris? | How is he going to Paris? |
| Pourquoi est-elle à Paris? | Why is she in Paris? |
| Quand partez-vous? | When are you leaving? |

| Que faites-vous? | What are you doing? |
| Qui connaissez-vous? | Who do you know? |
| Combien de chambres avez-vous? | How many bedrooms do you have? |

You can also use **est-ce que** after the question words and then you don't need to invert the subject and the verb.

| Où est-ce que vous allez? | Where are you going? |
| Comment est-ce qu'il va à Paris? | How is he going to Paris? |
| Pourquoi est-ce que vous allez à Paris? | Why are you going to Paris? |
| Quand est-ce que je dois partir? | When do I have to leave? |
| Qu'est-ce qu'il fait? | What is he doing? |
| Qui est-ce que vous connaissez déjà? | Who do you know already? |
| Combien de chambres est-ce qu'il y a? | How many rooms are there? |

 Use: **Qu'est-ce que …?**, **Où est-ce que …?** etc., if you are not happy with inverting the order.

**I**  Which question word would you use?

| **a** ___ habite M. Vincent? | Where does Mr Vincent live? |
| **b** ___ s'appelle sa femme? | What is his wife called? |
| **c** ___ partent-ils pour Londres? | When are they leaving for London? |
| **d** ___ va-t-il à Londres? | Why is he going to London? |
| **e** ___ va-t-il faire à Londres? | What is he going to do in London? |
| **f** ___ a-t-il rendez-vous à la banque? | When does he have a meeting at the bank? |
| **g** ___ de jours reste-t-il à Londres? | How many days is he staying in London? |
| **h** ___ connaît-il à Londres? | Who does he know in London? |

## 1.8.8  Since (*depuis*); to have just (*venir de*)

In these expressions, you use a different tense in French from the one you would expect to use in English.

### A  Depuis – *since*

In English, when we want to say we have been doing something for a certain length of time, we use the past tense. In French, they say they have been doing it since a year, etc. and still are, so they use the present tense.

| | |
|---|---|
| J'habite ici depuis six ans. | I have lived here for six years. |
| Il apprend le français depuis deux ans. | He has been learning French for two years. |
| J'ai cette voiture depuis un an. | I have had this car a year. |
| Ils attendent depuis une heure. | They have been waiting an hour. |
| Je suis ici depuis deux jours. | I have been here two days. |

**I** How would you answer these questions? Remember to use the present tense in your answers.

**a** Depuis quand habitez-vous ici?
**b** Depuis combien de temps apprenez-vous le français?
**c** Depuis combien de temps connaissez-vous votre meilleur ami/votre meilleure amie?

## B Venir de – *to have just*
(lit: to come from doing something)

Instead of using the past tense and saying *I have just seen him,* in French you use the verb **venir** and say *I come from seeing him.*

| | |
|---|---|
| Je viens de rentrer. | I have just got in. |
| Il vient de téléphoner. | He has just rung. |

**II** How would you say:

| | |
|---|---|
| **a** Il ___ rentrer. | He has just got back. |
| **b** Mon copain ___ me téléphoner. | My friend has just rung me. |
| **c** Nous ___ regarder un film épouvantable. | We have just seen a dreadful film. |
| **d** Mes parents ___ vendre leur maison. | My parents have just sold their house. |
| **e** Je ___ finir mon travail. | I have just finished my work. |

## 1.8.9 ▶Fast track: Useful expressions with verbs

## A Special uses of *avoir*
In French there are some expressions where you use **avoir** where we use the verb *to be* in English. The most common ones are:

| | |
|---|---|
| J'ai … ans | I am … (years old) |
| J'ai besoin de | I need |
| J'ai envie de | I would like |
| J'ai peur de | I am afraid of |
| J'ai chaud/froid | I am hot/cold |
| J'ai faim/soif | I am hungry/thirsty |

J'ai raison/tort · I am right/wrong
Il y a · There is/there are
Il y avait · There was/there were

## B How to say 'I know'

To know someone, a place, etc., is **connaître**:

Je connais Avignon. · I know Avignon.

To know a fact, or how to do something, is **savoir**:

Je sais le faire. · I know how to do it.

## C How to say 'bring/take/fetch'

prendre · to take – *je prends le bus*
amener · to take/bring (someone over here)
emmener · to take (someone away)
apporter · to bring (something over here)
emporter · to take (something away)

## D How to say 'remember'

In French you say **se souvenir de** (lit: to remind yourself of someone or something).

Je me souviens de lui. · I remember him.

## E Negatives

**Ne** is put in front of the verb and **pas**, **rien**, **personne**, **jamais**, **plus** and **que** come after the verb.

The **ne** is a 'marker' to let the listener know that there is going to be a negative. It is sometimes left out in colloquial speech, e.g. **Je sais pas**.

ne ... pas · not
Je ne sais pas. · I don't know.
ne ... rien · nothing
Il ne fait rien. · He isn't doing anything.
ne ... personne · nobody
Je n'ai vu personne. · I didn't see anyone.
ne ... jamais · never
Je n'ai jamais fait de ski. · I have never skied.
ne ... plus · no longer
Théo ne fait plus de plongée. · Théo doesn't go diving any more.
ne ... que · only
Je n'ai que vous. · I only have you.

F   Questions words

To avoid inverting the subject and verb you can use:

| | |
|---|---|
| Est-ce que …? | Is it that …? |
| Est-ce que vous allez au cinéma? | Are you going to the cinema? |

You can use a question word and **est-ce que** …:

| | |
|---|---|
| Qu'est-ce que …? | What? |
| Qu'est-ce que vous allez faire? | What are you going to do? |
| Pourquoi est-ce que vous restez à la maison? | Why are you staying home? |

These words introduce a question:

| | |
|---|---|
| Quand? | When? |
| Pourquoi? | Why? |
| Combien? | How much/many? |
| Combien de temps? | How long? |
| Que …? | What …? |
| Qui? | Who? |

The subject and verb are inverted after a question word.

Quand va-t-il?
Où allez-vous?

G   Depuis – *since*

You use **depuis** to answer the question *how long*. It uses the present tense.

| | |
|---|---|
| Depuis combien de temps habitez-vous en Écosse? | How long have you lived in Scotland? |
| J'y habite depuis dix ans. | I have lived there ten years. (lit: I live there since ten years.) |

In French you use the present tense providing you still live there.

H   Venir de – *to have just*

| | |
|---|---|
| Je viens d'arriver. | I have just arrived. (lit: I come from arriving.) |
| il vient de le faire. | He has just done it. (lit: He comes from doing it.) |

In French you use the present tense because you 'come from doing it'.

# 2 NOUNS AND DETERMINERS

## How to recognise nouns

▶▶ **If you know what a noun and a determiner are, go on to 2.2.**

Nouns are 'naming' words. They tell you who somebody is (e.g. *he is a soldier, she is a dentist*) or what something is (e.g. *it is a table, it is a rainbow*).

 You can recognise nouns because you can say 'the' or 'a' in front of them, e.g. a pencil, the dog, the house, the postman.

Sometimes the same word can be a noun or a verb.

*to drive – the drive*
*to cook – the cook*

**I** There are ten nouns in this text. Can you find them all?

My sister has her own restaurant. She goes to the market each morning to buy fresh vegetables to make the soup for lunch. The other dishes she has prepared the night before and left ready to cook in the fridge.

**II** A determiner is a word which comes in front of a noun to tell you (determine) which one it is: *the coat, **a** coat, **some** coats, **my** coat, **your** coat, **this** coat, **which** coat?*

## 2.1 Nouns and gender

▶▶ **If you know about the gender of nouns, go on to 2.2.**

In French all nouns are either masculine or feminine.

The word for *house* – **maison** – is a feminine word.

The word for *garden* – **jardin** – is a masculine word.

Feminine words are usually indicated by *nf* in the dictionary (n – noun f – feminine) and masculine words by *nm*.

# **2.2** Nouns and the word for 'the': *le* and *la*

The word *the* is a determiner. It is also called the definite article because it refers to a definite thing, e.g. *the* pen (which you are using) and not just any pen.

▶▶ **If you know about le and la and the gender of nouns, go on to 2.3.**

- The word for *the* in front of masculine nouns is **le**.
  le garçon                  the boy
  le journal                 the newspaper
- The word for *the* in front of feminine nouns is **la**.
  la fille                   the girl
  la porte                   the door

It is not always so easy to tell which words are going to be masculine or feminine. When you look a word up in the dictionary, it usually tells you the gender of the word in brackets after it: **maison** (nf) *house*; **appartement** (nm) *flat*.

I   Put the correct form (**le** or **la**) in front of these.

   **a** _la_ voiture (f)                car
   **b** _la_ valise (f)                suitcase
   **c** _le_ sac (m)                  bag
   **d** _le_ portable (m)             laptop or mobile phone
   **e** _la_ calculette (f)            calculator
   **f** _le_ fichier (m)              file, folder
   **g** _la_ carte bancaire (f)        bank card
   **h** _la_ réservation (f)           reservation
   **i** _le_ manteau (m)              coat
   **j** _le_ billet (m)               ticket (for train/plane/ferry/theatre, etc.)
   **k** _le_ ticket (m)               ticket (for bus/cinema)

II  Now do the same for these places.

   **a** _la_ maison (f)                house
   **b** _la_ station-service (f)        petrol station
   **c** _la_ gare (f)                 station
   **d** _la_ rue (f)                  street
   **e** _le_ boulevard (m)            boulevard
   **f** _la_ station de métro (f)      underground station
   **g** _le_ magasin (m)              shop

**h** _la_ banque (f)           bank
**i** _la_ poste (f)           post office
**j** _le_ pont (m)           bridge

If the word begins with a vowel or silent **h**, you use **l'** for
both masculine and feminine words as it makes them easier
to say.

hôtel (m) l'hôtel           hotel
avenue (f) l'avenue           avenue

**III**   Fill in the gaps with **le**, **la** or **l'**.

**a** _l'_ appartement (m)           flat
**b** _le_ château (m)           castle
**c** _l'_ école (f)           school
**d** _l'_ hôpital (m)           hospital
**e** _l'_ église (f)           church
**f** _la_ mairie (f)           town hall
**g** _l'_ immeuble (m)           block of flats
**h** _l'_ hôtel (m)           hotel
**i** _l'_ avenue (f)           avenue
**j** _l'_ entrée (f)           entrance
**k** _l'_ arbre (m)           tree
**l** _le_ bébé (m)           baby
**m** _l'_ eau (f)           water
**n** _l'_ enfant (m)           child
**o** _l'_ homme (m)           man
**p** _l'_ horloge (f)           clock
**q** _la_ rivière (f)           river
**r** _la_ route (f)           road (through country)
**s** _la_ ville (f)           town
**t** _le_ village (m)           village

# 2.3   Nouns and the word for 'the' in the plural: *les*

▶▶   **If you know about the plural, go on to 2.4.**

In the plural, the word for *the* becomes **les** for ALL nouns,
both masculine and feminine.

| singular | plural |
|---|---|
| la maison | les maisons |
| le studio | les studios |
| l'appartement | les appartements |

To make the plural of the noun in English, we usually add an **-s**. In French, most words make their plural in the same way, by adding **-s**.

la maison → les maisons; le chien → les chiens; la rue → les rues

 The **-s** is not pronounced, so the singular and plural sound the same.

## 2.3.1 Common irregular plurals

The following categories form their plurals differently.

- Most words which end in **-al** form their plural with **-aux** (pronounced 'o').
  un journal – a newspaper → deux journaux – two newspapers
  un cheval – a horse → deux chevaux – two horses
  un animal – an animal → trois animaux – three animals
- Most words which end in **-au**, **-eau** and **-eu** add **-x**.
  un manteau – a coat → cinq manteaux – five coats
  un neveu – a nephew → trois neveux – three nephews
  BUT le pneu – the tyre → les pneus – the tyres
- Seven words ending in **-ou** add **-x**: genou – knee, caillou – pebble, bijou – jewel, joujou – (baby word for) toy, hibou – owl, chou – cabbage, pou – louse.
  un genou → deux genoux
- Other words ending in **-ou** form their plural with **-s**.
  le trou – the hole → les trous – the holes
- Words which already end in **-s**, **-x**, or **-z** don't change in the plural.
  le bras – the arm → les bras – the arms
  le prix – the price → les prix – the prices
  le nez – the nose → les nez – the noses

- Initialisms don't add an **-s**.
  le CD – the CD → les CD – the CDs

Two words are mostly used in the plural:
un cheveu – a (single) hair → les cheveux – hair
un œil – an eye → les yeux – the eyes

**I** Put these words into the plural.

| | | |
|---|---|---|
| **a** l'animal | the animal |
| **b** l'oiseau | the bird |
| **c** le genou | the knee |
| **d** le cheval | the horse |
| **e** le bateau | the boat |
| **f** le journal | the newspaper |
| **g** le château | the castle |
| **h** le neveu | the nephew |
| **i** le cadeau | the present, gift |

**II** Write out the plural forms of these words. Check what they already end in first!

**a** le fils           the son
**b** le Français       the Frenchman
**c** l'Anglais        the Englishman
**d** la croix         the cross
**e** le repas        the meal
**f** le feu          the fire
**g** le pneu         the tyre
**h** le chou         the cabbage
**i** le bois         the wood
**j** la souris       the mouse

# 2.4 Nouns and the word for 'a': *un* and *une*

The word *a* is a determiner. It is also called the indefinite article because it refers to any one item and not a specific one: *a* bottle of red wine, not the particular bottle that you have chosen specifically.

▶▶ **If you know all about un and une, go on to 2.5.**

- The word for *a* (or *an*) in front of a masculine noun is **un**.
  un verre            a glass
- The word for *a* (or *an*) in front of a feminine noun is **une**.
  une bouteille       a bottle

**I** Imagine you are talking about your family. How would you say you have one of all these?

J'ai …

**a** ___ frère           **f** ___ tante
**b** ___ sœur         **g** ___ beau-père
**c** ___ grand-père    **h** ___ cousine
**d** ___ grand-mère   **i** ___ belle-mère
**e** ___ oncle         **j** ___ chien

In French, you omit the indefinite article when saying what 'job' you do:

Il est étudiant.           He is a student.
Elle est vétérinaire.      She is a vet.
M. Brown est médecin.    Mr Brown is a doctor.
Mme Gibbs est professeur   Mrs Gibbs is an art teacher.
de dessin.

Some nouns, often for jobs, have masculine and feminine forms. The feminine is usually made by adding **-e** to the masculine.

| | |
|---|---|
| un ami → une amie | a friend |
| un employé → une employée | an employee |
| employé(e) de banque | bank employee |
| un étudiant → une étudiante | a student |
| un avocat → une avocate | a lawyer |
| un voisin → une voisine | a neighbour |
| un cousin → une cousine | a cousin |

Some nouns change:

| | |
|---|---|
| un acteur → une actrice | an actor/an actress |
| un directeur → une directrice | a director |
| un copain → une copine | a friend (m)/a friend (f) |
| la copine de Marc | Mark's girlfriend |
| un chanteur → une chanteuse | a singer |

**II** How would you say the following?

**a** Marilène is a director.
**b** Arthur is a student.
**c** Murielle is employed in a bank.
**d** Lucien is an actor.
**e** Thomas is a singer.
**f** Véronique is a lawyer.
**g** She is Patrice's girlfriend.

**Un** or **une** is used with a singular noun and has no plural:

J'ai une chaise.

If you are talking about more than one thing (some/any chair), you use **des**:

J'ai des chaises.

After a negative, e.g. if you are saying you haven't any chairs, you use **de**:

Je n'ai pas de chaises.

| | singular | plural |
|---|---|---|
| **Il a** – He has | **un jardin** – a garden<br>**une pelouse** – a lawn | **des arbres** – some trees<br>**des fleurs** – some flowers |
| **Il n'a pas de**<br>– He hasn't got | **jardinier** – a gardener<br>**tondeuse** – a lawn mower | **légumes** – any vegetables<br>**roses** – any roses |

**a** Mon copain habite dans ___ grand immeuble.
**b** Il a ___ petit appartement au cinquième étage.
**c** Il n'a pas ___ salle à manger.
**d** Il a ___ balcon où il range son vélo.
**e** Sur le balcon il y a aussi ___ plantes mortes dans ___ pots de fleurs.
**f** Dans sa chambre, il a ___ poste de télévision, ___ ordinateur et ___ lit.
**g** Il a ___ CD (**several**) et ___ jeux vidéo mais il n'a pas ___ DVD.
**h** Il y a ___ ascenseur, mais il est toujours en panne.

# 2.5 How to tell if a noun is masculine or feminine

As it is not always possible to tell whether a word is masculine or feminine in French, it is helpful to learn the **le** or **la** when you learn the word. However, there are a few groups of words which are all masculine or all feminine.

If you hear **le** or **un** being used in front of the word it is masculine.

If you hear **la** or **une** being used in front of the word it is feminine.

If you hear **les** or **des** in front of the word it is plural and you can't tell whether it's masculine or feminine.

These words are all **masculine**:

- words for male relations and male job-holders: **le père** (*father*), **le garçon** (*boy*), **le boulanger** (*baker*)
- days, months, seasons, weights and measures, and languages: **le deux** (*the number two*), **le mercredi** (*Wednesday*), **l'hiver** (*winter*), **le kilo** (*kilo*), **le français** (*the French language*)
- most words which have been adopted from English: **le short** (*shorts*), **le jean** (*jeans*), **le walkman** (*walkman*), **le blues** (*the blues*), **le parking** (*car park*)
- countries, rivers, vegetables and fruit not ending in *-e*: **le Japon** (*Japan*), **le chou** (*cabbage*), **le citron** (*lemon*)
- nouns which end in *-c*: **le lac** (*lake*); *-é*: **le passé** (*the past*); *-eau*\*: **le bateau** (*boat*) (but **l'eau** (*water*) and **la peau** (*skin*) are feminine); *-ou*: **le trou** (the hole)
- nouns which end in *-ème*: **le système**, **un problème**
- most words which end in *-eur*: **le bonheur** (*happiness*) (but **la fleur**, **la couleur** are feminine)

These words are all **feminine**:

- female relations and female job-holders: **la mère** (*mother*), **la tante** (*aunt*), **la boulangère** (*baker*)
- most countries, rivers, vegetables and fruits ending in *-e*: **la Russie** (*Russia*), **la Seine** (*the Seine*), **la carotte** (*carrot*), **la poire** (*pear*) (but **le Rhône** (*the Rhone*), **le pamplemousse** (*grapefruit*) are masculine)
- shops that end in *-ie* or *-ique*: **la boutique** (*small shop*), **la boulangerie** (*the baker's*)
- most words which end in *-sion* and *-tion*: **option**, **ambition**, **condition**, **émission**.

**I**   Using the above rules to help you, put **le** or **la** in front of these words.

| | | | |
|---|---|---|---|
| **a** \_\_\_ dimanche | | **k** \_\_\_ boucherie | |
| **b** \_\_\_ salade | | **l** \_\_\_ lundi | |
| **c** \_\_\_ Canada | | **m** \_\_\_ pâtisserie | |
| **d** \_\_\_ Loire | | **n** \_\_\_ France | |
| **e** \_\_\_ gâteau | | **o** \_\_\_ parking | |
| **f** \_\_\_ printemps | | **p** \_\_\_ marché | |
| **g** \_\_\_ litre | | **q** \_\_\_ Dordogne | |
| **h** \_\_\_ réception | | **r** \_\_\_ sweat-shirt | |
| **i** \_\_\_ tennis | | **s** \_\_\_ château | |
| **j** \_\_\_ ski | | **t** \_\_\_ français | |

# **2.6** How to say: my, your, his, her, etc.

▶▶ **If you know all about these words, go on to 2.7.**

These are determiners that tell you to whom something belongs: *my coat*, ***his*** *umbrella*, ***your*** *briefcase*, ***their*** *house*, ***our*** *cat*, etc.

In English, we only have one form of each: *my, your, his, her, our, their*. In French, the word has to agree with the noun it is describing.

| | masculine | feminine | plural |
|---|---|---|---|
| my | mon | ma | mes |
| your (tu) | ton | ta | tes |
| his/her/its | son | sa | ses |
| our | notre | notre | nos |
| your (vous) | votre | votre | vos |
| their | leur | leur | leurs |

## 2.6.1 My (mon, ma, mes)

The word for *my* agrees with the person or thing it is
describing. This means that you use the masculine form
(**mon**) with masculine nouns:

| | |
|---|---|
| mon frère | my brother |
| mon portable | my mobile/laptop |
| mon ami | my (male) friend |

*My* in front of feminine nouns is **ma**:

| | |
|---|---|
| ma sœur | my sister |
| ma voiture | my car |

But you use **mon** in front of feminine nouns which begin
with a vowel. This is because it is easier to say. However, if
there is another word between them, e.g. **petite**, it goes
back to being **ma**.

| | |
|---|---|
| mon amie | my (female) friend |
| ma petite amie | my girlfriend |

You use the plural form **mes** with plural nouns:

| | |
|---|---|
| mes parents | my parents |
| mes amis, mes amies | my friends |

**I**  **Mon, ma** or **mes**?

**a** ___ ordinateur       **f** ___ dossier
**b** ___ clés             **g** ___ serviette
**c** ___ portable         **h** ___ carte bancaire
**d** ___ agenda           **i** ___ ticket de bus
**e** ___ crayon           **j** ___ porte-monnaie

**II**  Now do the same for your clothes …

**a** ___ pantalon         **f** ___ anorak
**b** ___ chemise          **g** ___ manteau
**c** ___ pull             **h** ___ écharpe
**d** ___ chaussettes      **i** ___ gants
**e** ___ chaussures       **j** ___ parapluie

**III**  … and your family. Imagine you are showing someone
photographs of your family. What would you say?

*C'est mon/ma …/Ce sont mes …*

**a** ___ enfants          **g** ___ frères
**b** ___ mari             **h** ___ grands-parents
**c** ___ femme            **i** ___ cousin
**d** ___ père             **j** ___ fils (one)
**e** ___ mère             **k** ___ fille
**f** ___ sœur

## 2.6.2 Your (*ton, ta, tes*)

You can only use **ton, ta, tes** when speaking to a child or someone that you know very well and would address as **tu**.

▶▶ **If you are not going to need this form (it behaves just like the mon form), go on to 2.6.3.**

The words for *your* (**ton, ta, tes**) rhyme with the words for *my* (**mon, ma, mes**) and behave in the same way.

**I** Put the correct form of **ton, ta** or **tes** in front of these words.

*C'est ton/ta …/Ce sont tes …*

| | | | |
|---|---|---|---|
| **a** ___ enfants | | **f** ___ grands-parents |
| **b** ___ père | | **g** ___ fille |
| **c** ___ mère | | **h** ___ deux fils |
| **d** ___ sœurs | | **i** ___ chiens |
| **e** ___ frère | | **j** ___ chat |

**II** How would you ask what they are called?

*Comment s'appelle ton/ta …?/Comment s'appellent tes …?*

| | | | |
|---|---|---|---|
| **a** ___ collègues | | **f** ___ amies |
| **b** ___ collègue | | **g** ___ ami |
| **c** ___ copain | | **h** ___ amie |
| **d** ___ copines | | **i** ___ petite amie |
| **e** ___ amis | | **j** ___ petit ami |

## 2.6.3 His, her and its (*son, sa, ses*)

The words for *his/her* also rhyme with **mon, ma, mes** and **ton, ta, tes** and are used in the same way.

Notice that:

- **son frère** means both *his brother* and *her brother*
- **sa sœur** means both *his sister* and *her sister*
- **ses parents** means both *his parents* and *her parents*.

▶▶ **If you know all about son, sa and ses, go on to 2.6.4.**

**I** Tell me about Thomas by filling in the right word (**son, sa, ses**).

**a** ___ amie s'appelle Juliette.
**b** ___ cousin s'appelle Auban.
**c** ___ frère est grand.
**d** ___ mère est sculpteur.
**e** ___ père travaille à la BCE (Banque Centrale Européenne).

**f** ____ sœur est chercheuse en cardiologie.
**g** ____ petit frère n'a que dix ans.
**h** ____ sport préféré est le tennis.
**i** ____ plat préféré est la pizza «quatre saisons».
**j** ____ couleur préférée est le rouge coquelicot.

> Not sure whether 'couleur' is (m) or (f)? Look for a clue in the sentence: préférée.

**II** Now do the same for Charlotte's family and friends.

**a** ____ amie s'appelle Jennifer.
**b** ____ petit ami s'appelle Benjamin.
**c** ____ frère s'appelle Nicolas.
**d** ____ sœur s'appelle Isabelle.
**e** Comment s'appellent ____ parents?
**f** ____ scooter est noir et jaune.
**g** ____ passion, c'est le théâtre.
**h** ____ couleur préférée est le bleu.
**i** ____ plat préféré est le filet de veau Marengo.
**j** ____ boisson préférée est un cocktail à base de champagne.

## 2.6.4 Our (notre, nos)

▶▶ **If you know all about notre and votre, go on to 2.6.6.**

The word for *our* is **notre**. It is the same for both masculine and feminine, but changes to **nos** in the pural: **notre appartement**, **notre maison**, **nos enfants**.

**I** How would you say these are our things?

*C'est notre …/Ce sont nos …*

**a** ____ maison
**b** ____ appartement
**c** ____ chiens
**d** ____ cave
**e** ____ vins

**f** ____ garage
**g** ____ voiture
**h** ____ jardin
**i** ____ arbres
**j** ____ pelouse

## 2.6.5 Your (votre, vos)

The word for *your* (**vous** form) is easy to remember because it rhymes with **notre** and **nos** and behaves in the same way: **votre appartement**, **votre maison**, **vos enfants**.

**I** Ask if these are your things.

*C'est votre …?/Ce sont vos …?*

**a** ___ bureau
**b** ___ chaise
**c** ___ ordinateur
**d** ___ papiers
**e** ___ manteau

**f** ___ gants
**g** ___ parapluie
**h** ___ affaires
**i** ___ portefeuille
**j** ___ clés

## 2.6.6 Their (*leur, leurs*)

The word for *their* is **leur**. It adds an **-s** in the plural: **leur appartement, leur maison, leurs enfants**.

**I** Say these are their things.

*C'est leur …/Ce sont leurs …*

**a** ___ voiture
**b** ___ garage
**c** ___ vélos
**d** ___ jardin
**e** ___ fleurs

**f** ___ plantes
**g** ___ maison
**h** ___ porte
**i** ___ fenêtres
**j** ___ balcon

## 2.6.7 ▶**Fast track:** nouns and determiners

All nouns in French are either masculine or feminine.

- The word for *the* with masculine nouns is **le**.
- The word for *the* with feminine nouns is **la**.
- If the noun begins with a vowel or silent **h**, **le** and **la** both become **l'**.
- The word for *the* with plural nouns (masculine and feminine) is **les**.

- The word for *a* with masculine nouns is **un**.
- The word for *a* with feminine nouns is **une**.
- When you are talking about jobs you omit the *a* in French:

Je suis fiscaliste.          I am a tax lawyer.

- *A* does not have a plural of its own. The plural of *a* is *some*.
- The French word for *some* is **des**:

Je dois acheter des chaussettes.    I have to buy some socks.

- If you want to say you haven't *any* you use **de**:

Je n'ai pas de chaussettes.    I haven't any socks.

It is a good idea to learn French nouns with the **le** and **la**: **la maison; le jardin**.

How to translate *my, your*, etc.:

|  | with masculine nouns | with feminine nouns | with plural nouns |
|---|---|---|---|
| my | mon | ma | mes |
| your (**tu** form) | ton | ta | tes |
| his/her/its | son | sa | ses |
| our | notre | notre | nos |
| your (**vous** form) | votre | votre | vos |
| their | leur | leur | leurs |

If a female noun begins with a vowel, you use **mon/ton/son** instead of **ma/ta/sa**.

**Son**, **sa** and **ses** mean *his, hers*, and *its*.

# 2.7 More determiners

Remember determiners are words which come before the noun and say which one it is. You already know some but there are some more.

Ones you already know: ***the*** *table,* ***a*** *table,* ***some*** *tables,* ***my*** *table,* ***your*** *table.*

Other determiners include: ***which*** *table,* ***all*** *tables,* ***the same*** *table,* ***several*** *tables,* ***every*** *table.*

If you do not think you need these yet, leave them and come back to them later.

| le, la; les | the |
|---|---|
| un, une; des | a; some |
| mon, ma, mes | my |
| ce, cet, cette; ces | this; these |
| quel, quelle; quels, quelles? | which? |
| autre(s) | other |
| certain(e)(s) | certain |
| chaque | each/every |
| même(s) | same |
| plusieurs | several |
| quelques | some |
| tout, toute; tous, toutes | all |

**Tout** (etc.) can be used to express *every*:
Je me lève tous les matins à sept heures. *I get up every morning at 7.00.*

## 2.7.1 This, that, these: *ce, cet, cette* and *ces*

**Ce**, etc. is used to point to a particular thing or things: *this page, that book, these clothes.*

| singular | | plural |
|----------|----------|--------|
| **masculine** | **feminine** | |
| ce (cet*) | cette | ces |

* You use **cet** before a masculine noun which begins with a vowel or silent **h: cet homme**.

**I** Put the correct form (**ce**, **cet**, **cette** or **ces**) in front of these words.

**a** Je vous conseille ____ hôtel.  I recommend this hotel.

**b** Derrière ____ maison, il y a un jardin japonais.  Behind this house there is a Japanese garden.

**c** Dans ____ jardin poussent surtout des plantes exotiques.  In this garden grow mostly exotic plants.

**d** ____ personnes travaillent dans le jardin.  These people work in the garden.

**e** ____ fleurs sont rares.  These flowers are rare.

**f** ____ arbre est très vieux.  This tree is very old.

**g** ____ porte est réservée aux visiteurs.  This door is reserved for visitors.

**h** ____ dépliants sont gratuits.  These brochures are free.

**i** ____ homme prend des photos.  This man is taking photographs.

**j** ____ printemps il y a beacoup de jonquilles.  This spring there are lots of daffodils.

## 2.7.2 Which: *quel, quelle, quels* and *quelles*

There are four forms of **quel**. They agree with the noun in these ways:

| singular | | plural | |
|----------|----------|--------|---------|
| **masculine** | **feminine** | **masculine** | **feminine** |
| quel | quelle | quels | quelles |

**I** Put in the correct form: **quel**, **quelle**, **quels** or **quelles**.

**a** Vous préférez ____ hôtel?  Which hotel do you prefer?

**b** Vous préférez ____ chambre?  Which room do you prefer?

**c** Vous préférez ____ table?  Which table do you prefer?

**d** Vous préférez ____ fleurs?  Which flowers do you prefer?

**e** Je l'envoie à \_\_\_\_ adresse?     Which address should I send it to?

**f** Vous habitez dans \_\_\_\_ appartement?     Which flat do you live in?

**g** Je ne sais pas \_\_\_\_ manteau porter.     I don't know which coat to wear.

**h** \_\_\_\_ chaussures allez-vous porter?     Which shoes are you going to wear?

## 2.7.3   Some, other, certain, every, etc.

These adjectives agree as normal with the noun (but note that some, such as **plusieurs** and **quelques**, are only used in the plural).

### autre, autres (*other*)

Je vais prendre une autre route.     I am going to take another road.

Connaissez-vous d'autres histoires?     Do you know any other stories?

### certain, certaine, certains, certaines (*certain*)

Cette opération demande un certain savoir-faire.     This procedure requires a certain competence.

Il y a une certaine personne dans ce quartier que je n'aimerais pas rencontrer.     There is a certain individual in this neighbourhood whom I would very much dislike bumping into.

### chaque (*each/every*)

chaque jour, *or* tous les jours     each day/every day

chaque fois     every time

### même, mêmes (*same*)

en même temps     at the same time

Je vois les mêmes gens au bureau tous les jours.     I see the same people in the office every day.

### plusieurs (*some*)

J'y suis allé plusieurs fois.     I have been (there) several times.

### quelques (*a few*)

Avez-vous quelques minutes?     Have you got a few minutes?

## tout, toute, tous, toutes (*all/every*)

| | |
|---|---|
| tout le temps | all the time |
| toute ma famille | all my family |
| tous les autres | all the others/everyone else |
| toutes les fleurs | all the flowers/every flower |
| tous les jours | every day |
| toutes les semaines | every week |

# 3 PRONOUNS

## What is a pronoun?

A pronoun is a word which stands in for a noun. Instead of saying:

- *Mr Jones*, you can say *he:* **il**
- *the lady*, you can say *she:* **elle**
- *my husband/wife and I*, you can say *we:* **nous**
- *M. et Mme Gérard* you can say *they:* **ils/elles**.

In English instead of saying *table* we say *it*. In French everything is either masculine or feminine so *the table* is *she* (**elle**) and *the book* is *he* (**il**).

## 3.1 *Je, tu, il/elle*, etc.: subject pronouns

▶▶ **If you know what a subject pronoun is, go on to 3.2.**

The subject is the person or thing that does the action: *I* run, *you* play, *he* eats, *she* drinks, *it* shuts, *we* live, *you* swim, *they* talk.

The subject pronouns in French are as follows:

|  | singular | plural |
|---|---|---|
| **first person** | **je** – I | **nous** – we |
| **second person** | **tu** – you | **vous** – you |
| **third person** | **il** – he/it<br>**elle** – she/it<br>**on** – one/we | **ils** – they<br>**elles** – they |

### 3.1.1 *Je – I*: the first person singular
You use the first person singular when you are talking about yourself.

| je lis | I am reading |
|---|---|
| je dors | I am sleeping |
| je suis | I am |

In front of a word beginning with a vowel or silent **h**, **je** becomes **j'**.

| | |
|---|---|
| j'écoute | I am listening |
| je m'appelle Monsieur Smith | I am called Mr Smith |
| et j'habite … | and I live … |

**Je** (**j'**) is only written with a capital letter at the beginning of a sentence, unlike *I* in English.

After **je** the verb usually ends in **-e** or **-s** in the present tense.

### 3.1.2 *Tu* – you: the second person singular

You use **tu** when you are talking to someone you know very well, someone who has invited you to do so, or to a child. There is a special verb which means *to call someone **tu** –* **tutoyer**.

| | |
|---|---|
| Tu as un chien? *or* As-tu un chien? | Have you got a dog? |
| Tu es allé en ville? *or* Es-tu allé en ville? | Did you go to town? |

After **tu** the verb usually ends in **-es** or **-s** in the present tense.

### 3.1.3 *Il/elle* – he/she/it: the third person singular

You use **il/elle** when you are talking about someone or something else. It translates *he, she* and *it*.

Remember that in French everything is either masculine or feminine. *A chair* is feminine, so if you want to say anything about *it*, you have to use **elle** (*she*); similarly, *a book* is masculine so if you want to refer to *it*, you have to say **il** (*he*).

| | |
|---|---|
| La voiture! Elle est en panne. | The car! **It** has broken down. |
| Regarde le livre de ma grand-mère. Il est très vieux. | Look at my grandmother's book. **It** is very old. |

After **il/elle** the verb usually ends in **-e** or **-t** in the present tense.

### 3.1.4 *Nous* – we: the first person plural

You use **nous** to talk about yourself and someone else. You use it when you would use *we* in English.

| | |
|---|---|
| Nous préférons partir tôt. | We prefer to leave early. |
| Mon mari et moi, nous allons au théâtre demain soir. | My husband and I (we) are going to the theatre tomorrow evening. |

After **nous** the verb usually ends in **-ons** in the present tense.

> **On** (one) is often used in conversation instead of **nous**. It is followed by the third person singular of the verb (the *he/she/it* form). After **on** the verb usually ends in **-e** or **-t** in the present tense.
>
> On va au théâtre demain soir. *We're going to the theatre tomorrow evening.*

## 3.1.5 *Vous* – you: the second person plural

You use **vous** when you are talking to someone else. It translates *you*.

**Vous** is often referred to as the 'polite' form, as it is used not only in the plural but also when talking to someone older than you or to a stranger, even if there is only one person.

The verb which means *to call someone **vous*** is **vouvoyer**.

After **vous** the verb usually ends in **-ez** in the present tense.

## 3.1.6 *Ils/elles* – they: the third person plural

You use **ils/elles** when you are talking about more than one person or thing. It translates *they*.

You use **ils** to refer to:

• more than one masculine person or thing
• a mixture of masculine and feminine people or things.

You use **elles** only if all the people or things are feminine.

| | |
|---|---|
| Mes copains, ils vont à Paris. | My friends are going to Paris |
| Mes copines, elles restent ici. | My girlfriends are staying here. |

After **ils/elles** the verb usually ends in **-ent** or **-ont** in the present tense.

**I** Which subject pronoun should you use?

**a** I am going to the cinema tonight.
**b** After the cinema we are going to a restaurant.
**c** My girlfriends will be there.
**d** The boys are going to a football match.
**e** Luc is playing.
**f** Isabelle is going to watch.
**g** Where are you going, Mr Jones?

**II** Which subject pronoun would you use in these sentences?

**a** Jean habite en France. ___ habite dans le Nord.
**b** Paul et Marianne habitent dans le Sud. ___ habitent à Marseille.
**c** Moi? ___ habite à Paris.
**d** Où habitez-___?
**e** J'habite à Paris avec mes amis. ___ habitons dans un grand immeuble, boulevard Haussmann.
**f** Séverine et Emmanuelle habitent dans la banlieue nord. ___ ont un petit appartement.
**g** Ma sœur habite à Lyon. ___ fait ses études à l'université de Lyon.
**h** Mes grands-parents habitent en Auvergne. ___ ont une ferme.
**i** Où habites-___?
**j** Mon frère joue au tennis. ___ joue très bien.

## 3.1.7 ▶**Fast track:** Subject pronouns

A pronoun is a word which stands for a noun: *I* run, *you* play, *he* eats, *she* drinks, *it* shuts, *we* live, *you* swim, *they* talk.

The subject is the person or thing does the action.

You use **je** (first person singular) when you are talking about yourself: **je lis** – *I am reading.* In front of a word beginning with a vowel or silent **h**, **je** becomes **j'**: **j'écoute** – *I am listening.*

You use **tu** (second person singular) when you are talking to someone you know very well, someone who has invited you to do so, or to a child.

Tu dois ranger ta chambre.             You've got to tidy your room.

You use **il/elle** (third person singular) to translate *he, she* and *it.* In French everything is either masculine or feminine so *the table* is *she* (**elle**) and *the book* is *he* (**il**).

Il ne vient pas.                         He/it is not coming.

You use **nous** (first person plural) to talk about yourself and someone else. You use it when you would use *we* in English.

Nous allons au cinéma.                   We are going to the cinema.

After **nous** the verb usually ends in **-ons** in the present tense.

**On** (*one*) is often used in conversation instead of **nous**. It is followed by the third person singular of the verb (the *he/she/it* form): **nous allons** or **on va** – *we are going*.

After **on** the verb usually ends in **-e** or **-t** in the present tense.

You use **vous** (second person plural) to translate *you*. **Vous** is often referred to as the 'polite' form, as it is used not only in the plural but also when talking to someone older than you or to a stranger, even if there is only one person.

After **vous** the verb usually ends in **-ez**.

You use **ils/elles** (third person plural) to translate *they*.

You use **ils** to refer to:

• more than one masculine person or thing
• a mixture of masculine and feminine people or things.

You use only **elles** if all the people or things are feminine.

After **ils/elles** the verb usually ends in **-ent** or **-ont** in the present tense.

# 3.2 *Le, la, les,* etc.: direct object pronouns

▶▶ **If you know what a direct object pronoun is and how to use it, go on to 3.3.**

*Him, her* and *it* are object pronouns. They stand in for the person or object to which an action is done:

I saw John/*him*.
John saw Karen/*her*.
I bought the watch/*it*.
I like Paul/*him*.
He likes Isabelle/*her*.
She doesn't like the boys/*them*.

In English it is easy to recognise the direct object as it always comes straight after the verb.

**I** Which is the direct object? (It may be a noun or a pronoun.)

**a** I bought a new car.
**b** My husband drove it home for me.
**c** A dog chased a cat across the road.
**d** He swerved and hit a tree.
**e** He broke the wing mirror.
**f** He bought a bunch of flowers for his girlfriend.
**g** He took the car to the garage to be repaired.

The object pronouns in French are as follows:

|  | **singular** | **plural** |
|---|---|---|
| **first person** | **me** – me | **nous** – us |
| **second person** | **te** – you | **vous** – you |
| **third person** | **le** – him/it<br>**la** – her/it | **les** – them |

## **3.2.1** *Le, la, les* – him, her, it, them

In French, the **le**, **la** and **les** come in front of the verb:

Je le vois.      I see him/it. (lit: I him see)
Je ne les vois pas.      I don't see them.
     (lit: I them don't see)

You use **l'** if the following verb begins with a vowel:

Je l'ai fini.      I have finished it.
Il l'a cassé.      He broke it.
Je ne les ai pas vus.      I didn't see them.

**I** Mme Robert buys a new dress (*la robe*). What is the pronoun?

**a** She sees it.      Elle ____ voit.
**b** She tries it on.      Elle ____ essaie.
**c** She buys it.      Elle ____ achète.
**d** She takes it home.      Elle ____ rapporte à la maison.
**e** She wears it that evening.      Elle ____ porte ce soir-là.
**f** Monsieur Robert finds it old-fashioned.      M. Robert ____ trouve démodée.
**g** She takes it back to the shop.      Elle ____ rapporte à boutique.

Marcel bought some socks. *Marcel a acheté des chaussettes.*

**h** He put them in his bag.  Il ___ a mises dans son sac.
**i** On the way home, he left  En rentrant, il ___ a laissées dans
them on the bus.  le bus.

## 3.2.2 *Me, te, nous, vous* – me, you, us

These pronouns also come in front of the verb. The **me**
and **te** change to **m'** and **t'** before a vowel.

| | |
|---|---|
| John called *me*. | Il m'a appelé(e). |
| He sees *you*. | Il te voit. |
| Elisabeth sees *us*. | Elle nous voit. |
| We see *you*. | Nous vous voyons. |

**I** Put the correct pronoun in these sentences: **me**, **te**, **le**, **la**,
**nous**, **vous**, **les**.

**a** He sees me every day.  Il ___ voit tous les jours.
**b** He saw us in town  Il ___ a vus en ville hier.
yesterday.
**c** We saw you on the bus.  Nous ___ avons vu dans le bus.
**d** He contacted me last  Il ___ a contacté la semaine
week.  dernière.
**e** He's invited us to dine  Il ___ a invités à dîner chez eux
with them tonight.  ce soir.

## 3.2.3 Past participle agreement with object pronouns

You need this mainly for written French. It only alters the
pronunciation when the past participle ends in a
consonant: e.g. *fait → faite*.

▶▶ **If you are not going to need it, go on to 3.2.4.**

In the perfect tense, the past participle 'agrees' with a
direct object pronoun. 'Agreement' means adding the
following endings to the past participle:

• feminine objects: **-e**
• plural objects: **-s**
• feminine plural objects: **-es**

| | |
|---|---|
| Je l'ai vu. | I saw him/it. |
| Je l'ai vue. | I saw her/it. |
| Je les ai achetés. | I bought them. (masculine objects) |
| Je les ai achetées. | I bought them. (feminine objects) |

**I** Add an ending to the past participle where necessary.

Example: Martin a vu *son amie.* Il l'a *vue.*

| | |
|---|---|
| **a** Il a vu son ami. | Il l'a ____. |
| **b** Il a vu ses amis. | Il les a ____. |
| **c** Il a vu ses copines. | Il les a ____. |
| **d** Il a perdu son sac. | Il l'a ____. |
| **e** Il a perdu son portable. | Il l'a ____. |
| **f** Il a perdu ses clés (fpl). | Il les a ____. |
| **g** Il a perdu son porte-monnaie. | Il l'a ____. |
| **h** Il a perdu ses cartes bancaires (fpl). | Il les a ____. |
| **i** Il a perdu son agenda (m). | Il l'a ____. |
| **j** Il a perdu ses lunettes. | Il les a ____. |

## 3.2.4 ▶Fast track: Direct object pronouns

*Le, la, les* – him, her, it, them

In English the direct pronoun (e.g. *it*) always comes straight after the verb.

In French, the direct pronoun (e.g. **le**, **la**, **les**) comes in front of the verb.

| | |
|---|---|
| Je le vois. | I see him/it. (lit: I him see) |
| Je ne les vois pas. | I don't see them. (lit: I them don't see) |

You use **l'** instead of **le** or **la** if the following verb begins with a vowel.

*Me, te, nous, vous* – me, you, us

| | |
|---|---|
| John called *me.* | Il m'a appelé(e). |
| He sees *you.* | Il te voit. |
| Elisabeth sees *us.* | Elle nous voit. |
| We see *you.* | Nous vous voyons. |

You use **m'** and **t'** instead of **me** and **te** before a vowel.

Past participle agreement with object pronouns

You need this mainly for written French. It only alters the pronunciation when the past participle ends in a consonant: e.g. *fait → faite.*

In the perfect tense, the past participle 'agrees' with a direct object pronoun. 'Agreement' means adding endings to the past participle as follows:

| singular | | plural | |
|---|---|---|---|
| **masculine** | **feminine** | **masculine** | **feminine** |
| – | -e | -s | -es |

# 3.3 *Me, lui, leur,* etc.: Indirect object pronouns

▶▶ **If you know what an indirect object pronoun is and how to use it, go on to 3.4.**

In English, an indirect object pronoun is the same word as a direct object pronoun but has (or can have) *to* or *for* in front of it.

- *I bought her it. I bought it* (direct object – it is the thing that you bought) *for her* (indirect object).
- *Give me it. Give it* (direct object – the thing which is being given) *to me* (indirect object).
- *They showed him it. They showed it* (direct object – the thing which is being shown) *to him* (indirect object).

Indirect pronouns are used with verbs such as: give, send, write, show, buy, offer, tell, lend, etc. where you do something *to* or *for* someone/something.

The indirect object pronouns are as follows:

| | singular | plural |
|---|---|---|
| **first person** | **me** – (to) me | **nous** – (to) us |
| **second person** | **te** – (to) you | **vous** – (to) you |
| **third person** | **lui** – (to) him/her | **leur** – (to) them |

Notice that **me**, **te**, **nous** and **vous** are the same as the direct object pronouns, so you only have to remember **lui** – (to) him/her and '**leur**' – (to) them.

I  Identify the indirect object pronouns in these English sentences.

 Try saying *to/for* in front of the pronoun to see if it is indirect.

**a** Pascal sent me a text message.
**b** I could not read it. My friend could. I showed her it.
**c** She translated it for me.
**d** I wrote him a reply.
**e** She sent it to him.
**f** He sent her a new message.
**g** She did not show me it.
**h** She sent him a photo of herself.
**i** He sent her another message.
**j** She sent him a reply.
**k** He texted her.
**l** She did not tell me what he said.
**m** She gave me my phone back and went.

## **3.3.1** Word order when using the indirect object

In French, you always put the indirect object pronoun in front of the verb.

| | |
|---|---|
| Il me donne des fleurs. | He gives (to) me flowers. |
| Je vous passerai un coup de fil. | I'll give you a call. |
| Je lui envoie un fax. | I am sending him/her a fax. |
| Nous leur avons donné les billets. | We have given them the tickets. |
| Vous ne nous avez pas donné les clés. | You haven't given us the keys. |

I  Fill in the missing pronouns.

**a** Il ___ prête son stylo. (her)
**b** Je ___ envoie une lettre. (them)
**c** Il ___ raconte une histoire. (me)
**d** Nous ___ achetons un cadeau. (them)
**e** Vous ___ donnez une invitation. (us)
**f** M. Bertrand ___ présente sa femme. (you)
**g** Nous ___ offrons des fleurs. (her)
**h** Elle ___ remercie. (us)
**i** Je ___ dis «Bon anniversaire!» (him)
**j** On ___ offre une bouteille de cognac. (them)
**k** Ma femme ___ a téléphoné hier. (you)
**l** Le médecin ___ a donné rendez-vous pour ce matin. (us)
**m** Je ___ ai envoyé un mél. (her)
**n** Il ___ a raconté l'histoire. (me)

▶▶ **If you don't want to know about this yet, go on to 3.3.3.**

If you have more than one pronoun in front of the verb, they always go in the following order:

| je<br>tu<br>il/elle/on<br>nous<br>vous<br>ils/elles | (ne) | me<br>te<br>se<br>nous<br>vou | le<br>la<br>les | lui<br>leur | verb | (pas) |
|---|---|---|---|---|---|---|

In the perfect tense the pronouns always come before the part of **avoir**:

Il me l'a prête. He lent it to me.

**I** How would you say the following?

**a** He gave it to me. (*le numéro de téléphone de l'entreprise*)
**b** I gave it to her.
**c** She gave it to them.
**d** They gave it to you.
**e** You gave it to us.
**f** She bought him it. (*le livre*)
**g** He read it.
**h** He gave it to us.
**i** We gave it to you.
**j** They read it to them.
**k** She lent it to me.
**l** I won't lend it to you!

 Choose one phrase to learn by heart to use as a pattern: **Je le lui ai donné** – *I gave it to him*.

▶▶ **If you have had enough of pronouns, move on to Chapter 4 on Adjectives and come back later.**

### 3.3.3 ▶**Fast track:** Indirect object pronouns

In English, an indirect object pronoun is the same word as a direct object pronoun but has (or can have) *to* or *for* in front of it.

Indirect pronouns are only used with verbs such as: give, send, write, show, buy, offer, tell, lend, etc. where you do something *to* or *for* someone.

In French, you always put the indirect object pronoun in front of the verb.

Most of the indirect object pronouns are the same as the direct object pronouns so you only have to remember **lui** – (*to*) *him/her* and **leur** – (*to*) *them*.

# 3.4 Y: there

▶▶ **If you know about y, go on to 3.5.**

You already know the expression **il y a** so you already know that *y* comes before the verb.

If that is all you want to know at the moment choose a phrase to memorise as a pattern and come back later.

| | |
|---|---|
| J'y suis allé(e). | I have been there. |
| On y va? | Let's go (there). |
| Vous y êtes allés? | Have you been there? |

The word **y** (there) stands for a place that you have already mentioned. It always goes in front of the verb.

| | |
|---|---|
| John est allé en Grèce. | John has been to Greece. |
| Il y est allé deux fois. | He has been (there) twice. |
| Y êtes-vous déjà allé? | Have you been (there)? |

Sometimes we would miss it out in English, but you need to put it in in French.

| | |
|---|---|
| Il va en ville. | He is going to town. |
| J'y vais aussi. | I am going (there) too. |
| Alors … Allons-y! | So … Let's go (there)! |

**I** In the following sentences, replace the name of the place (shown in italics) with the pronoun **y**. For example:

Bénédicte va à Paris. → Bénédicte y va.

**a** Monique habite *à Lyon*.
**b** Je vais *en ville*.

**c** Nous allons *au cinéma* au moins trois fois par mois.
**d** Êtes-vous jamais allés *en Écosse*?
**e** Ils mangent souvent *au restaurant*.
**f** Il a écouté le Requiem de Mozart *à la phonotèque*.
**g** Nous achetons nos fruits et nos légumes *au marché*.
**h** Nous avons fait toutes nos études *à Paris*.
**i** Je suis allée *en Italie* la semaine dernière.
**j** Il faisait un temps splendide *à Rome*.

In French some verbs are followed by **à**: **s'intéresser à** – *to be interested in*; **penser à** – *to think of*. **Y** is also used to translate **à** + a pronoun: *in it/them, about it/them*, etc.

| | |
|---|---|
| Je ne m'intéresse pas à vos affaires. | I am not interested in your business. |
| Je ne m'y intéresse pas. | I am not interested (in it/them). |
| Je ne pense jamais à ce qu'il a fait. | I never think about what he has done. |
| Je n'y pense jamais. | I don't ever think about it/them. |

If you want to know more about this go to *French Grammar and Usage*, R. Hawkins and R. Towell, 1996/2001, 2nd edn.

# 3.5  *En*: of it/of them

**En** refers to something you have already mentioned, and stands for *of it* or *of them*.

If that is all you want to know about **en** at the moment choose a phrase to memorise as a pattern and come back later.

| | |
|---|---|
| J'en ai trop mangé. | I've eaten too much/many (of it/them). |
| Je n'en veux pas. | I don't want any (of it/them). |
| Combien en avez-vous? | How many (of them) do you have? |
| J'en ai beaucoup. | I've got a lot (of them). |
| Les escargots? J'en mange souvent. | Snails? I often eat some (of them). |
| Je n'en mange pas. | I don't eat (any of) them. |

Like **y** (*there*) we often miss out **en** (of it/them) in English, but you must include it in French.

| | |
|---|---|
| Des photos de Liam, en avez-vous? | The photos of Liam? Have you any (of them)? |
| J'en ai beaucoup. | I've got a lot (of them). |
| Je n'en ai pas. | I haven't any (of them). |

In French some verbs are followed by **de**: **parler de** – *to talk about/of*; **s'occuper de** – *to look after*; **avoir besoin de** – *to have need of.* **En** is also used to translate **de** + a pronoun: *of it/them*, etc.

| | |
|---|---|
| Je veux parler de mon idée. | I want to talk about my idea. |
| Je veux en parler. | I want to talk about/of it. |
| Lou s'occupe de son petit frère. | Lou is looking after her little brother. |
| Lou s'en occupe. | Lou is looking after him. |
| J'ai besoin de monnaie. | I (have) need (of) some change. |
| J'en ai besoin. | I (have) need (of) it. |

For more about this go to *French Grammar and Usage*, R. Hawkins and R. Towell, 1996/2001, 2nd edn.

**I**  Rephrase these sentences using **en** instead of the words in italics. Remember to put **en** in front of the verb!

**a** J'ai beaucoup *de CD*.
**b** Il n'a pas *d'ordinateur*.
**c** Il a trois *stylos*.
**d** Combien *de livres* avez-vous?
**e** Nous avons beaucoup *de vins différents*.
**f** Avez-vous *des cigarettes*?
**g** Ils ont trois *chiens*.
**h** Avez-vous *une voiture*?
**i** Oui, j'ai *une voiture*.
**j** Mon ami n'a pas *de voiture*.

**I**  Which pronoun would you use instead of the words in italics.

**a** Nous sommes allés *à la plage*.
**b** Ils nous ont accompagnés *à l'aéroport*.
**c** J'ai acheté *des huîtres** et des langoustines*.
**d** J'ai jeté tous *les journaux qui traînaient*.
**e** Vous nous avez déjà rendu *la cisaille**.
**f** Elle lui a acheté *le livre qu'il avait vu chez le libraire*.
**g** Il n'a pas fini de lire *le livre qu'elle lui a acheté*.
**h** Il nous a prêté *ses roller-blades*.

**i** Nous vous avons donné *des graines de pavot*\* l'année dernière.

**j** Elle lui a raconté *l'histoire* en entier une deuxieme fois pour lui faire plaisir.

\*huîtres – oysters; cisaille – shears; graines de pavot – poppy seeds

# 3.6 More about word order

If you have more than one pronoun in front of the verb, they always go in the following order.

You are not likely to need to use more than two pronouns together.

| je<br>tu<br>il/elle/on<br>nous<br>vous<br>ils/elles | **(ne)** | me<br>te<br>se<br>nous<br>vous | le<br>la<br>les | lui<br>leur | **y** | **en** | verb | **(pas)** |
|---|---|---|---|---|---|---|---|---|

Remember **en** is always the last pronoun.

Choose a sentence to memorise to help you remember the sound of the phrases:

Je ne le lui ai pas donné.     I didn't give him it.

Il ne me les a pas données.     He didn't give me them.

You can easily avoid having to use more than one pronoun by repeating one of the nouns!

Je ne lui ai pas donné son cadeau.     I haven't given him his present.

Il ne m'a pas rendu mes lettres.     He didn't give me back my letters.

**I** Put the sentences into French. The pronouns 'it' and 'them' stand for masculine objects, here.

**a** We saw them at the market.
**b** He bought me some.
**c** You saw them.
**d** I took them there.
**e** She didn't see them.
**f** They weren't there.
**g** She bought me some.
**h** I put them there.
**i** He told me it.
**j** There weren't any.

**II** How would you say the following?

**a** He saw her at the sweetshop (*la confiserie*).
**b** She didn't notice him there.
**c** She wanted to buy him some.
**d** He went back later.
**e** He bought her some.
**f** She didn't eat any.
**g** She gave them to her friend.
**h** She didn't eat them either.
**i** She kept them there.
**j** She gave him them for his birthday.

**3.6.1** Pronouns with *devoir, pouvoir, savoir, vouloir* and *falloir*

These verbs are usually used together with another verb, e.g. *I have to leave*; *I am able to come*; *I know how to sail*; *I want to go*; *I need to hurry*. The pronoun comes in front of the verb it refers to (which will be the second verb or the infinitive).

| | |
|---|---|
| Je dois *les* surveiller. | I have to keep an eye on them. |
| Il ne peut pas *y* aller. | He can't go there. |
| Vous savez *le* faire. | You know how to do it. |
| Elle veut *en* avoir. | She wants to have some. |
| Il faut *le* finir. | We/You have to finish it. |

**I** Put the pronoun in the correct place in the sentence.

**a** Nous ne pouvons pas aller. (**y**)
**b** Je dois payer. (la)
**c** Vous savez comment utiliser. (l')
**d** Elle veut acheter une pour la fête des mères. (**en**)
**e** Il faut aller. (**y**)
**f** Il peut lire maintenant. (le)

**g** Nous devons aller. (**y**)
**h** Ils ne peuvent pas accompagner. (**nous**)
**i** Ils faut dire au revoir. (**vous**)
**j** Je ne sais pas faire. (**le**)

▶▶ **If you have had enough of pronouns, move on to Chapter 4 on Adjectives and come back later.**

# 3.7 Moi, etc.: Emphatic pronouns

Emphatic pronouns are only used when talking about people or animals.

They are used:

• for emphasis: *Who, me? No, him!* – **Qui, moi? Non, lui!**
• after prepositions: *with me*; *for us* – **avec moi**; **pour nous**
• after instructions (in the imperative): *Wait for me!* – **Attends-moi! Attendez-moi!**

|  | singular | plural |
|---|---|---|
| **first person** | **moi** – me | **nous** – us |
| **second person** | **toi** – you | **vous** – you |
| **third person** | **lui** – him <br> **elle** – her | **eux** – them (m) <br> **elles** – them (f) |

## 3.7.1 Using pronouns for emphasis

**I** How would you give these answers in French?

*Who is there?*

**a** Me!
**b** Us!
**c** You! (the child)
**d** Her!
**e** Them! (the lads)
**f** Him!
**g** Them! (the girls)
**h** You!

**II** Replace the names with the pronouns.

**a** C'est Marc! C'est ___!
**b** C'est ton père! C'est ___!
**c** C'est sa mère! C'est ___!
**d** Ce sont ses parents! Ce sont ___!
**e** Ce sont ses sœurs! Ce sont ___!
**f** Ce sont ses copains! Ce sont ___!

## 3.7.2 Emphatic pronouns and prepositions

The same pronouns are used after prepositions:

**à moi** (*to me*), **avec moi** (*with me*), **sans lui** (*without him*),
**pour eux** (*for them*), **selon moi** (*in my opinion*, lit: *according to me*), **chez toi** (*at your house*), etc.

| | |
|---|---|
| C'est à moi. | It's mine./It belongs to me. |
| Il est avec moi. | He's with me. |
| Nous achetons un cadeau pour elle. | We're buying a present for her. |
| Il est parti sans elle. | He went without her. |

**I**  Replace the people in italics with a pronoun.

**a** Ce stylo est à *Jean-Pierre*.
**b** Maurice est allé en ville sans *sa femme*.
**c** Elle est sortie avec *ses amies*.
**d** M. Bertrand a acheté un cadeau pour *sa fille*.
**e** Le sac bleu est à *Sylvain*, et le sac rouge est à *Isabelle*.
**f** Il a mangé avec *mes enfants et moi*.
**g** C'est *sa mère*!
**h** Nous sommes partis sans *nos enfants*.
**i** On a acheté des glaces pour *toi et tes copains*.
**j** Je sors avec *Gilles*.

**II**  How would you say the following?

**a** Are you coming with me?   Vous venez avec _____?
**b** I am going with him.   Je vais avec _____.
**c** He went without us.   Il est parti sans _____.
**d** We will leave without her.   Nous partirons sans _____.
**e** We are buying it for you.   Nous l'achetons pour _____.
**f** In his opinion, we are too old.   Selon _____, nous sommes trop vieux.
**g** In my opinion, he is wrong.   Selon _____, il a tort.
**h** We are going without him.   Nous y allons sans _____.
**i** They are going without her.   Ils y vont sans _____.
**j** She is coming with us.   Elle vient avec _____.

# **3.8** Pronouns and the imperative

▶▶ **If you are not going to be telling people what to do, leave this out and go on to 3.9.**

You probably already know the parts of this you are likely to need. Check that it sounds familiar and then move on.

Attendez-moi! | Wait for me!

| singular | plural |
|----------|--------|
| attendez-moi | attendez-nous |
| attendez-le | attendez-les |
| attendez-la | |

**I** How would you say: Wait ...?

Attendez-

**a** for us      **d** for her
**b** for him      **e** for me
**c** for them

## **3.8.1** Pronouns with reflexive verbs

| singular | plural |
|----------|--------|
| assieds-toi | asseyez-vous |

| | |
|---|---|
| s'asseoir | to sit down (sit yourself down) |
| se dépêcher | to hurry (hurry yourself up) |
| se débrouiller | to manage on your own (sort yourself out) |

**I** How would you say the following?

**a** Sit down!      Assieds- ___!
**b** Sit down!      Asseyez- ___!
**c** Hurry up!      Dépêche- ___!
**d** Hurry up!      Dépêchez- ___!
**e** Manage on your own!      Débrouille- ___!
**f** Manage on your own!      Débrouillez- ___!

## **3.8.2** Order of pronouns in the imperative

The pronouns come after the verb and are hyphenated to it.

 This is easy to remember, as the order is just the same as it is in English!

| Regardez-moi. | Look at me. |
| Tenez-le. | Hold it. |
| Choisissez-le. | Choose it. |
| Donne-le-moi. | Give it to me. |
| Restez-y. | Stay there. |
| Achetez-en. | Buy some. |
| Mangez-les. | Eat them. |
| Donnez-le-moi. | Give it to me. |

| le | moi | en |
|---|---|---|
| la | toi | y |
| les | lui | |
| | nous | |
| | vous | |
| | leur | |

## 3.9 Qui? Que?: Interrogative pronouns

An interrogative pronoun is used to ask the question *who?* or *what?* In French you use **Qui ...?** (*who?*) when talking about a person and **Que ...?** (*what?*) when talking about a thing.

▶▶ **If you know all about qui and que, go on to 3.10.**

You can use the short form ...

| Qui? | Who? |
| Qui dit ça? | Who says that? |
| Que ...? | What ...? |
| Que dit-il? | What is he saying? |

... or the long form.

| Qui est-ce qui ... ? | Who (is it that) ... ? |
| Qui est-ce qui dit ça? | Who (is it that) says that? |
| Qu'est-ce que ... ? | What (is it that) ... ? |
| Qu'est-ce qu'il dit? | What is (it that) he (is) saying? |

Note that with the short form, you have to invert the subject and the verb. With the long form, the word order stays the same.

**Qui?** can stand on its own to ask just **Who?** But if you want just to ask **What?** you say **Quoi?** The word **Que** has to be followed by something else.

### 3.9.1 *Qui* or *que*?

**I** **Qui** or **que**? Which question word would you use to ask about the person or thing in italics? For example:

*Michel* arrive en premier. → Qui (arrive en premier)?

**a** Jean-Luc porte *un pantalon rouge et un pull bleu*.
**b** *Thomas* joue au basket.
**c** *Nous* mangeons du pain grillé.
**d** Jérôme fait *sa déclaration d'impôts*.
**e** Tu veux *un billet aller-retour*.
**f** Vous buvez *de l'eau*.
**g** *Elvire* va au cinéma.
**h** *Mes parents* dînent au restaurant.
**i** Vous lisez *Le Monde*.
**j** *Mon copain* fait du roller.

# 3.10 *Le mien, la mienne,* etc.: Possessive pronouns

▶▶ **If you want to avoid using the possessive pronouns for the moment you can say 'C'est à moi', etc. (see section 3.7). Go on to 3.11.**

|          | singular      |              | plural         |               |
|----------|---------------|--------------|----------------|---------------|
|          | **masculine** | **feminine** | **masculine**  | **feminine**  |
| mine     | le mien       | la mienne    | les miens      | les miennes   |
| yours    | le tien       | la tienne    | les tiens      | les tiennes   |
| his/hers | le sien       | la sienne    | les siens      | les siennes   |
| ours     | le nôtre      | la nôtre     | les nôtres     | les nôtres    |
| yours    | le vôtre      | la vôtre     | les vôtres     | les vôtres    |
| theirs   | le leur       | la leur      | les leurs      | les leurs     |

Possessive pronouns translate the English *mine, yours, his, hers, ours, yours, theirs.* They have to agree with the noun they are replacing.

Regardez cette voiture, c'est la mienne.

Look at this car, it's mine.

**(la mienne to agree with la voiture)**
Alternative:
Regardez cette voiture, c'est à moi.

Ce porte-monnaie, c'est le sien.     This purse is his/hers.
(**le sien** to agree with **le porte-monnaie**)
Alternative:
Ce porte-monnaie, c'est à elle.     … it's hers.
… c'est à lui.                       … it's his.

**I**   Replace the nouns in italics with the correct form of the pronoun (**le mien, la mienne, les miens, les miennes**).

   **a**  *Ce livre* est à moi. C'est ____.
   **b**  *Ces journaux* (mpl) sont à moi. Ce sont ____.
   **c**  *Cette chaise* est à moi. C'est ____.
   **d**  *Ces papiers* (mpl) sont à moi. Ce sont ____.
   **e**  *Ce message* est à moi. C'est ____.
   **f**  *Ces CD* (mpl) sont à moi. Ce sont ____.
   **g**  *Ces photos* (fpl) sont à moi. Ce sont ____.
   **h**  *Cette voiture* est à moi. C'est ____.

**II**  Replace the nouns in italics with the correct form of the pronoun (**le sien**, etc., or **le leur**, etc.).

   **a**  Ce sont *les lunettes* de Hugo? Ce sont ____?
   **b**  Ce sont *les tennis* de Paul et Théo? Ce sont ____?
   **c**  Ce sont *les chaussettes* de Pascal? Ce sont ____?
   **d**  C'est *le sac* de Sarah? C'est ____?
   **e**  C'est *la robe* de Mathilde? C'est ____?
   **f**  C'est *le pull* de Manon? C'est ____?
   **g**  C'est *le maillot* de Catherine? C'est ____?
   **h**  Ce sont *les serviettes* de Théo et Noé? Ce sont ____?

> Remember that the relative pronoun agrees with the noun it stands in for, not with the person who owns the object.

**III**  Replace the nouns in italics with the correct form of the pronoun (**le vôtre, la vôtre, les vôtres; le leur, la leur, les leurs**).

   **a**  *Ce billet* est à vous? C'est ____?
   **b**  *Ces journaux* sont à eux? Ce sont ____?
   **c**  *Cette montre* est à vous? C'est ____?
   **d**  C'est *la voiture* de mes parents? C'est ____?
   **e**  *Ce message* est à vous? C'est ____?
   **f**  *Ces nouvelles revues* sont à elles? Ce sont ____?
   **g**  *Cette moto* est à vous? C'est ____?
   **h**  *Ces frites* sont à eux? Ce sont ____?
   **i**  Ce sont *vos glaces*? Ce sont ____?
   **j**  C'est *votre pantalon*? C'est ____?

# 3.11 *Qui, que, dont*: Relative pronouns

► ► **If you can recognise a relative pronoun, go on to 3.11.1.**

Relative pronouns are the words *who, which* and *whose* when they are used to refer to someone already mentioned.

| | |
|---|---|
| la femme *qui* habite à côté | the lady *who* lives next door |
| le chien *qui* aboie toute la nuit | the dog *which* barks all night |
| mon portable *qui* ne marche plus | my mobile *which* doesn't work any more |
| le livre *que* nous venons d'acheter | the book *which* we have just bought |
| l'homme *dont* la voiture est toujours garée devant notre maison | the man *whose* car is always parked in front of our house |

## 3.11.1 *Qui, que, dont*: Who, which, whose

### A *Qui* – who/which

**Qui** always refers to the subject of the sentence.

> Remember the subject is the person or thing that 'does' the action. In the sentences below, it is the woman who is *wearing*; and the bottle which doesn't *have* a label: they are the subjects.

| | |
|---|---|
| la femme *qui* porte un tailleur-pantalon bleu | the woman *who* is wearing a blue trouser suit |
| la bouteille *qui* n'a pas d'étiquette | the bottle *which* doesn't have a label |

### B *Que* – whom/which

**Que** refers to the object of the sentence.

> The object is the person or thing that has the action done to him/it. In this case it was I and John who did the seeing and the breaking. The man and the bottle are the objects.

| | |
|---|---|
| l'homme *que* j'ai vu traverser la rue | the man (*whom*) I saw crossing the road |
| la bouteille *que* Jean a cassée | the bottle (*which*) John broke |

The past participle also agrees with the object if the object comes before the subject and the relative pronoun **que**:

| | |
|---|---|
| Le temps qu'il a perdu … | The time that he has lost … |
| La maison que j'ai vue … | The house that I have seen … |
| Les courses qu'elle a faites … | The shopping that she did … |
| Les verres qu'il a cassés … | The glasses that he broke … |

**I**   Add an ending to the past participle, where necessary.

**a** La femme qu'il a aimé.

**b** Les livres qu'il a lu.

**c** Les émissions qu'il a regardé.

**d** La voiture qu'il a conduit.

**e** Les papiers qu'il a signé.

**f** Les mensonges qu'il a inventé.

**g** L'ami qu'il a trahi.

C   *Dont* – whose/of whom/of which

| | |
|---|---|
| la femme *dont* je connais le mari | the lady *whose* husband I know |
| la maison *dont* j'ai oublié le numéro | the house *whose* number I have forgotten |

**II**   Which relative pronoun would you use?

**a** The man who is wearing a suit and tie is called Mr Bertrand.
L'homme ____ porte un costume-cravate s'appelle M. Bertrand.

**b** The man whom I met last year at the conference in New York is the one wearing sunglasses.
L'homme ____ j'ai rencontré l'année dernière au congrès de New York est celui qui porte des lunettes de soleil.

**c** The person whose car is parked in the drive is kindly asked to come to the front desk.
La personne ____ la voiture est garée dans l'allée est priée de bien vouloir se présenter à l'accueil.

**d** The person for whom I am waiting hasn't arrived yet.
La personne ____ j'attends n'est pas encore arrivée.

**e** The person whose address you gave me isn't at that address any more.
La personne ____ vous m'avez donné l'adresse n'habite plus à cette adresse.

**f** The person who wants to buy our flat has already put in an offer.
La personne ____ veut acheter notre appartement a déjà fait une offre.

**g** Mr Botton, whose wife is seriously ill, will not be coming.
M. Botton, ____ la femme est gravement malade, ne viendra pas.

**h** What is the name of the man who is sitting in the third row?
Comment s'appelle l'homme ____ est assis au troisième rang?

**i** You haven't given me back the pen I lent you.

**j** It's a man whose name I have forgotten.

Vous ne m'avez pas rendu le stylo ____ je vous ai prêté.

C'est un homme ____ j'ai oublié le nom.

# 3.12 *Lequel?*: Which one?

| singular | | plural | |
|---|---|---|---|
| masculine | feminine | masculine | feminine |
| lequel | laquelle | lesquels | lesquelles |

Nous avons six chiots. *Lequel* voulez-vous?

Regardez les maisons à louer. *Laquelle* préféreriez-vous?

Essayez nos nouveaux parfums. *Lesquels* aimez-vous?

*Lesquelles* de ces chemises préférez-vous?

We have six puppies. Which one would you like?

Look at the houses to let. Which would you prefer?

Try our new perfumes. Which ones do you like?

Which (ones) of these shirts do you prefer?

# 3.13 *Celui, celle*: The one which/whose

These pronouns are followed by **qui**/**que** or a preposition.

| singular | | plural | |
|---|---|---|---|
| masculine | feminine | masculine | feminine |
| celui | celle | ceux | celles |

J'ai donné la photo à mon cousin: *celle* de ma tante le jour de son mariage.

Avez-vous vu mon stylo, *celui* que mon père m'a donné pour mon bac?

Il faut changer les fleurs: *celles* du vase la salle à manger.

Achetez des haricots, *ceux* qui sont bicolores.

I gave the photo to my cousin – the one of my aunt on her wedding day.

Have you seen my pen – the one my father gave me for passing my A levels?

You must change the flowers – the ones in the vase in the dining-room.

Buy some beans – the ones which are two colours.

### 3.13.1 *Celui-ci, celui-là*: This one, that one

If you want to be more specific and say *this one (here)* or *that one (there)*, you can add **-ci** (*here*) or **-là** (*there*) to **celui, celle,** etc. **Celui-ci** can also mean *the former* and **celui-là** *the latter*.

|  | singular | | plural | |
|---|---|---|---|---|
|  | **masculine** | **feminine** | **masculine** | **feminine** |
| this/these one(s) (here) | celui-ci | celle-ci | ceux-ci | celles-ci |
| that/those one(s) (there) | celui-là | celle-là | ceux-là | celles-là |

| | |
|---|---|
| Quelle bague préférez-vous? | Which ring do you prefer? |
| Je préfère *celle-ci*. | I prefer this one (here). |
| Vous préférez *celle-là*. | You prefer that one (there). |
| Quel porte-monnaie préférez-vous? | Which purse do you prefer? |
| Je préfère *celui-là*. | I prefer that one (there). |
| Vous préférez *celui-ci*. | You prefer this one (here). |

**I** Say you want to order *these* things (here).

Je voudrais commander …

**a** des gants (m)  
**b** une bague  
**c** un porte-monnaie  
**d** des chaussures (f)  
**e** une veste  
**f** un pantalon  
**g** un pull  
**h** des livres (m)  
**i** un pyjama  
**j** et des boucles d'oreilles (f)

**II** Say you want to order *those* trees and flowers (there)

**a** des géraniums (m)  
**b** une rose  
**c** un érable  
**d** un olivier  
**e** des jonquilles (f)  
**f** des œillets (m)  
**g** des tulipes (f)  
**h** un marronier  
**i** un sapin  
**j** des pensées (f)

## 3.14 ▶Fast track: Pronouns

A pronoun is a word which stands in for a noun.

A Subject pronouns: I, you, he, etc.

The subject pronoun is the person or thing that does the action: *I, you*, etc. You use them in front of a verb to replace a person or thing you have already mentioned or whose identity is known.

They are:

| singular | plural |
|----------|--------|
| je – I | nous – we |
| tu – you | vous – you |
| il – he | ils – they |
| elle – she | elles – they (f) |
| on – one (we) | |

B  Direct object pronouns: me, you, etc.

The direct object pronoun stands in for the person or object that has the action done to him/it.

They are:

| singular | plural |
|----------|--------|
| me – me | nous – us |
| te – you | vous – you |
| le – him | les – them |
| la – her | |

In English they come after the verb. In French they come in front of the verb.

| I see him. | Je le vois. (I him see.) |
|------------|-------------------------|
| She sees me. | Elle me voit. (She me sees.) |
| I see him/it. | Je le vois. (I him see.) |
| We don't see them. | Nous ne les voyons pas. |
| | (We them don't see.) |

C  Indirect object pronouns: to me, to him, etc.

In English, an indirect object pronoun is the same as a direct object pronoun but has (or can have) *to* or *for* in front of it.

 **Me**, **te**, **nous** and **vous** are the same as the direct object pronouns (see above) so you only have to remember '**lui**' – *(to) him/her* and '**leur**' – *(to) them*.

## D  *Y – there*

**Y** stands for a place that you have already mentioned. It always goes in front of the verb.

*Mon copain est allé en ville. J'y suis allé hier.*

## E  *En – of it/of them*

**En** refers to something you have already mentioned and stands for *of it* or *of them*.

| | |
|---|---|
| *J'en ai trop mangé.* | I've eaten too many (of them). |

## F  Order of pronouns

If you have more than one pronoun in front of the verb, they always go in the following order.

| je<br>tu<br>il/elle/on<br>nous<br>vous<br>ils/elles | (ne) | me<br>te<br>se<br>nous<br>vous | le<br>la<br>les | lui<br>leur | y | en | verb | (pas) |
|---|---|---|---|---|---|---|---|---|

 In the perfect tense the pronouns always come before the part of **avoir**. Choose one phrase to learn by heart to use as a pattern: **Je le lui ai donné** – *I gave it to him*.

### *Moi! Me!*

These are called emphatic pronouns.

They are used

- for emphasis: *Who, me? No, him!* – Qui, moi? Non, lui!
- after prepositions: *with me, for us* – avec moi, pour nous

| | singular | | plural | |
|---|---|---|---|---|
| **first person** | moi | me | nous | us |
| **second person** | toi | you | vous | you |
| **third person** | lui | him | eux | them (m) |
| | elle | her | elles | them (f) |

They are also used after the imperative:

| | |
|---|---|
| *Attendez-moi!* | Wait for me! |
| *Attendez-le!* | Wait for him! |
| *Attendez-les!* | Wait for them! |

## F  Qui? Que …? Who? What …?

These are called interrogative pronouns. They are used to
ask the question *Who?* or *What …?* You use **Qui …?** (*who?*)
when talking about a person and **Que …?** (*what?*) when
talking about a thing.

## G  Le mien, la mienne – mine

These are called possessive pronouns. They translate the
English *mine, yours, his, hers, ours, yours, theirs.* They have to
agree with the noun they are replacing.

## H  Qui, que, dont – who, which, whose

These are called relative pronouns. They translate *who,
which* and *whose* when they are used to refer to
someone/something already mentioned.

**Qui** always refers to the subject of the sentence.

**Que** refers to the object of the sentence.

**Dont** translates: *whose/of whom/of which.*

## I  Some more pronouns

| | |
|---|---|
| Lequel, Laquelle? | Which one? |
| Lesquels, Lesquelles? | Which ones? |
| celui, celle, ceux, celles | the one(s) (which/whose) |
| celui-ci, celle-ci | this one |
| ceux-ci, celles-ci | these ones |
| celui-là, celle-là | that one |
| ceux-là, celles-là | those ones |

# 4 ADJECTIVES

## What is an adjective?

▶▶ **If you know what an adjective is, go on to 4.2.**

Adjectives are 'describing' words; you use them to say what something or someone is like.

**I** Highlight the adjectives in these sentences.

**a** Jack is tall and good-looking.
**b** He has short, dark hair and blue-grey eyes.
**c** He has just bought a new car.
**d** He likes to wear smart clothes when he goes to work and casual clothes at the weekend.
**e** His house is quite modern and has a big garden.
**f** His girlfriend is small and bubbly.
**g** She manages a large bank.
**h** He has an older brother and a younger sister.
**i** His favourite dish is tagliatelle alla carbonara.
**j** He likes his coffee very hot and very black.

## 4.1 Adjectival agreement: *grand(e) et petit(e)*

In French the adjective 'agrees' with the noun, i.e. it usually adds **-e** if the noun is feminine and **-s** if the noun is plural.

As you don't pronounce **-e** or **-s** at the end of a word, adjectives mostly sound the same, whatever the ending.

▶▶ **If you know about adjectival agreement, go on to 4.3 Fast track.**

- If the noun is feminine singular, **grand** and **petit** add **-e**: **grande, petite.**
- If the noun is masculine plural, **grand** and **petit** add **-s**: **grands, petits.**
- If the noun is feminine plural, **grand** and **petit** add **-es**: **grandes, petites.**

|  | singular | | plural | |
|---|---|---|---|---|
|  | **masculine** | **feminine** | **masculine** | **feminine** |
| big small | grand petit | grande petite | grands petits | grandes petites |

**I** Fill in the correct form: **grand, grande, grands** or **grandes**:

**a** un ___ bâtiment      **c** des ___ bâtiments
**b** une ___ maison      **d** des ___ maisons

and **petit, petite, petits** or **petites**:

**e** un ___ train      **g** des ___ trains
**f** une ___ barrière      **h** des ___ barrières

## **4.1.1** Regular adjectives

Most adjectives add **-e** for the feminine unless they already
end in **-e** (**timide** – *shy*) and **-s** or **-es** for the plural.

 In French, most endings are not pronounced, so many adjectives
sound the same in all forms BUT if the adjective ends in **-d**, **-s** or
**-t**, the added **-e** and **-es** will mean that you have to pronounce
the final **-d/-s/-t**. So **grand** is pronounced gr-aa-n, but
**grande** is pronounced gr-aa-nd; similarly **petit** = pe-ti and
**petite** = pe-teet; and **gris** is pronounced gri, but **grise** sounds
something like greaze.

**I** Fill in the missing forms. Check your answers and then try
saying them aloud and note which ones will sound different.

| | meaning | singular | | plural | |
| | | masculine | feminine | masculine | feminine |
|---|---|---|---|---|---|
| **a** | happy | content | | | |
| **b** | sad | triste | | | |
| **c** | short | court | | | |
| **d** | tall/big | grand | | | |
| **e** | weak | faible | | | |
| **f** | strong | fort | | | |
| **g** | intelligent | intelligent | | | |
| **h** | stupid | stupide | | | |
| **i** | pretty | joli | | | |
| **j** | ugly | laid | | | |
| **k** | fun/funny | marrant | | | |
| **l** | naughty | méchant | | | |
| **m** | bad | mauvais | | | |
| **n** | young | jeune | | | |
| **o** | wide | large | | | |
| **p** | thin | mince | | | |
| **q** | modern | moderne | | | |
| **r** | clean | propre | | | |
| **s** | dirty | sale | | | |
| **t** | friendly | aimable | | | |

**II**  Which form of the adjective in brackets would you use to complete these sentences?

**a**  John a les cheveux ____. (court)
**b**  Il est ____. (content)
**c**  Il a une ____ sœur qui s'appelle Louise. (petit)
**d**  Et deux ____ frères qui s'appellent Yann et Serge. (grand)
**e**  Louise est ____. (joli)
**f**  Yann et Serge sont ____. (mince)
**g**  Ils ont les cheveux ____. (noir)
**h**  Louise est très ____. (intelligent)
**i**  Mais elle est souvent ____. (méchant)
**j**  Yann et Serge sont ____. (marrant)
**k**  Patrice habite dans une ____ ville. (petit)
**l**  Il habite dans un quartier ____. (calme)
**m**  Le lotissement où il habite est ____. (moderne)
**n**  Les maisons sont assez ____. (grand)
**o**  Il a un ____ jardin. (petit)
**p**  Le salon est ____. (grand)
**q**  La cuisine est plutôt ____. (petit)
**r**  Et les chambres ne sont pas ____ non plus. (grand)
**s**  Il a une ____ vue de son bureau. (joli)
**t**  Il préfère les maisons ____. (moderne)

On these pages you will find some adjectives sitting before the noun, and some after it. If you want to find out about this, see section 4.2.

## **4.1.2**  Irregular adjectives

### A  Adjectives which end in -f
These make the feminine by replacing the **-f** with **-ve**.

|  | singular | | plural | |
|---|---|---|---|---|
| **meaning** | **masculine** | **feminine** | **masculine** | **feminine** |
| active | actif | active | actifs | actives |
| sporty | sportif | sportive | sportifs | sportives |
| new | neuf | neuve | neufs | neuves |

## B   Adjectives which end in -x

These make the feminine by replacing the **-x** with **-se**. In the masculine plural no **-s** is added.

| | singular | | plural | |
|---|---|---|---|---|
| **meaning** | **masculine** | **feminine** | **masculine** | **feminine** |
| dreadful | affreux | affreuse | affreux | affreuses |
| ambitious | ambitieux | ambitieuse | ambitieux | ambitieuses |
| boring | ennuyeux | ennuyeuse | ennuyeux | ennuyeuses |
| generous | généreux | généreuse | généreux | généreuses |
| happy | heureux | heureuse | heureux | heureuses |
| joyful | joyeux | joyeuse | joyeux | joyeuses |
| serious | sérieux | sérieuse | sérieux | sérieuses |

## C   Other adjectives which end in -x

These form the feminine in different ways.

| | singular | | plural | |
|---|---|---|---|---|
| **meaning** | **masculine** | **feminine** | **masculine** | **feminine** |
| old | vieux (vieil*) | vieille | vieux | vieilles |
| soft/sweet | doux | douce | doux | douces |
| false/wrong | faux | fausse | faux | fausses |

\* You use **vieil** before masculine nouns beginning with a vowel or silent **h**.

**I**   Choose the right form of the adjectives in brackets.

**a**   M. Barnard est très ____. (actif)

**b**   Mme Barnard n'est pas ____. (sportif)

**c**   Les filles Barnard sont ____. (sportif)

**d**   Leurs fils, Étienne et Marc, sont ____. (paresseux)

**e**   Mme Dubois n'est pas ____. (vieux)

**f**   Son fils, Nicolas, est très ____. (ambitieux)

**g**   Ses filles, Marianne et Laurence, ne sont pas ____. (heureux)

**h**   Le film était ____. (ennuyeux)

**i**   Les chiens sont ____. (heureux)

**j**   Mon chat est ____. (paresseux)

**k**   Marilène est ____. (sérieux)

**l**   Sa peau est ____. (doux)

**m**   Ses parents sont ____. (ambitieux)

**n**   La pollution est ____. (affreux)

**o**   Mes grands-parents sont ____. (vieux)

**p**   La réponse est ____. (faux)

**q**   Ma tante n'est pas ____. (généreux)

**r**   Ces histoires sont ____. (ennuyeux)

**s**   Mes notes sont ____. (affreux)

**t**   ____ Noël! (joyeux)

D   Adjectives which end in *-s, -n* or *-l*

These usually double the final consonant before adding **-e**. In the masculine plural of words ending in **-s**, no extra **-s** is added

| meaning | singular | | plural | |
|---|---|---|---|---|
| | **masculine** | **feminine** | **masculine** | **feminine** |
| low | bas | basse | bas | basses |
| fat/big | gros | grosse | gros | grosses |
| good | bon | bonne | bons | bonnes |
| old | ancien | ancienne | anciens | anciennes |
| kind/nice | gentil | gentille | gentils | gentilles |
| natural | naturel | naturelle | naturels | naturelles |

E   Adjectives which end in *-eau*

| meaning | singular | | plural | |
|---|---|---|---|---|
| | **masculine** | **feminine** | **masculine** | **feminine** |
| beautiful/ good-looking | beau (bel*) | belle | beaux | belles |
| new | nouveau (nouvel*) | nouvelle | nouveaux | nouvelles |

* Before masculine nouns beginning with a vowel or silent **h**, **beau** becomes **bel** and **nouveau** becomes **nouvel**: **un bel/nouvel hôtel**.

F   Adjectives which are irregular

| meaning | singular | | plural | |
|---|---|---|---|---|
| | **masculine** | **feminine** | **masculine** | **feminine** |
| long | long | longue | longs | longues |
| mad | fou | folle | fous | folles |

**II**   Give the right form of the adjectives in brackets.

**a**   Mon oncle est ____. (gros)
**b**   Ma tante n'est pas ____. (gros)
**c**   Ma petite sœur est ____. (gentil)
**d**   Mes parents ne sont pas ____. (gentil)
**e**   Ma grande sœur est ____. (beau)
**f**   Son ami n'est pas ____. (beau)
**g**   Mes amies sont ____. (bon)
**h**   Mes grands-parents sont ____. (bon)

**i**  Buvez de l'eau ___! (naturel)

**j**  Les images sont ___! (naturel)

**k**  Avignon est une ville ___. (ancien)

**l**  M. Hibert est un ___ professeur de géographie. (ancien)

**m**  Amsterdam est la capitale des Pays- ___. (bas)

**n**  La chaise est trop ___. (bas)

**o**  C'est un ___ livre. (nouveau)

**p**  Il y a un ___ hôtel dans cette rue. (nouveau)

**q**  Les ___ maisons sont dans la rue Lecourbe. (nouveau)

**r**  Quelle ___ vue! (beau)

**s**  Nous avons une ___ voiture. (nouveau)

**t**  Mes notes sont ___. (bon)

## G  Adjectives which end in *-er*

The feminine forms take a grave accent: **è**.

| | singular | | plural | |
|---|---|---|---|---|
| **meaning** | **masculine** | **feminine** | **masculine** | **feminine** |
| dear/ expensive | cher | chère | chers | chères |
| proud | fier | fière | fiers | fières |
| last | dernier | dernière | derniers | dernières |
| first | premier | première | premiers | première |

## H  Adjectives which end in *-c*

| | singular | | plural | |
|---|---|---|---|---|
| **meaning** | **masculine** | **feminine** | **masculine** | **feminine** |
| dry | sec | sèche | secs | sèches |
| white | blanc | blanche | blancs | blanches |
| Greek | grec | grecque | grecs | grecques |
| public | public | publique | publics | publiques |

**III**  Give the right form of the adjectives in brackets.

**a**  C'est le ___ jour des vacances. (premier)

**b**  C'est la ___ fois que je vais en France. (premier)

**c**  La semaine ___ nous sommes allés à New York. (dernier)

**d**  Avez-vous vu le ___ film de Gérard Depardieu? (dernier)

**e**  Mes cheveux sont trop ___. (sec)

**f**  J'ai les mains ___. (sec)

**g**  Il préfère le vin ___. (blanc)

**h**  Elle porte des sandales ___. (blanc)

**i**  Sa chemise est ___. (blanc)

**j**  La Maison ___. (blanc)

**k** Mes ___ amis. (cher)
**l** Ma ___ amie. (cher)
**m** Mon ami est très ___ de sa moto. (fier)
**n** Ses parents sont très ___ de lui. (fier)
**o** C'est la ___ tarte aux fraises. (dernier)
**p** Il a mangé le ___ croissant. (dernier)
**q** On a trouvé un ancien vase ___. (grec)
**r** Les îles ___ sont très belles. (grec)
**s** On va au jardin ___. (public)
**t** La piscine ___ n'est pas encore ouverte. (public)

## **4.1.3** Colours

Most adjectives of colour agree in the same way as other
adjectives, and they always come after the noun they
describe: *a red car* becomes *a car red* – **une voiture rouge**; *the
White House* becomes *the House White* – **la Maison Blanche**.

> Choose a phrase to memorise to help you remember the order:
> **un chat noir**; **un oiseau bleu**; etc.

> Remember that the plural **-s** is not pronounced and most forms of
> the adjectives of colour will sound the same except for
> **vert/verte**, **gris/grise** and **blanc/blanche.**

Most adjectives of colour form their agreements in the
same way as other adjectives, including those which end in
**-e** and **-c** (see 4.1.1).

| | singular | | plural | |
| --- | --- | --- | --- | --- |
| **meaning** | **masculine** | **feminine** | **masculine** | **feminine** |
| black | noir | noire | noirs | noires |
| blue | bleu | bleue | bleus | bleues |
| green | vert | verte | verts | vertes |
| red | rouge | rouge | rouges | rouges |
| yellow | jaune | jaune | jaunes | jaunes |
| white | blanc | blanche | blancs | blanches |

**I** Complete the sentences with the right form of the colour
given in brackets.

**a** Sandrine porte une jupe ___. (rouge)
**b** Ses sandales sont ___. (vert)
**c** Matthias porte une chemise ___. (gris)
**d** Sa gabardine est ___. (bleu)
**e** Kathy porte une robe du soir ___. (bleu)

**f** Ses chaussures sont ___. (rouge)
**g** Simon porte un tee-shirt ___. (jaune)
**h** Ses espadrilles sont ___. (rouge)
**i** Jennifer porte un tailleur-pantalon ___. (bleu)
**j** Ses bottes en caoutchouc sont ___. (jaune)

## 4.1.4 Colours that don't change

These colours never change, regardless of the noun they are describing:

- adjectives made up of two words:

| | |
|---|---|
| bleu marine | navy blue |
| bleu pâle | pale blue |
| bleu clair | light blue |
| bleu foncé | dark blue |

- nouns which are being used as adjectives:

| | |
|---|---|
| marron | brown (chestnut) |
| ivoire | ivory |
| parme | (parma) violet |
| chocolat | chocolate |
| orange | orange |
| turquoise | turquoise |
| bordeaux | wine-coloured |
| crème | cream |

 When two colour words are used together, they are hyphenated. **bleu-vert**, **bleu-gris**. These colours don't change either.

**I**  Add the correct form of the adjective given in brackets.

**a** Séverine a les yeux ___ (bleu-vert)
**b** ... et des cheveux ___. (marron)
**c** Elle porte un sarong ___ (bleu marine)
**d** ... un bustier ___ (ivoire)
**e** ... et un cardigan ___. (parme)
**f** Ses mocassins sont ___ (bleu clair)
**g** ... et ses chaussettes sont ___. (blanc)
**h** Les murs de son atelier de peintre sont ___ (rose pâle)
**i** ... les rideaux sont ___ (rose foncé)
**j** ... et la porte est ___. (turquoise)

# **4.2** The position of adjectives

In English, adjectives come in front of the noun they are describing: *a large house, a fast car*. In French, most adjectives (including all adjectives of colour) come after the noun:

| | |
|---|---|
| la maison moderne, le garçon paresseux | the modern house, the lazy boy |

The adjectives which do come in front of the noun are: **beau, bon, demi, grand, gros, jeune, joli, long, mauvais, nouveau, petit, prochain,\* vieux** and all ordinal numbers (**premier deuxième**).

| | |
|---|---|
| la petite maison, le grand bâtiment | the little house, the large building |

**I** Put these adjectives in the right place.

**a** une entreprise (jeune)
**b** une jacinthe (bleue)
**c** un enfant (sage)
**d** un bijou (petit)
**e** une femme (belle)
**f** un après-midi (paresseux)
**g** un château (vieux)
**h** une idée (bonne)
**i** un chat (petit, noir)
**j** un rat (gros)

**k** une histoire (intéressante)
**l** une couleur (jolie)
**m** une femme (grosse)
**n** un philosophe (moderne)
**o** un film (ennuyeux)
**p** un voyage (long)
**q** une expérience (mauvaise)
**r** une ville (grande)
**s** des falaises (blanches)
**t** un penseur (nouveau)

\* When used with days of the week, months and years, *prochain(e)* comes after the noun. See 4.4 for other adjectives that can be placed before or after the noun.

# **4.3** ▶**Fast track:** Adjectives

## Agreement

Adjectives are 'describing' words. They agree with the noun they describe, i.e. they usually add **-e** for a feminine noun (unless they already end in **-e**: **timide, stupide,** etc.) and they add **-s** (or **-es**) for a plural noun.

| singular | | plural | |
|---|---|---|---|
| **masculine** | **feminine** | **masculine** | **feminine** |
| un pantalon noir | une chemise noire | des pantalons noirs | des chemises noires |

In French most endings are not pronounced so the adjectives usually sound the same in all forms. These all sound the same:

joli, jolie, jolis, jolies
jeune, jeune, jeunes, jeunes

The **-d**, **-t** or **-s** at the end of a word is not usually pronounced but when **-e** is added it is pronounced. If you are talking about something feminine you may have to remember to pronounce the ending: **il est petit** but **elle est petite**.

The two singulars and two plurals still sound the same as the **-s** is not pronounced:

petit, petits; petite, petites

Some adjectives change the spelling to make them easier to pronounce.

Look for patterns. Adjectives with the same endings usually change in the same way:

paresseux → paresseuse; nerveux → nerveuse; ennuyeux → ennuyeuse

actif → active; sportif → sportive; neuf → neuve

beau → belle; nouveau → nouvelle

bon → bonne; moyen → moyenne

## Word order

Most adjectives come after the word they are describing: **une femme sérieuse** – *a serious woman*; **un ami généreux** – *a generous friend*; **un bâtiment moderne** – *a modern building*.

But these ones usually come in front: **beau/belle**; **bon/bonne**; **grand/grande**; **gros/grosse**; **jeune/jeune**; **joli/jolie**; **long/longue**; **mauvais/mauvaise**; **nouveau/nouvelle**; **petit/petite**; **premier/première** (and other ordinal numbers); **vieux/vielle**.

une belle maison; un vieil ami; un petit village

## Colours

All adjectives of colour come after the word they are describing: **un chien noir** – *a black dog*.

Most colours take the same endings as other adjectives:

bleu, bleue, bleus, bleues

 **Blanc** becomes **blanche** in the feminine:
blanc, blanche, blancs, blanches

Some colours don't change. They are colours made up of two words: **bleu-gris** – *blue-grey*; and most words which are nouns used as adjectives: **chocolat**, **ivoire**, **orange**, etc.

# **4.4** Adjectives with two meanings

Some adjectives have a completely different meaning depending on whether they are used in front of or after the noun.

- un cher ami                           a dear friend
  un pullover cher                    an expensive pullover
- un ancien acteur                   a former actor
  une ville ancienne                 an old town
- mes propres mains             my own hands
  des mains propres               clean hands
- Ce pauvre enfant!               That poor child! (unfortunate)
  une famille pauvre               a poor family (lacking money)
- le seul homme au monde   the only man in the world
  un homme seul.                    a lonely man

**I**  Put the adjective in the right place in the sentence according to the context.

   **a** M. Gilbert l'a vu de ses yeux. (propres)
   **b** Je vais vous présenter, auditeurs, un auteur contemporain. (chers)
   **c** Jérôme est un élève de mon lycée. (ancien)
   **d** Je n'ai plus de chaussettes. (propres)
   **e** La voiture est une Ferrari. (chère)
   **f** Mon oncle nous a montré la ville. (ancienne)
   **g** Des millions de cailles sont tuées chaque année pendant la saison de la chasse. (pauvres)
   **h** Les gens habitent dans des bidonvilles. (pauvres)
   **i** La solution, c'est d'aller voir par vous-même. (seule)
   **j** L'homme qui attend le bus, c'est M. Robert. (seul)

# **4.5** Big, bigger, biggest: the comparative and superlative

The *comparative* is the form you use when you are comparing two things and say, for example, that something is bigger, smaller, newer, older, etc.

The *superlative* is the form you use when you say something is the best, biggest, smallest, best of all.

| adjective | comparative | superlative |
|---|---|---|
| big<br>*grand* | bigger<br>plus grand | biggest<br>le plus grand |
| small<br>*petit* | smaller<br>plus petit | smallest<br>le plus petit |

 As **grand** and **petit** are adjectives they still have to agree with the noun they describe: **une voiture plus grande** – *a bigger car*; **la plus grande voiture** – *the biggest car*.

## 4.5.1 Comparing two people or things

In French, you put **plus** (*more*) in front of the adjective.

| | |
|---|---|
| M. Bertrand est important, mais le P.D.G. est plus important. | Mr Bertrand is important but the MD is more important. |
| Marc est petit, mais sa sœur est encore plus petite! | Marc is small but his sister is even smaller. |
| Fabien est intelligent, mais son frère est plus intelligent que lui. | Fabien is intelligent but his brother is more intelligent than him. |

**I**  Say the second things are all 'more' than the first.

**a** Nicolas est timide, mais sa sœur est ___.
**b** Notre maison est grande, mais votre maison est ___.
**c** Cet exercice est difficile, mais l'exercice suivant est ___.
**d** L'article du *Nouvel économiste* est intéressant, mais l'émission est ___.
**e** Le mont Blanc est déjà très haut, mais le mont Everest est encore ___.
**f** La Seine est longue, mais le Rhône est ___.

To say something is *less* you use **moins** instead of **plus**.

| | |
|---|---|
| Nicolas est moins grand que son frère. | Nicholas is less tall than his brother. |

**II**  Say these things are more (+) or less (−).

**a** (+) La Ferrari est ___ rapide que la Lotus.
**b** (+) Une Mercedes est ___ chère qu'une Renault.
**c** (−) Nicolas est ___ désordonné que sa sœur.
**d** (+) La vipère est ___ dangereuse que la couleuvre.*
**e** (−) L'ours noir est ___ grand que l'ours brun.
**f** (+) La station de ski de Tignes est ___ haute que la station d'Avoriaz.
**g** (−) L'île de La Réunion est ___ grande que l'île Maurice.

* grass snake

**h** (+) Calais se trouve ____ au nord que Vancouver.

**i** (−) L'argent est ___ précieux que l'or.

**j** (+) Le président de la République française est ____ connu que son premier ministre.

### 4.5.2 The superlative: 'the most ...' and 'the least ...'

To say something is *the most* or *the least* use **le**, **la** or **les** before **plus** or **moins**.

le plus, la plus, les plus ...
le moins, la moins, les moins ...

**I** Say these things are the most (+) or the least (−).

*Au monde des animaux.*

**a** (+) Le loup de Tasmanie est l'animal ____ rare qui existe.

**b** (+) La chauve-souris ___ dangereuse est connue sous le nom de 'vampire'.

**c** (+) L'éléphant est le ____ gros de tous les mammifères.

**d** (+) L'insecte ___ dangereux est le moustique porteur de la malaria.

**e** (+) Les girafes sont les animaux ____ grands du monde.

**f** (+) Les serpents ____ venimeux se trouvent en Australie.

**g** (+) L'araignée ____ venimeuse s'appelle la veuve noire.

**h** (−) (+) Les méduses* ___ grandes sont ___ mortelles.

* jellyfish

**II** Complete these sentences with 'the most' (+) or 'the least' (−) and the correct form of the adjective.

**a** Le lac naturel ___ de France s'appelle le lac du Bourget et il se trouve en Savoie. (+ grand)

**b** La montagne ____ s'appelle le mont Blanc. (+ haut)

**c** Le fleuve ____ est la Loire. (+ long)

**d** La grotte ____ s'appelle le puits d'Aphanize. (+ profond)

**e** La stalagmite ___ se trouve dans Armand. (+ grand)

**f** Le réseau de grottes ____ s'appelle Félix Tombe et s'étend sur 70km. (+ long)

**g** Le glacier____ s'appelle le glacier d'Argentière. (+ long)

**h** L'acteur français ___ s'appelle Gérard Depardieu. (+ connu)

**i** La commune ____ s'appelle Saint-Véran et elle se trouve dans les Hautes-Alpes. (+ haut)

**j** La ville ____ de France est Marseille: elle a été fondée vers 600 av. J.-C. (+ ancien)

### 4.5.3 Saying 'as (big) as'

If you are comparing two things which are similar, you use the expression **aussi (grand) que** *as (big) as.*

Il est aussi grand que son père.     He is as tall as his father.
Il est aussi étrange que son frère.     He is as strange as his brother.

**I**    Say these places are (1) bigger, (2) less big or (3) as big as … (Remember to make **grand** agree with the noun where necessary.)

**a** L'Hôtel Bellevue est ___ l'Hôtel Bijou. (3)
**b** L'agglomération de Paris est ___ l'agglomération de Lyon. (1)
**c** Le port de Nantes est ___ le port de Marseille. (2)
**d** Les hypermarchés Champion sont ___ les hypermarchés Continent. (2)
**e** Le lac d'Annecy est ___ le lac du Bourget. (2)
**f** La Tour Eiffel est ___ que Blackpool Tower. (1)

**II**    Make these things (1) more, (2) less or (3) just as … as.

**a** Le mont Everest est ___ le Kilimanjaro. (1 haut)
**b** La Seine est ___ la Loire. (2 long)
**c** En Afrique, il fait ___ en Europe. (1 chaud)
**d** La vue de la montagne est ___ la vue du lac. (3 beau)
**e** Le footing est ___ le yoga. (1 fatigant)

## 4.5.4   Good, better, best: irregular comparisons

*Good, better, best* are adjectives and have to agree with the noun.

| meaning | singular | | plural | |
| --- | --- | --- | --- | --- |
| | masculine | feminine | masculine | feminine |
| good | bon | bonne | bons | bonnes |
| better | meilleur | meilleure | meilleurs | meilleures |
| best | le meilleur | la meilleure | les meilleurs | les meilleures |

**I**    How would you say these things are *better*?

**a** Ce bourgogne est bon, mais le bordeaux que vous avez acheté hier est ___.
**b** Mon fils a eu de ___ notes cette année que l'année dernière.
**c** Un café, c'est bon, mais un chocolat, c'est encore ___.
**d** Cette reproduction est presque ___ que l'original.
**e** Le climat de La Martinique est ___ que le climat en France.
**f** La plage du Lavandou est ___ que la plage de Calais.

**II**    How would you say these are *the best*, according to M. Picard?

*Selon M. Picard …*

**a** Le bourgogne est ___ vin de France.
**b** Les voitures françaises sont ___ voitures.

**a** Les Alpes sont ___ montagnes d'Europe.
**d** Paris est ___ ville du monde.
**e** Les Français sont ___ sportifs d'Europe.
**f** La France est ___ pays d'Europe.
**g** Air France est ___ ligne aérienne d'Europe.
**h** La cuisine française est ____ cuisine d'Europe.

### 4.5.5 *Meilleur* and *mieux*

These two are often confusing as we use the same words for both in English.

**Meilleur** – *better* and **le meilleur** – *best* are used as adjectives and describe a noun or pronoun.

| | |
|---|---|
| Patrice est fort en maths. | Patrice is good at maths. |
| Julien est meilleur que lui. | Julien is better than him. |
| Hugo est le meilleur. | Hugo is the best. |
| Il est le meilleur de sa classe. | He is the best in his class. |

**Mieux** – *better* and **le mieux** – *best* are used as adverbs and describe a verb (in this case – *to cook*).

| | |
|---|---|
| Je cuisine bien. | I cook well. |
| Ma mère cuisine mieux. | My mother cooks better. |
| C'est mon père qui cuisine le mieux de nous trois. | My father is the one who cooks best of us three. |

When you are not sure whether you need **meilleur** or **mieux** for *better*, try substituting a word in English that you know is an adverb (e.g. well, slowly, carefully) and see if the sentence still makes sense: *she cooks well/more slowly/more carefully than me*. If it does then you need **mieux**.

# 4.6 ►Fast track: Comparative and superlative

### A The comparative

The comparative is the form you use when you are comparing two things and say, for example, that something is bigger, smaller, newer, older, etc.

In English we can either add *-er* or use the word *more*.

green → *greener* or *more green*
healthy → *healthier* or *more healthy*
tired → *tireder* or *more tired*

In French there is only one way: you add the word **plus –** *more* or **moins –** *less*:

plus vert, plus sain, moins fatigué

As the word is an adjective it must still agree with the noun.

| | |
|---|---|
| L'herbe est plus verte … | The grass is greener … |
| Elle est moins fatiguée que moi. | She is less tired than I. |

B   The superlative

When you are talking about *the most* or *the least* you use the superlative.

In French the superlative is made by inserting **le**, **la** or **les** before the **plus** or **moins**.

le/la plus vert(e), le/la plus sain(e), le/la moins fatigué(e)

As the word is an adjective it must still agree with the noun.

l'enfant le plus terrible
la fille la moins intelligente
les histoires les plus intéressantes

C   Good, better, best
These are irregular:

bon, meilleur, le meilleur

| | |
|---|---|
| J'ai eu une bonne idée. | I had a good idea. |
| Nina a eu de meilleures idées. | Nina had some better ideas. |
| Mais c'est Arthur qui a eu la meilleure idée. | But Arthur had the best idea. |

 All comparatives and superlatives are adjectives so they have to agree with the noun.

D   Well, better, best
These are **adverbs** and describe an action.

bien, mieux, le mieux

In English we use *better* and *best* for both the adjective **meilleur** (**le meilleur**) and the adverb **mieux** (**le/la/les mieux**).

Being adverbs, **bien**, **mieux** and **le mieux** describe a verb, in this case **jouer –** *to play*:

| | |
|---|---|
| Maurice a bien joué. | Maurice played well. |
| Louis a joué encore mieux. | Louis played even better. |
| Mais c'est Hugo qui a joué le mieux. | But Hugo played best. |

# 5 ADVERBS

## What is an adverb?

Adverbs are words that describe a verb:

She drives *fast*. He speaks *loudly*.

Some adverbs can qualify an adjective or adverb, e.g. *very* (fast), *quite* (loudly), *too* (hard).

# 5.1 Formation of adverbs

## 5.1.1 Regular adverbs

Most French adverbs are formed by adding **-ment** to the feminine form of the adjective.

| | |
|---|---|
| doux/douce → doucement | quietly/softly |
| lent/lente → lentement | slowly |
| traditionnel/traditionelle → traditionnellement | traditionally |
| normal/normale → normalement | normally/usually |
| regulier/regulière → regulièrement | regularly |

But if the masculine form ends in a vowel, **-ment** is added to the masculine.

| | |
|---|---|
| sage → sagement | wisely |
| poli → poliment | politely |
| absolu → absolument | absolutely |

An exception is:

fou → follement

**I** Make these adjectives into adverbs.

| | | | |
|---|---|---|---|
| **a** | sec | **f** | franc |
| **b** | aisé | **g** | rare |
| **c** | simple | **h** | heureux |
| **d** | rapide | **i** | vrai |
| **e** | naturel | **j** | sérieux |

## 5.1.2 Adjectives ending in -ent and -ant

These change the ending from **-ent** to **-emment** or from **-ant** to **-amment**. The only exception is **lent** (see 5.1.1).

| | |
|---|---|
| évident → évidemment | evidently |
| constant → constamment | constantly |
| récent → récemment | recently |

| adjective | adverb |
|---|---|
| bon | bien – well |
| meilleur | mieux – better |
| mauvais | mal – badly |
| énorme | énormément – enormously |
| gentil | gentiment – kindly |

# 5.2 Adjectives used as adverbs

Some adjectives can be used as adverbs in certain contexts:

- when talking about speaking/singing/playing an instrument

| fort | loud/strong |
|---|---|
| parler fort | to talk loudly |
| haut | high |
| chanter haut | to sing high |
| bas | low |
| parler bas | to speak in a low voice |

- when talking about prices

| cher | expensive |
|---|---|
| Ça coûte cher. | It is expensive. |

- when used after **c'est**, e.g.

| vrai | true |
|---|---|
| C'est vrai. | It's true. |
| faux | false |
| C'est faux. | It's wrong/false. |
| dur | hard |
| C'est dur. | It's hard/difficult. |

- in certain other situations

| court | short |
|---|---|
| couper court | to cut short |
| net | neat/tidy |
| refuser net | to refuse point blank |

**I** How would you say the following?

**a** Speak more quietly, please! Parlez plus ___, s'il vous plaît!
**b** He refused point blank.
**c** That's not true!
**d** It's very expensive.
**e** Sing more loudly, please.

# 5.3 Other useful adverbs

The following adverbs are very common, so it's worth learning them.

| | |
|---|---|
| très | very |
| assez | quite |
| trop | too |
| beaucoup | a lot |
| peu | a little |
| souvent | often |
| toujours | always |
| quelquefois | sometimes |

# 5.4 ▶Fast track: Adverbs

Adverbs are words which describe an action: *well, fast, slowly,* etc.

In English most words which end in *-ly* are adverbs: *naturally, romantically, sadly,* etc.

In French most adverbs are made by adding **-ment** to the feminine form of the adjective:

douce → doucement

unless the masculine form already ends in a vowel:

simple → simplement
vrai → vraiment

Words which already end in **-ent** or **-ant** change the ending to **-emment** or **-amment**:

évident → évidemment
constant → constamment

Some useful adverbs:

| | |
|---|---|
| C'est bien | It's good |
| mal | bad (ly) |
| peu | a little |
| mieux | better |
| fort | loud/strong |
| vraiment | really |
| souvent | frequently/often |

These words are used with another adverb or adjective:

| | | | |
|---|---|---|---|
| très | **very** | très cher | **very expensive** |
| assez | **quite** | assez grand | **quite big** |
| trop | **too** | trop petit | **too small** |

## Recognising prepositions

▶▶ **If you know what a preposition is, go on to 6.1.**

Prepositions are words such as *in, on* and *under*. Unlike verbs and adjectives, most prepositions do not change. They are usually used before a noun or pronoun, e.g. *in the cupboard*, **near** *the station*, **for** *her*, **with** *me*. Prepositions show the relationship between a noun/pronoun and what comes before.

Prepositions can tell you:

- **where** a person or thing is:
  | | |
  |---|---|
  | l'assiette *sur* la table | the plate on the table |
  | il était *sous* le pont | he was under the bridge |

- **how** it is:
  | | |
  |---|---|
  | *avec* du beurre | with butter |
  | *sans* eau | without water |

- **when** it is:
  | | |
  |---|---|
  | *dans* une minute | in a minute |
  | *après* le dîner | after dinner |

- **for whom** it is:
  | | |
  |---|---|
  | *pour* moi | for me |

## 6.1 The preposition à

**À** is a very useful preposition, although it does change according to the noun (see 6.1.1). It can be used to convey where, how, when, etc., according to the context in which it is used.

### Where?

| | |
|---|---|
| Il habite à la campagne. | He lives in the country. |
| Je vais à la gare. | I am going to the station. |
| J'ai mal au genou. | My knee hurts. (lit: I have pain at the knee.) |

## How? What kind of?

| | |
|---|---|
| un sandwich au jambon | a ham sandwich |
| un homme aux cheveux longs | a man with long hair |

## When?

| | |
|---|---|
| Le train part à 10h45. | The train leaves at 10.45. |

## Whose?

| | |
|---|---|
| C'est à moi! | It's mine! |

### 6.1.1 À and the definite article

When **à** is used in front of the definite article, it changes in the masculine and plural.

- **à** + **le** becomes **au**
- **à** + **les** becomes **aux**
- before words beginning with a vowel or silent **h**, you use **à l'**

| masculine | feminine | plural |
|---|---|---|
| au (à l') | à la (à l') | aux |

### 6.1.2 Where? Où?

**À** and the definite article translate *at the* or *to the*. This is usually in answer to the question **où**? (*where?*).

| | |
|---|---|
| Je suis à la maison. | I am at home. |
| Je vais au bureau. | I am going to the office. |

**I**  How would you say you were going to these places?

Je vais …

| | | | |
|---|---|---|---|
| **a** | la plage | **f** | le cinéma |
| **b** | l'hôtel | **g** | le théâtre |
| **c** | la piscine | **h** | la station-service |
| **d** | l'hôpital | **i** | la banque |
| **e** | le musée | **j** | le distributeur (**cash point**) |

**II**  How would you ask the way to these places in Rouen?

Excusez-moi, pourriez-vous m'indiquer comment aller …?

| | | | |
|---|---|---|---|
| **a** | l'église St-Ouen | **f** | le musée du Théâtre |
| **b** | la cathédrale Jeanne d'Arc | **g** | l'office du tourisme |
| **c** | le Gros Horloge | **h** | la Seine |
| **d** | l'Hôtel de Ville | **i** | la Place du marché |
| **e** | la chapelle des Capucines | **j** | les toilettes publiques |

À is also used to mean *at/to/in* with:

- the names of all towns and cities:

  à Madrid, au Mans

- the names of countries which are masculine, unless they begin with a vowel:

  au Canada, au Luxembourg

- the names of all countries and regions which include 'les' in their name:

  aux États-Unis

**III** How would you say where these places are?

**a** La Tour Eiffel est ___ Paris.
**b** Buckingham Palace est ___ Londres.
**c** L'Empire State Building est ___ États-Unis.
**d** Montréal est ___ Canada.
**e** Tokyo est ___ Japon.
**f** La Cour européenne de justice se trouve ___ Luxembourg.
**g** La Haye est ___ Pays-Bas.
**h** La Guadeloupe est ___ Antilles.
**i** On parle français ___ Québec.
**j** Lisbonne est ___ Portugal.

**IV** How would you say you are going to these places?

Je vais à/au …

**a** Le Havre
**b** Le Mans
**c** les Champs-Élysées
**d** les Deux-Alpes
**e** le Lavandou
**f** le Louvre
**g** les Menuires
**h** la Cité des Sciences et de l'Industrie

# 6.1.3 What kind of? *Quel genre de?*

À is used to say *what kind of* where we don't need a word in English.

| | |
|---|---|
| un sandwich au fromage | a cheese sandwich |
| une glace au chocolat | a chocolate ice cream |

**I** What flavour? **Quel parfum?** Say what sort of ice cream you would like.

Je voudrais une glace …

**a** la vanille
**b** le citron
**c** la pistache
**d** le cassis
**e** l'abricot
**f** le chocolat
**g** la banane
**h** la fraise
**i** l'orange
**j** la mangue

**II** Now say what sort of sandwich you would like.

Je voudrais un sandwich …

**a** le jambon            **e** la sardine
**b** le poulet              **f** le thon
**c** le saucisson        **g** les rillettes
**d** le fromage         **h** le camembert

> Remember that the final **-x** in **aux** is not pronounced …
> *une tarte aux fraises, une glace aux fruits rouges, une omelette aux fines herbes*
> … unless it is followed by a word beginning with a vowel, and then it sounds like an 's' at the beginning of the next word.
> *un flan aux‿asperges, une quiche aux‿épinards, un gâteau aux‿amandes*

**À** is also used to talk about how something is powered:

| | |
|---|---|
| un moteur à essence | a petrol engine |
| un moulin à vent | a windmill |
| une voiture à propulsion nucléaire | a nuclear-powered car |

## 6.1.4 When? *Quand?*
When used in expressions of time, **À** means *at*.

| | |
|---|---|
| À quelle heure partez-vous? | What time are you leaving? |
| Le train part à 10h20. | The train will depart at 10.20 am. |
| Je me suis couché(e) hier à onze heures et demie. | I went to bed last night at half past eleven. |

## 6.1.5 Whose? *C'est à qui?*
**À** is used to say to whom something belongs:

| | |
|---|---|
| C'est à moi! | It's mine. |
| Le manteau est à Jean-Luc et le parapluie est à Nicolas. | The coat belongs to Jean-Luc and the umbrella belongs to Nicolas. |

## 6.1.6 What's wrong? *Qu'est-ce qu'il y a?*
**À** is used in expressions of pain to say which part of the body is hurting.

| | |
|---|---|
| J'ai mal à la tête. | I have a headache. |
| As-tu mal à la jambe? | Does your leg hurt? |
| Il a mal aux dents. | He has toothache. |
| Nous avons mal aux pieds. | We have sore feet. |
| Avez-vous mal à la tête? | Have you got a headache? |
| Ils ont mal au cœur. | They feel sick. |

Parts of the body which might hurt!

| singular | plural | meaning |
|----------|--------|---------|
| un œil | les yeux | eye(s) |
| une oreille | les oreilles | ear(s) |
| la dent | les dents | tooth/teeth |
| la main | les mains | hand(s) |
| le doigt | les doigts | finger(s) |
| le bras | les bras | arm(s) |
| la jambe | les jambes | leg(s) |
| le pied | les pieds | foot/feet |
| le dos | | back |

**La cœur** is *heart* but **J'ai mal au cœur** means *I feel sick.*

**Mal au ventre** (*stomach*) is used to refer to *stomach ache* or *heartburn.*

**I** How would you say the following?

**a** I have a headache.
**b** Have you got toothache?
**c** Her foot hurts.
**d** My arms ache.
**e** His knee hurts.
**f** Have you got a headache?
**g** She has earache.
**h** Do you feel sick?
**i** Does your back hurt?
**j** He has backache.

## 6.1.7 ▶Fast track: à

When **à** is used together with the definite article, **à + le** and **à + les** combine to become **au** and **aux**.

| masculine | feminine | plural |
|-----------|----------|--------|
| au (à l') | à la (à l') | aux |

**À** is used in some expressions to say where you are or where you are going:

Je suis à Paris. Je vais à l'hôtel.

**À** translates *at* when talking about time:

à six heures
à midi

À is used to say what kind of:

une tarte aux pommes
un bateau à vapeur

À is used to say where it hurts:

J'ai mal à la tête.

À is used to say to whom something belongs:

C'est à Philippe.

## **6.2** The preposition *de*

**De** is used in different ways. It can mean:

- *of*
  C'est le vieux centre de la ville.    It's the old centre of the town.

- *from*
  M. Bériot arrive de la gare.    Mr Bériot is coming from the station.

- *with/in*
  La voiture est couverte de boue.    The car is covered in mud.

### **6.2.1** *De* and the definite article

When **de** is used in front of the definite article:

- **de + le** becomes **du** and **de + les** becomes **des**.
- **de l'** is used before both masculine and feminine nouns which begin with a vowel or a silent **h**.

| masculine | feminine | plural |
|---|---|---|
| du (de l') | de la (de l') | des |

**I**   Complete these sentences using **de** and the phrase in brackets.

a Les touristes arrivent ___. (le Japon)
b Ils descendent ___. (le train)
c Ils font un tour ___. (les monuments)
d Ils visitent le musée ___. (le Louvre)
e Ils traversent la place ___. (la Concorde)
f Ils prennent le pont ___. (Bir-Hakeim)
g Ils prennent des photos ___. (la Tour Eiffel)
h Leur hôtel est près ___. (la place du Trocadéro)

## 6.2.2 De meaning some or any: *du, de la* or *des*

**De** with the definite article refers to an unspecified quantity, e.g. **le sucre** (*the sugar*) → **du sucre** (*some/any sugar*).

Je voudrais du pain.      I would like some bread.
Avez-vous du pain?      Have you got any bread?

▶▶ **If you know how to use du, de la and des as *some*, go on to 6.2.3.**

**I** How would you ask for 'some' of the following?

Avez-vous …?

**a** ___ sucre (m)      **f** ___ cognac (m)
**b** ___ huile d'olives (f)      **g** ___ eau minérale (f)
**c** ___ crème fraîche (f)      **h** ___ pommes (pl)
**d** ___ pain de campagne (m)      **i** ___ œufs (pl)
**e** ___ petits pains (pl)      **j** ___ pizza (f)

 In English, we sometimes miss out the word *some* or *any*, but in French you must put it in: **Je mange de la salade**.

**II** Put in the correct form: **du, de la** or **de l'**.

Je bois … (I drink)

**a** ___ bière (f)      **f** ___ café (m)
**b** ___ vin (m)      **g** ___ thé (m)
**c** ___ limonade (f)      **h** ___ jus d'orange (m)
**d** ___ Coca-Cola (m)      **i** ___ eau (f)
**e** ___ lait (m)      **j** ___ champagne (m)

**III** **…, s'il vous plaît.** How would you ask for these?

**a** ___ croissants      **f** ___ confiture
**b** ___ café      **g** ___ céréales
**c** ___ lait chaud      **h** ___ thé
**d** ___ beurre      **i** ___ fromage
**e** ___ miel      **j** ___ jambon

## 6.2.3 De and how to say 'not any'

When *any* follows a negative statement (e.g. *I don't have any/I don't drink any*), you use **de** for both masculine and feminine words. You always need to use **de** in French, even when you drop the *any* in English.

Je ne veux pas de café.      I don't want any coffee.
Je ne mange pas de salade.      I don't eat salad.

**I**  Say what is not available. Use **Il n'y a pas** … (There isn't any …).

| | |
|---|---|
| **a** ketchup | **f** beurre |
| **b** confiture | **g** fromage |
| **c** mayonnaise | **h** soupe |
| **d** sucre | **i** jus d'orange |
| **e** lait | **j** yaourt |

**II**  Now say that you don't eat these things. Use **Je ne mange pas** …

**a** noix – walnuts
**b** cacahuètes – peanuts
**c** sucreries – sweet things
**d** viande – meat
**e** poisson – fish
**f** laitue – lettuce
**g** tomates – tomatoes
**h** légumes – vegetables
**i** pain – bread
**j** escargots – snails

## 6.2.4  Other expressions with *de* or *d'*

The following expressions are very common, so it's worth learning them.

| | |
|---|---|
| beaucoup de | a lot of |
| assez de | enough (of) |
| trop de | too much/many (of) |
| un peu de | a little |
| plus de | more |
| moins de | less |

**I**  How would you say you have lots of the following?

| | |
|---|---|
| **a** livres | **c** CD |
| **b** cartes postales | **d** photos |

**II**  Now say that you have enough of the following.

| | |
|---|---|
| **a** essence | **d** temps |
| **b** argent | **e** catalogues |
| **c** informations | |

**III**  Finally, say that you have too much/many of the following.

| | |
|---|---|
| **a** travail | **d** bagages |
| **b** invitations | **e** papiers |
| **c** déplacements | |

### 6.2.5 *De* in expressions of quantity

In these expressions, the **de** does not change.

| | |
|---|---|
| un kilo de | a kilo of |
| un kilo de pommes de terre | a kilo of potatoes |
| une bouteille de | a bottle of |
| une bouteille de ketchup | a bottle of ketchup |
| une boîte de | a tin/can of |
| une boîte de sardines | a tin of sardines |
| un lot de | a pack of/special offer of |
| un lot de trois savons | a pack of three soaps |
| un litre de | a litre of |
| un litre de lait | a litre of milk |

## 6.3 Prepositions of 'position'

These prepositions tell you where something or somebody is:

| | |
|---|---|
| dans | in |
| dans la maison | in the house |
| derrière | behind |
| derrière la porte | behind the door |
| devant | in front of |
| devant le cinéma | in front of the cinema |
| entre | between |
| entre le cinéma et le café | between the cinema and the café |
| sous | under |
| sous le pont | under the bridge |
| sur | on |
| sur la table | on the table |

**I**  Match the pictures with the sentences.

**a** Il est sous la douche.
**b** Il est derrière la porte de la salle de bains.
**c** Il est devant la glace.
**d** Il est entre la cuisine et la salle à manger.
**e** Il est dans son lit.
**f** Il est dans un fauteuil.

**II**  What would you say to tell someone where the telephone is?

Il y a un téléphone ...

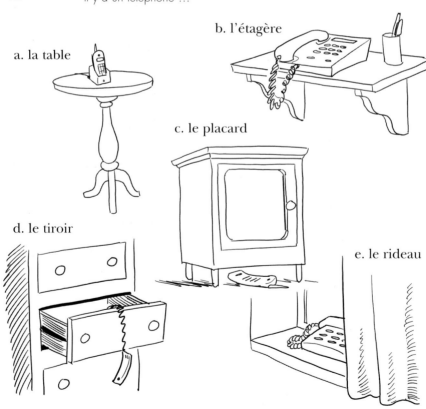

a. la table
b. l'étagère
c. le placard
d. le tiroir
e. le rideau

# 6.4 The prepositions *en* and *chez*

**En** translates *in* or *to* when you are talking about countries which are feminine or begin with a vowel.

| | |
|---|---|
| Elle habite en Chine. | She lives in China. |
| Vous allez en Iran? | Are you going to Iran? |

**Chez** is a special preposition which means *at the house of*. It is followed by the person's name or the relevant emphatic pronoun (**moi, toi, lui, elle, nous, vous, elles, eux**: see 3.7.2).

| | |
|---|---|
| chez moi | at my house |
| chez lui | at his/her house |
| chez les Martin | at the Martins |

# 6.5 Useful prepositional phrases

Some prepositions of 'position' are phrases, i.e. they are made up of more than one word. For example, *in front of* is a prepositional phrase in English because it is made up of three words.

| | |
|---|---|
| en face de | opposite |
| près de | near |
| loin de | far from |
| à côté de | beside/next to |
| au-dessus de | above |
| au-dessous de | below/beneath |
| autour de | around |

The following useful expressions tell you where someone or something is in a building.

| | |
|---|---|
| en haut | upstairs |
| en bas | downstairs |
| au rez-de-chaussée | on the ground floor |
| au premier/deuxième étage | on the first/second floor |
| au sous-sol | in the basement |

# 6.6 Expressions of time

These prepositions are used when saying when something happened.

| | |
|---|---|
| à | at |
| à dix heures | at ten o'clock |
| après | after |
| après le petit déjeuner | after breakfast |
| avant | before |
| avant d'aller au bureau | before going to the office |
| pendant | during/for (in the past) |
| pendant la journée | during the day |
| pendant un an | for a year (in the past) |
| pour | for |
| pour une semaine | for a week (in the future) |
| vers | about |
| vers dix heures | about/towards ten o'clock |

With the preposition **depuis** (*since*), remember to be careful with the verb tense.

| | |
|---|---|
| Je t'attends depuis ce matin. | I've been waiting for you since this morning. |
| Il habite ici depuis trois ans. | He has been living here for three years. |
| Depuis combien de temps prenez-vous des cours de français? | How long have you been studying French (and you still are)? |
| Je prends des cours de français depuis deux ans. | I have been studying French (and I still am) for two years. |

I  How would you answer these questions, using the information given in brackets?

Depuis combien de temps ...

**a** ... Marc prend-il des cours d'espagnol? (deux ans)
**b** ... habite-t-il à Paris? (cinq ans)
**c** ... M. Proudhon habite-t-il à Paris? (deux mois)
**d** ... joue-t-il de la guitare? (un an)
**e** ... travaille-t-il dans cette boulangerie? (six mois)
**f** ... joue-t-il aux échecs? (son enfance)
**g** ... Constance est-elle végétarienne? (l'âge de treize ans)
**h** ... fait-elle du ski? (cinq ans)
**i** ... font-ils de la planche? (l'été dernier)
**j** ... sortent-ils ensemble? (six mois)

# 7 CONJUNCTIONS AND OTHER USEFUL WORDS

## 7.1 Conjunctions

Here are some useful words for joining two parts of a sentence or filling in gaps in a conversation.

| | |
|---|---|
| et | and |
| mais | but |
| puis | then |
| alors | then, so |
| en tout cas | anyway |
| eh bien … | well, er . . . |
| et voilà | and there you are |
| voici | here is |
| oh là là | oh dear |
| C'est tout! | That's all! |

## 7.2 Useful phrases

These are useful phrases:

| | |
|---|---|
| Ne quittez pas. | Please hold on. *(on the telephone)* |
| Veuillez patienter. | Please wait. *(on the telephone)* |
| Attendez. | Wait. |
| Je n'en sais rien. | I don't know anything about it. |
| Je m'en doutais. | I thought as much. |
| Ça m'étonnerait. | I find that surprising. (I would be surprised if that were true.) |

# **7.3** Help with understanding spelling and numbers

Letters which can be difficult:

a   sounds ah
e   sounds uh
i   sounds ee
g   sounds jay
j   sounds gi in Gigi

é   e accent aigu
è   accent grave
ê   accent circonflexe
à   accent grave
â   accent circonflexe
ç   c cédille

-   tiret
,   comma
.   point
?   point d'interrogation
/   barre (oblique)
@   arobase

## Other useful words

capital (b) – (b) majescule
small (d) – (d) miniscule
next word – plus loin
underline – souligner

## Days and dates

les jours – the days
lundi mardi mercredi jeudi vendredi samedi dimanche

## les mois – the months

janvier février mars avril mai juin juillet août septembre
octobre novembre décembre

## Some difficult numbers

soixante – 60
soixante-dix – 70
soixante-onze – 71
soixante-quinze – 75
quatre-vingts – 80
quatre vingt dix – 90
quatrevingt dix neuf – 99

mille neuf cent quatre-vingt – 1986
deux mille six – 2006

# VERB TABLES

## Avoir and être

| Infinitive | Present tense | | Perfect<br>Imperfect | Future<br>Conditional<br>Subjunctive |
|---|---|---|---|---|
| **avoir**<br>to have | j'ai<br>tu as<br>il a | nous avons<br>vous avez<br>ils ont | j'ai eu<br>j'avais | j'aurai<br>j'aurais<br>que j'aie |
| **être**<br>to be | je suis<br>tu es<br>il est | nous sommes<br>vous êtes<br>ils sont | j'ai été<br>j'étais | je serai<br>je serais<br>que je sois |

## Regular -er, -ir and -re verbs

| Infinitive | Present tense | | Perfect<br>Imperfect | Future<br>Conditional<br>Subjunctive |
|---|---|---|---|---|
| **parler**<br>to speak | je parle<br>tu parles<br>il parle | nous parlons<br>vous parlez<br>ils parlent | j'ai parlé<br>je parlais | je parlerai<br>je parlerais<br>que je parle |
| **finir**<br>to finish | je finis<br>tu finis<br>il finit | nous finissons<br>vous finissez<br>ils finissent | j'ai fini<br>je finissais | je finirai<br>je finirais<br>que je finisse |
| **répondre**<br>to reply | je réponds<br>tu réponds<br>il répond | nous répondons<br>vous répondez<br>ils répondent | j'ai répondu<br>je répondais | je répondrai<br>je répondrais<br>que je réponde |

# Common irregular verbs

| Infinitive | Present tense | | Perfect<br>Imperfect | Future<br>Conditional<br>Subjunctive |
|---|---|---|---|---|
| **acheter**<br>to buy | j'achète<br>tu achètes<br>il achète | nous achetons<br>vous achetez<br>ils achètent | j'ai acheté<br>j'achetais | j'achèterai<br>j'achèterais<br>que j'achète |
| **admettre**<br>to admit | see: mettre | | | |
| **aller**<br>to go | je vais<br>tu vas<br>il va | nous allons<br>vous allez<br>ils vont | je suis allé(e)<br>j'allais | j'irai<br>j'irais<br>que j'aille |
| **apercevoir**<br>to catch<br>sight of | j'aperçois<br>tu aperçois<br>il aperçoit | nous apercevons<br>vous apercevez<br>ils aperçoivent | j'ai aperçu<br>j'apercevais | j'apercevrai<br>j'apercevrais<br>que j'aperçoive |
| **apparaître**<br>to appear | see: paraître | | | |
| **apprendre**<br>to learn | see: prendre | | | |
| **s'asseoir**<br>to sit down | je m'assieds<br>tu t'assieds<br>il s'assied | nous nous<br>   asseyons<br>vous vous asseyez<br>ils s'asseyent | je me suis<br>assis(e)<br>je m'asseyais | je m'assiérai<br>je m'assiérais<br>que je m'asseye |
| **atteindre**<br>to reach | j'atteins<br>tu atteins<br>il atteint | nous atteignons<br>vous atteignez<br>ils atteignent | j'ai atteint<br>j'attegnais | j'atteindrai<br>j'atteindrais<br>que j'atteigne |
| **battre**<br>to beat | je bats<br>tu bats<br>il bat | nous battons<br>vous battez<br>ils battent | j'ai battu<br>je battais | je battrai<br>je battrais<br>que je batte |
| **boire**<br>to drink | je bois<br>tu bois<br>il boit | nous buvons<br>vous buvez<br>ils boivent | j'ai bu<br>je buvais | je boirai<br>je boirais<br>que je boive |
| **commencer**<br>to begin | je commence<br>tu commences<br>il commence | nous commençons<br>vous commencez<br>ils commencent | j'ai commencé<br>je commençais | je commencerai<br>je commencerais<br>que je commence |

| Infinitive | Present tense | | Perfect Imperfect | Future Conditional Subjunctive |
|---|---|---|---|---|
| **comprendre** to understand | see: prendre | | | |
| **conduire** to drive | je conduis tu conduis il conduit | nous conduisons vous conduisez ils conduisent | j'ai conduit je conduisais | je conduirai je conduirais que je conduise |
| **connaître** to know | je connais tu connais il connaît | nous connaissons vous connaissez ils connaissent | j'ai connu je connaissais | je connaîtrai je connaîtrais que je connaisse |
| **coudre** to sew | je couds tu couds il coud | nous cousons vous cousez ils cousent | j'ai cousu je cousais | je coudrai je coudrais que je couse |
| **courir** to run | je cours tu cours il court | nous courons vous courez ils courent | j'ai couru je courais | je courrai je courrais que je coure |
| **couvrir** to cover | see: ouvrir | | | |
| **craindre** to fear | je crains tu crains il craint | nous craignons vous craignez ils craignent | j'ai craint je craignais | je craindrai je craindrais que je craigne |
| **croire** to believe | je crois tu crois il croit | nous croyons vous croyez ils croient | j'ai cru je croyais | je croirai je croirais que je croie |
| **cueillir** to pick/ gather | je cueille tu cueilles il cueille | nous cueillons vous cueillez ils cueillent | j'ai cueilli je cueillais | je cueillerai je cueillerais que je cueille |
| **découvrir** to discover | see: ouvrir | | | |
| **décrire** to describe | see: écrire | | | |
| **devoir** to have to | je dois tu dois il doit | nous devons vous devez ils doivent | j'ai dû je devais | je devrai je devrais que je doive |

| Infinitive | Present tense | | Perfect Imperfect | Future Conditional Subjunctive |
|---|---|---|---|---|
| **dire** to say | je dis tu dis il dit | nous disons vous dites ils disent | j'ai dit je disais | je dirai je dirais que je dise |
| **dormir** to sleep | je dors tu dors il dort | nous dormons vous dormez ils dorment | j'ai dormi je dormais | je dormirai je dormirais que je dorme |
| **écrire** to write | j'écris tu écris il écrit | nous écrivons vous écrivez ils écrivent | j'ai écrit j'écrivais | j'écrirai j'écrirais que j'écrive |
| **envoyer** to send | j'envoie tu envoies il envoie | nous envoyons vous envoyez ils envoient | j'ai envoyé j'envoyais | j'enverrai j'enverrais que j'envoie |
| **espérer** to hope | j'espère tu espères il espère | nous espérons vous espérez ils espèrent | j'ai espéré j'espérais | j'espèrerai j'espèrerais que j'espère |
| **essayer** to try | j'essaie tu essaies il essaie | nous essayons vous essayez ils essaient | j'ai essayé j'essayais | j'essaierai j'essaierais que j'essaie |
| **faire** to do/make | je fais tu fais il fait | nous faisons vous faites ils font | j'ai fait je faisais | je ferai je ferais que je fasse |
| **falloir** to be necessary | il faut | | il a fallu il fallait | il faudra il faudrait qu'il faille |
| **introduire** to introduce | see: conduire | | | |
| **lever** to raise/lift | je lève tu lèves il lève | nous levons vous levez ils lèvent | j'ai levé je levais | je lèverai je lèverais que je lève |
| **lire** to read | je lis tu lis il lit | nous lisons vous lisez ils lisent | j'ai lu je lisais | je lirai je lirais que je lise |

| Infinitive | Present tense | | Perfect<br>Imperfect | Future<br>Conditional<br>Subjunctive |
|---|---|---|---|---|
| **manger**<br>to eat | je mange<br>tu manges<br>il mange | nous mangeons<br>vous mangez<br>ils mangent | j'ai mangé<br>je mangeais | je mangerai<br>je mangerais<br>que je mange |
| **mener**<br>to take | see: lever | | | |
| **mettre**<br>to put | je mets<br>tu mets<br>il met | nous mettons<br>vous mettez<br>ils mettent | j'ai mis<br>je mettais | je mettrai<br>je mettrais<br>que je mette |
| **mourir**<br>to die | je meurs<br>tu meurs<br>il meurt | nous mourons<br>vous mourez<br>ils meurent | je suis mort(e)<br>je mourais | je mourrai<br>je mourrais<br>que je meure |
| **naître**<br>to be born | je nais<br>tu nais<br>il naît | nous naissons<br>vous naissez<br>ils naissent | je suis né(e)<br>je naissais | je naîtrai<br>je naîtrais<br>que je naisse |
| **offrir**<br>to offer | j'offre<br>tu offres<br>il offre | nous offrons<br>vous offrez<br>ils offrent | j'ai offert<br>j'offrais | j'offrirai<br>j'offrirais<br>que j'offre |
| **ouvrir**<br>to open | j'ouvre<br>tu ouvres<br>il ouvre | nous ouvrons<br>vous ouvrez<br>ils ouvrent | j'ai ouvert<br>j'ouvrais | j'ouvrirai<br>j'ouvrirais<br>que j'ouvre |
| **paraître**<br>to appear/<br>seem | je parais<br>tu parais<br>il paraît | nous paraissons<br>vous paraissez<br>ils paraissent | j'ai paru<br>je paraissais | je paraîtrai<br>je paraîtrais<br>que je paraisse |
| **partir**<br>to leave | je pars<br>tu pars<br>il part | nous partons<br>vous partez<br>ils partent | je suis parti(e)<br>je partais | je partirai<br>je partirais<br>que je parte |
| **payer**<br>to pay | je paie<br>tu paies<br>il paie | nous payons<br>vous payez<br>ils paient | j'ai payé<br>je payais | je paierai<br>je paierais<br>que je paie |
| **permettre**<br>to permit | see: mettre | | | |
| **plaindre**<br>to complain | je me plains<br>tu te plains<br>il se plaint | nous nous plaignons<br>vous vous plaignez<br>ils se plaignent | je me suis plaint<br>je me plaignais | je me plaindrai<br>je me plaindrais<br>que je me plaigne |

| Infinitive | Present tense | | Perfect<br>Imperfect | Future<br>Conditional<br>Subjunctive |
|---|---|---|---|---|
| **pleuvoir**<br>to rain | il pleut | | il a plu<br>il pleuvait | il pleuvra<br>il pleuvrait<br>qu'il pleuve |
| **poursuivre**<br>to pursue | see: suivre | | | |
| **pouvoir**<br>to be able to | je peux<br>tu peux<br>il peut | nous pouvons<br>vous pouvez<br>ils peuvent | j'ai pu<br>je pouvais | je pourrai<br>je pourrais<br>que je puisse |
| **préférer**<br>to prefer | je préfère<br>tu préfères<br>il préfère | nous préférons<br>vous préférez<br>ils préfèrent | j'ai préféré<br>je préférais | je préférerai<br>je préférerais<br>que je préfère |
| **prendre**<br>to take | je prends<br>tu prends<br>il prend | nous prenons<br>vous prenez<br>ils prennent | j'ai pris<br>je prenais | je prendrai<br>je prendrais<br>que je prenne |
| **recevoir**<br>to receive | je reçois<br>tu reçois<br>il reçoit | nous recevons<br>vous recevez<br>ils reçoivent | j'ai reçu<br>je recevais | je recevrai<br>je recevrais<br>que je reçoive |
| **reconnaître**<br>to recognise | see: connaître | | | |
| **résoudre**<br>to solve/<br>resolve | je résous<br>tu résous<br>il résout | nous résolvons<br>vous résolvez<br>ils résolvent | j'ai résolu<br>je résolvais | je résoudrai<br>je résoudrais<br>que je résolve |
| **rire**<br>to laugh | je ris<br>tu ris<br>il rit | nous rions<br>vous riez<br>ils rient | j'ai ri<br>je riais | je rirai<br>je rirais<br>que je rie |
| **rompre**<br>to break (a<br>contract, etc.) | je romps<br>tu romps<br>il rompt | nous rompons<br>vous rompez<br>ils rompent | j'ai rompu<br>je rompais | je romprai<br>je romprais<br>que je rompe |
| **savoir**<br>to know | je sais<br>tu sais<br>il sait | nous savons<br>vous savez<br>ils savent | j'ai su<br>je savais | je saurai<br>je saurais<br>que je sache |
| **sentir**<br>to smell/feel | je sens<br>tu sens<br>il sent | nous sentons<br>vous sentez<br>ils sentent | j'ai senti<br>je sentais | je sentirai<br>je sentirais<br>que je sente |

| Infinitive | Present tense | | Perfect Imperfect | Future Conditional Subjunctive |
|---|---|---|---|---|
| **servir** to serve | je sers tu sers il sert | nous servons vous servez ils servent | j'ai servi je servais | je servirai je servirais que je serve |
| **sortir** to go out | je sors tu sors il sort | nous sortons vous sortez ils sortent | je suis sorti(e) je sortais | je sortirai je sortirais que je sorte |
| **souffrir** to suffer | je souffre tu souffres il souffre | nous souffrons vous souffrez ils souffrent | j'ai souffert je souffrais | je souffrirai je souffrirais que je souffre |
| **sourire** to smile | see: rire | | | |
| **suivre** to follow | je suis tu suis il suit | nous suivons vous suivez ils suivent | j'ai suivi je suivais | je suivrai je suivrais que je suive |
| **tenir** to hold | je tiens tu tiens il tient | nous tenons vous tenez ils tiennent | j'ai tenu je tenais | je tiendrai je tiendrais que je tienne |
| **vaincre** to defeat | je vaincs tu vaincs il vainc | nous vainquons vous vainquez ils vainquent | j'ai vaincu je vainquais | je vaincrai je vaincrais que je vainque |
| **valoir** to be worth | je vaux tu vaux il vaut | nous valons vous valez ils valent | j'ai valu je valais | je vaudrai je vaudrais que je vaille |
| **venir** to come | je viens tu viens il vient | nous venons vous venez ils viennent | je suis venu(e) je venais | je viendrai je viendrais que je vienne |
| **vivre** to live | je vis tu vis il vit | nous vivons vous vivez ils vivent | j'ai vécu je vivais | je vivrai je vivrais que je vive |
| **voir** to see | je vois tu vois il voit | nous voyons vous voyez ils voient | j'ai vu je voyais | je verrai je verrais que je voie |
| **vouloir** to want | je veux tu veux il veut | nous voulons vous voulez ils veulent | j'ai voulu je voulais | je voudrai je voudrais que je veuille |

# Verbs and prepositions

These verbs are followed by prepositions in English, but not in French.

| | |
|---|---|
| attendre | to wait for |
| J'attends le bus. | I'm waiting for the bus. |
| chercher | to look for |
| Il cherche son parapluie. | He's looking for his umbrella. |
| demander | to ask for |
| Je demande une réponse. | I'm asking for a reply. |
| écouter | to listen to |
| Elle écoute un CD de Céline Dion. | She's listening to a Céline Dion CD. |
| habiter | to live in/at |
| Mon collègue habite Paris. | My colleague lives in Paris. |
| or Mon collègue habite à Paris. | |
| mettre | to put (on) |
| Marianne met son imperméable. | Marianne puts on her raincoat. |
| payer | to pay for |
| Je paie les fleurs. | I pay for the flowers. |
| regarder | to look at/watch |
| Il regarde sa montre. | He's looking at his watch. |
| sortir | to go out |
| Elle sort. | She's going out. |

Some verbs which don't require a preposition in English are followed by **de** in French. These are some of the most commonly used ones.

| | |
|---|---|
| s'apercevoir de | to notice |
| Il s'est aperçu de l'heure. | He noticed the time. |
| changer de | to change |
| Elle a changé de robe. | She changed her dress. |
| discuter de | to discuss |
| Ils ont discuté des nouvelles. | They discussed the news. |
| douter de | to doubt |
| Elle doute de son intention. | She doubts his intention. |
| jouer de | to play (an instrument) |
| Elle joue du piano. | She plays the piano. |
| manquer de | to lack |
| Il manque d'humour. | He lacks humour. |
| se méfier de | to mistrust |
| Elle se méfie de son collègue. | She mistrusts her colleague. |
| se servir de | to use |
| Il se sert des idées de son ami. | He uses his friend's ideas. |
| se souvenir de | to remember |
| Je me souviens des vacances. | I remember the holidays. |
| se tromper de | to mistake |
| Il s'est trompé de route. | He mistook the way/took a wrong turn. |

These are some of the verbs which are followed by **à** in French.

| | |
|---|---|
| aider quelqu'un à | to help someone to |
| J'ai aidé mon père à classer. | I helped my father with sorting the papers. |
| | |
| s'apprêter à | to prepare to |
| Il s'est apprêté à aller à la réunion. | He prepared to go to the meeting. |
| arriver à | to manage to |
| Elle est arrivée à ouvrir la boîte. | She managed to open the tin. |
| assister à | to attend |
| J'ai assisté à deux réunions. | I attended two meetings. |
| commencer à | to begin to |
| Elle a commencé à chanter. | She began to sing. |
| demander à | to ask |
| J'ai demandé à mon collègue de m'aider. | I asked my colleague to help me. |
| obéir/désobéir à | to (dis)obey |
| L'enfant a obéi/désobéi à son père. | The child (dis)obeyed its father. |
| (dé)plaire à | to (dis)please |
| Elle fait tout pour plaire à ses enfants. | She does everything to please her children. |
| | |
| s'intéresser à | to be interested in |
| Je m'intéresse au cinéma comme métier. | I'm interested in a career in the cinema. |
| | |
| jouer à | to play (a sport) |
| Il joue au tennis. | He plays tennis. |
| penser à | to think about |
| Je pense à lui. | I'm thinking about him. |
| renoncer à | to renounce/give up |
| Il a renoncé à fumer. | He gave up smoking. |
| répondre à | to reply to |
| Il a répondu à mes questions. | He replied to my questions. |
| résister à | to resist |
| Il a résisté à ses cajoleries. | He resisted her coaxing. |
| ressembler à | to resemble |
| Il ressemble à son père. | He resembles his father. |
| réussir à | to succeed in |
| Il a réussi à envoyer le fax à temps. | He succeeded in sending the fax in time. |
| | |
| téléphoner à | to ring (up) |
| Il a téléphoné à son collègue. | He rang his colleague. |
| tenir à | to be determined to |
| Je tiens à y aller. | I'm determined to go (there). |

# ANSWERS

## 1.1

**I** **a** run **c** sleep **d** make **f** eat **i** think

**II** **a** **c** **f** **h** **i**

**III** **a** parler *to speak* **b** habiter *to live* **c** organiser *to organise* **d** entrer *to enter* **e** voyager *to travel* **f** porter *to carry/wear* **g** vérifier *to verify/check* **h** inviter *to invite* **i** laver *to wash* **j** arriver *to arrive*

**IV** **a** manger *to eat* **b** dîner *to dine* **c** déjeuner *to have lunch* **d** apprécier *to appreciate* **e** goûter *to taste/try* **f** souper *to have supper* **g** verser *to pour* **h** déguster *to taste/sample* **i** consommer *to consume* **j** assaisonner *to season (add salt and pepper, etc.)* **k** mélanger *to mix*

**VI** **a** 3/vend **b** 1/montr **c** 1/chant **d** 2/sort **e** 1/lav **f** 2/fin **g** 1/écout **h** 1/ferm **i** 2/part **j** 3/prend **k** 2/chois **l** 1/port **m** 1/rentr **n** 2/ven **o** 2/dorm

**VII** **a** *to know (something)* savoir **b** *to see* voir **c** *to have* avoir **d** *to go* aller **e** *to be able to* pouvoir **f** *to have to* devoir **g** *to want to* vouloir **h** *to take* prendre **i** *to be* être **j** *to do* faire

**VIII** **a** je **b** elle **c** il **d** nous **e** tu **f** vous **g** elles **h** ils

**IX** **a** il **b** elle **c** il **d** ils **e** elles **f** elles **g** je **h** ils **i** ils **j** nous

## 1.2

**I** **a** *downloading* **b** *ringing* **c** *accompanying* **d** *going* **e** *fetching* **f** *borrowing* **g** *flying* **h** *visiting* **i** *studying* **j** *dining*

**II** **a** parle **b** mange **c** porte **d** travaille **e** regarde **f** joue **g** aime **h** écoute **i** habite **j** décide

**III** **a** travaille **b** arrive **c** gare **d** entre **e** salue **f** monte **g** compose **h** entre **i** accroche **j** commence

**V** **a** vais **b** achète **c** appelle **d** préfère **e** paie
**f** envoie **g** espère **h** essaie **i** jette **j** lève

**VI** **a** parle **b** habite **c** vais **d** appelle **e** arrive
**f** entre **g** monte **h** déjeune **i** envoie **j** pose **k** joue
**l** gagne **m** téléphone **n** regarde

**VII** **a** remplir **b** finir **c** grossir **d** maigrir **e** choisir
**f** réfléchir **g** ralentir **h** applaudir **i** vieillir **j** rougir

**VIII** **a** je remplis **b** je finis **c** je grossis **d** je maigris
**e** je choisis **f** je réfléchis **g** je ralentis **h** j'applaudis
**i** je vieillis **j** je rougis

**X** **a** sors **b** finis **c** choisis **d** pars **e** grossis **f** dors
**g** ralentis **h** réfléchis **i** remplis **j** vieillis

**XI** **a** Je viens **b** J'offre **c** Je découvre **d** Je tiens **e** Je
couvre **f** J'ouvre

**XII** **a** J'ai **b** Je dois **c** Je sais **d** Je peux **e** Je dois
**f** Je veux **g** Je vois **h** Je sais **i** J'ai

**XIII** **a** Je vends **b** Je réponds **c** Je descends **d**
J'attends **e** J'entends **f** Je comprends

**XIV** **a** Je bois **b** J'écris **c** Je fais **d** Je lis **e** Je mets
**f** Je suis **g** Je dis **h** Je décris **i** Je crois **j** Je prends

**XV** **a** Je me réveille **b** Je me lève **c** Je me lave **d** Je me
douche **e** Je m'habille **f** Je m'assieds **g** Je me demande
**h** Je m'ennuie **i** Je me dispute **j** Je me couche

## 1.2.2

**I** **a** danses **b** aimes **c** habites **d** parles **e** regardes
**f** manges **g** écoutes **h** joues **i** laves **j** travailles

**II** **a** es **b** as **c** aimes **d** manges **e** regardes **f** habites
**g** parles **h** portes **i** fais **j** joues

**III** **a** ii **b** iv **c** v **d** iii **e** i

**IV** **a** Tu as **b** Tu pars **c** Tu prends **d** Tu arrives
**e** Tu dînes **f** Tu rentres

**V** **a** iii **b** vi **c** v **d** vii **e** i **f** ix **g** iv **h** ii **i** x **j** viii

## 1.2.3

**I** **a** joue **b** chante **c** surfe **d** aime **e** loue **f** vend
**g** désire **h** prête **i** prépare **j** signe

**II** **a** est **b** habite **c** va **d** prend **e** passe **f** arrive **g** a
**h** met **i** fait **j** retourne

**III**   **a** se réveille   **b** s'étire   **c** se lève   **d** se douche
**e** se fait   **f** se brosse   **g** se rase   **h** s'essuie   **i** s'habille
**j** se chausse   **k** prend   **l** sort

## 1.2.4

**I**   **a** Nous travaillons   **b** Nous jouons   **c** Nous sortons
**d** Nous dînons   **e** Nous rentrons   **f** Nous allons   **g** Nous
partons   **h** Nous arrivons   **i** Nous achetons   **j** Nous avons

**II**   **a** sommes   **b** parlons   **c** allons   **d** choisissons
**e** prenons   **f** changeons   **g** comprenons   **h** logeons
**i** mangeons   **j** travaillons   **k** finissons   **l** jouons

**III**   **a** Nous nous réveillons   **b** Nous nous levons   **c** Nous
nous couchons   **d** Nous nous douchons   **e** Nous nous
reposons   **f** Nous nous dépêchons   **g** Nous nous habillons
**h** Nous nous lavons   **i** Nous nous promenons   **j** Nous nous
séparons

**IV**   **a** *we have* nous avons   **b** *we are* nous sommes   **c** *we are
staying* nous logeons   **d** *we are eating* nous mangeons
**e** *we can* nous pouvons   **f** *we are not coming* nous ne venons
pas   **g** *we do not understand* nous ne comprenons pas   **h** *we
want* nous voulons   **i** *we are going* nous allons   **j** *we are
seeing* nous voyons   **k** *we are leaving* nous partons   **l** *we are
arriving* nous arrivons   **m** *we are coming* nous venons   **n** *we
are doing* nous faisons   **o** *we are reading* nous lisons

## 1.2.5

**I**   **a** Composez votre code   **b** Tirez   **c** Attendez le bip
sonore   **d** Parlez dans le micro   **e** Signez ici
**f** Compostez votre billet   **g** Poussez   **h** Ne quittez pas
**i** Patientez   **j** Appuyez sur le bouton

**III**   **a** lisez   **b** allez   **c** prenez   **d** dormez   **e** faites
**f** buvez   **g** devez   **h** avez

**IV**   **a** avez   **b** Allez   **c** Buvez   **d** Mangez   **e** Marchez
**f** Fumez   **g** Faites   **h** Allez   **i** Couchez   **j** Dormez

**VI**   **a** *Can you manage?* Vous vous en sortez?   **b** *Are you
interested in the firm?* Vous vous intéressez à la société?
**c** *Are you responsible for buying?* Vous vous occupez des
achats?   **d** *Are you making fun of me?* Vous vous moquez de
moi?   **e** *Do you get up early?* Vous vous levez tôt?   **f** *Do you
remember M. Pantin?* Vous vous rappelez M. Pantin?

## 1.2.6

**I  a** doivent  **b** ont  **c** vont  **d** garent  **e** font  **f** sortent
**g** trouvent  **h** cherchent  **i** trouvent  **j** appellent

**II  a** ils/elles se couchent  **b** ils/elles se douchent
**c** ils/elles s'étonnent  **d** ils/elles s'habillent  **e** ils/elles
s'intéressent à  **f** ils/elles se lavent  **g** ils/elles se lèvent
**h** ils/elles se réveillent

**III  a** se reposent  **b** se réveillent  **c** se lèvent
**d** se douchent  **e** se préparent  **f** sortent  **g** vont
**h** arrivent  **i** s'ennuient  **j** s'en vont

## 1.2.7

**I  a** ai  **b** suis  **c** vais  **d** prends  **e** descends  **f** sors
**g** traverse  **h** attends  **i** aime  **j** rentre

**II  a** as  **b** es  **c** vas  **d** prends  **e** descends  **f** sors
**g** traverses  **h** attends  **i** aimes  **j** rentres

**III  a** a  **b** est  **c** va  **d** prend  **e** descend  **f** sort
**g** traverse  **h** attend  **i** aime  **j** rentre

**IV  a** avons  **b** sommes  **c** allons  **d** prenons
**e** descendons  **f** sortons  **g** traversons  **h** attendons
**i** aimons  **j** rentrons

**V  a** Avez  **b** Êtes  **c** Allez  **d** Prenez  **e** Descendez
**f** Sortez  **g** Traversez  **h** Attendez  **i** Aimez  **j** rentrez

**VI  a** ont  **b** sont  **c** vont  **d** prennent  **e** descendent
**f** sortent  **g** traversent  **h** attendent  **i** aiment  **j** rentrent

## 1.3.1

**I  a** ne boivent pas  **b** n'écris pas  **c** ne lit pas
**d** n'achetons pas  **e** ne sais pas  **f** ne trouve pas
**g** ne viennent pas  **h** ne veux pas  **i** n'aimons pas
**j** ne mangez pas

## 1.3.2

**I  a** M. et Mme Leblanc habitent-ils en banlieue
parisienne?  **b** Partent-ils en vacances?  **c** Prennent-ils le
train?  **d** Vont-ils sur la côte d'Azur?  **e** Ont-ils une
résidence secondaire?  **f** Louent-ils une voiture?
**g** Jouent-ils au golf?  **h** Font-ils du ski nautique?  **i** Ont-ils
des amis qui habitent à St-Tropez?  **j** Dînent-ils au
restaurant le soir?

**II** **a** Où vont-ils? **b** Quand partent-ils? **c** Comment vont-ils à Paris? **d** Pourquoi sont-ils à Paris? **e** Que font-ils? **f** Avec qui ont-ils rendez-vous? **g** Combien de temps logent-ils à l'hôtel?

**III** **a** Où est-ce qu'ils vont? **b** Quand est-ce qu'ils partent? **c** Comment est-ce qu'ils vont à Paris? **d** Pourquoi est-ce qu'ils sont à Paris? **e** Qu'est-ce qu'ils font? **f** Avec qui est-ce qu'ils ont rendez-vous? **g** Combien de temps est-ce qu'ils logent à l'hôtel?

## 1.3.3

**I** (**vous** form) **a** Tournez **b** Montez **c** Prenez **d** Continuez **e** Allez **f** Regardez **g** Traversez **h** Prenez **i** Descendez **j** Envoyez
(**tu** form) **a** Tourne **b** Prends **c** Continue **d** Va **e** Regarde **f** Traverse **g** Prends **h** Descends **i** Envoie

**II** **a** Préchauffez **b** Émincez **c** Battez **d** Mettez **e** Ajoutez **f** Mélangez **g** Beurrez **h** Versez **i** Enfournez **j** Faites

**III** **a** Regardez **b** Mangez **c** Buvez **d** Faites **e** Fermez **f** Ouvrez **g** Présentez **h** Parlez **i** Venez

**IV** **a** Entrez **b** Mettez-vous **c** Trouvez **d** Courez **e** Écartez **f** Tendez **g** Rentrez **h** Baissez **i** Pliez **j** bougez

**V** **a** sortez **b** tournez **c** Prenez **d** Continuez **e** Traversez **f** Suivez **g** Tournez

**VI** **a** Ne fumez pas. **b** Ne marchez pas sur l'herbe. **c** Ne mangez pas dans le magasin. **d** Ne laissez pas vos bagages ici. **e** Ne traversez pas la rue. **f** Ne vous penchez pas par la fenêtre. **g** Ne buvez pas cette eau. **h** N'attendez pas ici. **i** Ne mettez pas vos chaussures de ski sur le comptoir. **j** Ne portez pas de noir. **k** N'ouvrez pas la porte.

## 1.4

**I** **a** perfect **b** perfect **c** perfect **d** imperfect **e** perfect **f** imperfect **g** imperfect **h** imperfect **i** perfect **j** imperfect

## 1.4.1

**I** **a** ai **b** as **c** avons **d** ont **e** a **f** a **g** avez **h** a **i** Avez **j** avons

**II** **a** avons **b** ai **c** a **d** As **e** ont **f** a **g** ont **h** Avez **i** a **j** ont

## 1.4.2

**I** **a** joué **b** mangé **c** fini **d** vendu **e** écouté **f** perdu **g** choisi **h** attendu **i** organisé **j** invité **k** lavé **l** demandé **m** fermé **n** poussé **o** tiré **p** oublié **q** sorti **r** entré **s** entendu **t** parti

**II** **a** joué **b** dîné **c** téléphoné **d** discuté **e** assuré **f** décidé **g** envoyé **h** changé **i** imprimé **j** regardé

**III** **a** vu **b** fait **c** écrit **d** entré **e** imprimé **f** vu **g** dû **h** été

**IV** **a** a gagné **b** a voulu **c** a vu **d** a acheté **e** a décidé **f** a mis **g** a pris **h** a vu **i** a cru **j** a suivi **k** a fait **l** out arrêté **m** a dû

**V** **a** Stéphanie a lu son dernier roman. **b** Avez-vous lu le livre? **c** Nous n'avons pas lu le livre. **d** Ils ont vu le film qui a été tiré du livre. **e** Stéphanie a vu le film hier. **f** Nous n'avons pas encore vu le film. **g** Avez-vous vu le film?

## 1.4.3

**I** **a** é **b** u **c** é **d** i **e** i **f** é **g** u **h** é **i** é **j** é **k** t **l** t

**II** **a** suis **b** est **c** sont **d** est **e** Es **f** est **g** est **h** est **i** Êtes **j** sommes

**III** **a** sommes **b** suis **c** Êtes **d** sont **e** est **f** es **g** est **h** sont **i** êtes **j** sommes

**IV** **a** allé **b** sorti **c** parti **d** arrivé **e** descendu **f** entré **g** monté **h** tombé **i** resté

**V** **a** est **b** est **c** suis **d** est **e** sommes **f** sommes **g** est **h** sont **i** suis **j** est

## 1.4.4

**I** **a** e **b** – **c** e **d** e **e** e **f** s **g** – **h** e **i** e **j** e

**II** **a** allé **b** allée **c** allés **d** allées **e** allés **f** allé **g** allés **h** allé **i** allé **j** allé/allée

## 1.4.5

**I** **a** me suis levé(e) **b** s'est levé **c** s'est levée **d** s'est levé **e** se sont levés **f** t'es levée **g** nous sommes levé(e)s **h** se sont levés **i** se sont levées **j** vous êtes levé(e)(s)/êtes-vous levé(e)(s)

**II** **a** nous sommes réveillés **b** nous sommes levés **c** nous sommes promenés **d** nous sommes trompés **e** nous sommes égarés **f** nous sommes arrêtés **g** nous sommes reposés **h** s'est énervée **i** s'est souvenue **j** me suis débrouillé

**III** **a** sommes **b** avons **c** avons **d** a **e** suis **f** sont **g** sommes **h** est **i** a **j** ont **k** êtes **l** avez

## 1.4.7

**I** **a** dormait **b** regardait **c** lisait **d** discutais **e** parlions **f** prenait **g** téléphonait **h** réparaient **i** jouaient

**II** **a** avait **b** avaient **c** avions **d** aviez **e** avais

**III** **a** était **b** étaient **c** étiez **d** était **e** étions

**IV** **a** attendais **b** écoutais **c** allions **d** lisait **e** attendait **f** sortait **g** étaient **h** faisait **i** regardiez **j** buvait

**V** **a** faisait **b** neigeait **c** avait **d** soufflait **e** brillait **f** pleuvait **g** se dissipait **h** faisait **i** avait **j** était

**VI** **a** était/habitait **b** étaient **c** avait **d** cultivait **e** travaillaient **f** cueillaient **g** faisaient **h** avait **i** cuisinait **j** devait **k** avait

## 1.4.8

**I** **a** habitaient/est née **b** était/a déménagé **c** avait/est né **d** a eu/avait **e** traversait/a grillé **f** a vu/attendait **g** avait/a passé **h** faisait/a décidé **i** suivait/a vu **j** travaillait/a rencontré **k** était/a posé **l** faisait/se sont mariés

## 1.5.1

**I** **a** vais **b** vas **c** va **d** allons **e** allez **f** vont **g** allez **h** vont **i** vais **j** vont

**II** **a** vont **b** va **c** va **d** vont **e** va **f** va **g** va **h** allons **i** va **j** allez

## 1.5.2

**I** **a** regarderons **b** prépareras **c** mettrez **d** mangeront **e** prendra **f** sortirez **g** arriveront **h** entrerons **i** partirai **j** portera

**II** **a** porterai **b** portera **c** portera **d** portera **e** porteront **f** porteront **g** porterons **h** porterez

**III** **a** irai  **b** viendrez  **c** feras  **d** aurons  **e** sera  **f** verra
**g** voudron  **h** devrons  **i** saurez  **j** tiendront  **k** faudra
**l** pourrez

**IV** **a** aurai  **b** irai  **c** ferai  **d** enverrai  **e** viendrez
**f** viendrez, ira  **g** pourrons, faudra, pleuvra  **h** aurai,
travaillerai

**V** **a** partirons  **b** prendrez  **c** attendra, emmènera
**d** pourra  **e** déjeunerez, voudrez  **f** pourrez  **g** fera,
devrez

## 1.5.3

**I** **a** je mangerais  **b** je boirais  **c** je dormirais  **d** je
parlerais  **e** j'habiterais  **f** j'achèterais  **g** je demanderais
**h** j'écouterais  **i** je regarderais

**II** **a** jouerais  **b** jouerait  **c** joueraient  **d** jouerions
**e** joueriez

**III** **a** préférerais  **b** préférerait  **c** préféreraient
**d** préférerions  **e** préféreriez

**IV** **a** aimerais  **b** aimerait  **c** aimerait  **d** aimeraient
**e** aimeriez

**V** **a** voudrais  **b** irais  **c** aurais  **d** verrais  **e** irais
**f** pourrais  **g** serais  **h** saurais  **i** devrais  **j** tiendrais

**VI** **a** pourrait  **b** pourrions  **c** pourrions  **d** pourrais
**e** pourriez  **f** pourrait  **g** pourraient  **h** pourrions
**i** pourriez  **j** pourraient

## 1.6.3

**I** **a** venir  **b** prendre  **c** faire  **d** être  **e** être  **f** avoir
**g** savoir  **h** pouvoir  **i** avoir  **j** vouloir

## 1.8.1

**I** **a** Nous avons raison.  **b** Vous avez tort.  **c** J'ai chaud.
**d** Il a soif.  **e** Ils ont faim.  **f** Nous avons froid.  **g** J'ai soif.
**h** J'ai besoin d'une bière.  **i** Nous avons besoin d'une
nouvelle voiture.  **j** J'ai raison.

**k** Ils ont tort.  **l** J'ai très froid.  **m** Ils ont chaud.  **n** Nous
avons soif.  **o** J'ai peur des araignées.  **p** Avez-vous soif?
**q** Avez-vous froid?  **r** Avez-vous chaud?  **s** Avez-vous faim?
**t** Avez-vous raison?  **u** Vous avez tort!  **v** Avez-vous peur?
**w** Je n'ai pas peur.  **x** Il n'a pas peur.  **y** Nous n'avons pas
peur.  **z** Il a toujours raison.

## 1.8.2

**I   a** n'y a pas; y a   **b** y a; n'y a pas   **c** n'y avait pas
**d** y avait; n'y a pas

## 1.8.3

**I   a** connais   **b** connaît   **c** savent   **d** connaissons
**e** connaît   **f** connaissent   **g** connaissent   **h** savons
**i** savent   **j** sait   **k** sais

## 1.8.5

**I   a** Je me souviens de John.   **b** Il se souvient de moi.
**c** Il se souvient de ma maison.   **d** Nous nous souvenons des
vacances.   **e** Je me souviens de sa femme.   **f** Je me souviens
de son sourire.   **g** Mes enfants se souviennent d'elle.

## 1.8.6

**I   a** ne … jamais   **b** n' … personne   **c** ne … plus
**d** n' … qu'   **e** n' … jamais   **f** ne … personne   **g** ne …
plus   **h** ne … que   **i** n' … qu'   **j** ne … jamais   **k** n' …
personne n' …   **l** n' … jamais   **m** n' … rien   **n** Personne
**o** n' … jamais   **p** n' … plus   **q** n' … qu'   **r** n' … rien
**s** n' … plus   **t** ne … jamais

**II   a** Nous n'avons rien à manger.   **b** Personne n'a fait les
courses.   **c** Je n'ai pas eu le temps d'aller en ville.   **d** Il n'y
a que du pain et du fromage.   **e** Vous n'allez jamais au
supermarché.   **f** Je n'ai plus d'argent.

## 1.8.7

**I   a** Où   **b** Comment   **c** Quand   **d** Pourquoi   **e** Que
**f** Quand   **g** Combien   **h** Qui

## 1.8.8

**I   a** J'habite ici depuis …   **b** J'apprends le français depuis
…   **c** Je le/la connais depuis …

**II   a** vient de   **b** vient de   **c** venons de   **d** viennent de
**e** viens de

## 2

**I**   sister, restaurant, market, morning, vegetables, soup,
lunch, dishes, night, fridge

## 2.2

**I   a** la   **b** la   **c** le   **d** le   **e** la   **f** le   **g** la   **h** la   **i** le   **j** le
**k** le

**II** **a** la **b** la **c** la **d** la **e** le **f** la **g** le **h** la **i** la **j** le

**III** **a** l' **b** le **c** l' **d** l' **e** l' **f** la **g** l' **h** l' **i** l' **j** l' **k** l' **l** le **m** l' **n** l' **o** l' **p** l' **q** la **r** la **s** la **t** le

## 2.3.1

**I** **a** les animaux **b** les oiseaux **c** les genoux **d** les chevaux **e** les bateaux **f** les journaux **g** les châteaux **h** les neveux **i** les cadeaux

**II** **a** les fils **b** les Français **c** les Anglais **d** les croix **e** les repas **f** les feux **g** les pneus **h** les choux **i** les bois **j** les souris

## 2.4

**I** **a** un **b** une **c** un **d** une **e** un **f** une **g** un **h** une **i** une **j** un

**II** **a** Marilène est directrice. **b** Arthur est étudiant. **c** Murielle est employée de banque. **d** Lucien est acteur. **e** Thomas est chanteur. **f** Véronique est avocate. **g** Elle est la copine de Patrice.

**III** **a** un **b** un **c** de **d** un **e** des, des **f** un, un, un **g** des, des, de **h** un

## 2.5

**I** **a** le **b** la **c** le **d** la **e** le **f** le **g** le **h** la **i** le **j** le **k** la **l** le **m** la **n** la **o** le **p** le **q** la **r** le **s** le **t** le

## 2.6.1

**I** **a** mon **b** mes **c** mon **d** mon **e** mon **f** mon **g** ma **h** ma **i** mon **j** mon

**II** **a** mon **b** ma **c** mon **d** mes **e** mes **f** mon **g** mon **h** mon **i** mes **j** mon

**III** **a** mes **b** mon **c** ma **d** mon **e** ma **f** ma **g** mes **h** mes **i** mon **j** mon **k** ma

## 2.6.2

**I** **a** tes **b** ton **c** ta **d** tes **e** ton **f** tes **g** ta **h** tes **i** tes **j** ton

**II** **a** tes **b** ton **c** ton **d** tes **e** tes **f** tes **g** ton **h** ton **i** ta **j** ton

### 2.6.3

**I** **a** Son **b** Son **c** Son **d** Sa **e** Son **f** Sa **g** Son
**h** Son **i** Son **j** Sa

**VII** **a** Son **b** Son **c** Son **d** Sa **e** ses **f** Son **g** Sa
**h** Sa **i** Son **j** Sa

### 2.6.4

**I** **a** notre **b** notre **c** nos **d** notre **e** nos **f** notre
**g** notre **h** notre **i** nos **j** notre

### 2.6.5

**I** **a** votre **b** votre **c** votre **d** vos **e** votre **f** vos
**g** votre **h** vos **i** votre **j** vos

### 2.6.6

**I** **a** leur **b** leur **c** leurs **d** leur **e** leurs **f** leurs
**g** leur **h** leur **i** leurs **j** leur

### 2.7.1

**I** **a** cet **b** cette **c** ce **d** Ces **e** Ces **f** Cet **g** Cette
**h** Ces **i** Cet **j** Ce

### 2.7.2

**I** **a** quel **b** quelle **c** quelle **d** quelles **e** quelle
**f** quel **g** quel **h** Quelles

### 3.1.6

**I** **a** je **b** nous **c** elles **d** ils **e** il **f** elle **g** vous or tu

**II** **a** Il **b** Ils **c** J' **d** vous **e** Nous **f** Elles **g** Elle
**h** Ils **i** tu **j** Il

### 3.2

**I** **a** a new car **b** it **c** a cat **d** a tree **e** the wing mirror
**f** a bunch of flowers **g** the car

### 3.2.1

**I** **a** la **b** l' **c** l' **d** la **e** la **f** la **g** la **h** les **i** les

### 3.2.2

**I** **a** me **b** nous **c** vous **d** m' **e** nous

### 3.2.3

**I** **a** vu **b** vus **c** vues **d** perdu **e** perdu **f** perdues
**g** perdu **h** perdues **i** perdu **j** perdues

## 3.3

I **a** me  **b** her  **c** me  **d** him  **e** him  **f** her  **g** me
**h** him  **i** her  **j** him  **k** her  **l** me  **m** me

## 3.3.1

I **a** lui  **b** leur  **c** me  **d** leur  **e** nous  **f** vous  **g** lui
**h** nous  **i** lui  **j** leur  **k** vous  **l** nous  **m** lui  **n** m'

## 3.3.2

I **a** Il me l'a donné.  **b** Je le lui ai donné.  **c** Elle le leur
a donné.  **d** Ils vous l'ont donné.  **e** Vous nous l'avez
donné.  **f** Elle le lui a acheté.  **g** Il l'a lu.  **h** Il nous l'a
donné.  **i** Nous vous l'avons donné.  **j** Ils le leur ont lu.
**k** Elle me l'a prêté.  **l** Je ne vous le prête pas!

## 3.4

I **a** Monique y habite.  **b** J'y vais.  **c** Nous y allons au
moins trois fois par mois.  **d** Y êtes-vous jamais allés?  **e** Ils
y mangent souvent.  **f** Il y a écouté le Requiem de Mozart.
**g** Nous y achetons nos fruits et nos légumes.  **h** Nous y
avons fait toutes nos études.  **i** J'y suis allée la semaine
dernière.  **j** Il y faisait un temps splendide.

## 3.5

I **a** J'en ai beaucoup.  **b** Il n'en a pas.  **c** Il en a trois.
**d** Combien en avez-vous?  **e** Nous en avons beaucoup.
**f** En avez-vous?  **g** Ils en ont trois.  **h** En avez-vous une?
**i** Oui, j'en ai (une).  **j** Mon ami n'en a pas.

II **a** Nous y sommes allés.  **b** Il nous y ont accompagnés.
**c** J'en ai acheté.  **d** Je les ai tous jetés.  **e** Vous nous
l'avez déjà rendue.  **f** Elle le lui a acheté.  **g** Il n'a pas fini
de le lire.  **h** Il nous les a prêtés.  **i** Nous vous en avons
donné …  **j** Elle la lui a racontée en entier …

## 3.6

I **a** Nous les avons vus au marché.  **b** Il m'en a acheté.
**c** Vous les avez vus.  **d** Je les y ai apportés.  **e** Elle ne les a
pas vus.  **f** Ils n'y étaient pas.  **g** Elle m'en a acheté.
**h** Je les y ai mis.  **i** Il me l'a dit.  **j** Il n'y en avait pas.

II **a** Il l'a vue à la confiserie.  **b** Elle ne l'y a pas
remarqué.  **c** Elle voulait lui en acheter.  **d** Il y est
retourné plus tard.  **e** Il lui en a acheté.  **f** Elle n'en a pas
mangé.  **g** Elle les a donné(e)s à son amie.  **h** Elle n'en a
pas mangé non plus.  **i** Elle les y a gardé(e)s.  **j** Elle les lui
a donné(e)s pour son anniversaire.

### 3.6.1

**III** **a** y aller **b** la payer **c** l'utiliser **d** en acheter une
**e** y aller **f** le lire **g** y aller **h** nous accompagner **i** vous
dire **j** le faire

### 3.7.1

**I** **a** Moi! **b** Nous! **c** Toi! **d** Elle! **e** Eux! **f** Lui!
**g** Elles! **h** Vous!

**II** **a** lui **b** lui **c** elle **d** eux **e** elles **f** eux

### 3.7.2

**I** **a** lui **b** elle **c** celles **d** elle **e** lui, elle **f** nous **g** elle
**h** eux **i** vous **j** lui

**II** **a** moi **b** lui **c** nous **d** elle **e** vous **f** lui **g** moi
**h** lui **i** elle **j** nous

### 3.8

**I** **a** Attendez-nous **b** Attendez-le **c** Attendez-les
**d** Attendez-la **e** Attendez-moi

### 3.8.1

**I** **a** toi **b** vous **c** toi **d** vous **e** toi **f** vous

### 3.9.1

**I** **a** Que **b** Qui **c** Qui **d** Que **e** Que **f** Que **g** Qui
**h** Qui **i** Que **j** Qui

### 3.10

**I** **a** le mien **b** les miens **c** la mienne **d** les miens
**e** le mien **f** les miens **g** les miennes **h** la mienne

**II** **a** les siennes **b** les leurs **c** les siennes **d** le sien
**e** la sienne **f** le sien **g** le sien **h** les leurs

**III** **a** le vôtre **b** les leurs **c** la vôtre **d** la leur
**e** le vôtre **f** les leurs **g** la vôtre **h** les leurs **i** les vôtres
**j** le vôtre

### 3.11.1

**I** **a** aimée **b** lus **c** regardées **d** conduite **e** signés
**f** inventés **g** trahi

**II** **a** qui **b** que **c** dont **d** que **e** dont **f** qui **g** dont
**h** qui **i** que **j** dont

## 3.13.1

**I** **a** ceux-ci **b** celle-ci **c** celui-ci **d** celles-ci **e** celle-ci
**f** celui-ci **g** celui-ci **h** ceux-ci **i** celui-ci **j** celles-ci

**II** **a** ceux-là **b** celle-là **c** celui-là **d** celui-là **e** celles-là
**f** ceux-là **g** celles-là **h** celui-là **i** celui-là **j** celles-là

## 4

**I** **a** tall, good-looking **b** short, dark, blue-grey **c** new
**d** smart, casual **e** modern, big **f** small, bubbly **g** large
**h** older, younger **i** favourite **j** hot, black

## 4.1

**I** **a** grand **b** grande **c** grands **d** grandes **e** petit
**f** petite **g** petits **h** petites

## 4.1.1

**I**

|   | singular | | plural | |
|---|---|---|---|---|
|   | **masculine** | **feminine** | **masculine** | **feminine** |
| **a** | content | contente | contents | contentes |
| **b** | triste | triste | tristes | tristes |
| **c** | court | courte | courts | courtes |
| **d** | grand | grande | grands | grandes |
| **e** | faible | faible | faibles | faibles |
| **f** | fort | forte | forts | fortes |
| **g** | intelligent | intelligente | intelligents | intelligentes |
| **h** | stupide | stupide | stupides | stupides |
| **i** | joli | jolie | jolis | jolies |
| **j** | laid | laide | laids | laides |
| **k** | marrant | marrante | marrants | marrantes |
| **l** | méchant | méchante | méchants | méchantes |
| **m** | mauvais | mauvaise | mauvais | mauvaises |
| **n** | jeune | jeune | jeunes | jeunes |
| **o** | large | large | larges | larges |
| **p** | mince | mince | minces | minces |
| **q** | moderne | moderne | modernes | modernes |
| **r** | propre | propre | propres | propres |
| **s** | sale | sale | sales | sales |
| **t** | aimable | aimable | aimables | aimables |

**II** **a** courts **b** content **c** petite **d** grands **e** jolie
**f** minces **g** noirs **h** intelligente **i** méchante **j** marrants
**k** petite **l** calme **m** moderne **n** grandes **o** petit
**p** grand **q** petite **r** grandes **s** jolie **t** modernes

## 4.1.2

**I** **a** actif **b** sportive **c** sportives **d** paresseux **e** vieille
**f** ambitieux **g** heureuses **h** ennuyeux **i** heureux
**j** paresseux **k** sérieuse **l** douce **m** ambitieux
**n** affreuse **o** vieux **p** fausse **q** généreuse **r** ennuyeuses
**s** affreuses **t** Joyeux

**II** **a** gros **b** grosse **c** gentille **d** gentils **e** belle
**f** beau **g** bonnes **h** bons **i** naturelle **j** naturelles
**k** ancienne **l** ancien **m** bas **n** basse **o** nouveau
**p** nouvel **q** nouvelles **r** belle **s** nouvelle **t** bonnes

**III** **a** premier **b** première **c** dernière **d** dernier
**e** secs **f** sèches **g** blanc **h** blanches **i** blanche
**j** Blanche **k** chers **l** chère **m** fier **n** fiers **o** dernière
**p** dernier **q** grec **r** grecques **s** public **t** publique

## 4.1.3

**I** **a** rouge **b** vertes **c** grise **d** bleue **e** bleue **f** rouges
**g** jaune **h** rouges **i** bleu **j** jaunes

## 4.1.4

**I** **a** bleu-vert **b** marron **c** bleu marine **d** ivoire
**e** parme **f** bleu clair **g** blanches **h** rose pâle **i** rose
foncé **j** turquoise

## 4.2

**I** **a** une jeune entreprise **b** une jacinthe bleue **c** un
enfant sage **d** un petit bijou **e** une belle femme **f** un
après-midi paresseux **g** un vieux château **h** une bonne
idée **i** un petit chat noir **j** un gros rat **k** une histoire
intéressante **l** une jolie couleur **m** une grosse femme
**n** un philosophe moderne **o** un film ennuyeux **p** un
long voyage **q** une mauvaise expérience **r** une grande
ville **s** des falaises blanches **t** un nouveau penseur

## 4.4

**I** **a** ses propres yeux **b** chers auditeurs **c** un ancien
élève *or* mon ancien lycée **d** de chaussettes propres **e** la
voiture chère **f** la ville ancienne **g** de pauvres cailles
**h** les gens pauvres **i** la seule solution **j** l'homme seul

## 4.5.1

**I** **a** plus timide **b** plus grande **c** plus difficile **d** plus
intéressante **e** plus haut **f** plus long

**II** **a** plus **b** plus **c** moins **d** plus **e** moins **f** plus **g** moins **h** plus **i** moins **j** plus

## 4.5.2

**I** **a** le plus **b** la plus **c** le plus **d** le plus **e** les plus **f** les plus **g** la plus **h** les moins, les plus

**II** **a** le plus grand **b** la plus haute **c** le plus long **d** la plus profonde **e** la plus grande **f** le plus long **g** le plus long **h** le plus connu **i** la plus haute **j** la plus ancienne

## 4.5.3

**I** **a** aussi grand que **b** plus grande que **c** moins grand que **d** moins grands que **e** moins grand que **f** plus grande que

**II** **a** plus haut que **b** moins longue que **c** plus chaud qu' **d** aussi belle que **e** plus fatigant que

## 4.5.4

**I** **a** meilleur **b** meilleures **c** meilleur **d** meilleure **e** meilleur **f** meilleure

**II** **a** le meilleur **b** les meilleures **c** les meilleures **d** la meilleure **e** les meilleurs **f** le meilleur **g** la meilleure **h** la meilleure

## 5.1.1

**I** **a** sèchement **b** aisément **c** simplement **d** rapidement **e** naturellement **f** franchement **g** rarement **h** heureusement **i** vraiment **j** sérieusement

## 5.2

**I** **a** bas **b** Il a refusé net. **c** Ce n'est pas vrai! **d** Ça coute très cher. **e** Chantez plus fort, s'il vous plaît.

## 6.1.2

**I** **a** à la plage **b** à l'hôtel **c** à la piscine **d** à l'hôpital **e** au musée **f** au cinéma **g** au théâtre **h** à la station-service **i** à la banque **j** au distributeur

**II** **a** à l'église St-Ouen **b** à la cathédrale Jeanne d'Arc **c** au Gros Horloge **d** à l'Hôtel de Ville **e** à la chapelle des Capucines **f** au musée du Théâtre **g** à l'office de tourisme **h** à la Seine **i** à la Place du marché **j** aux toilettes publiques

**III  a** à  **b** à  **c** aux  **d** au  **e** au  **f** au  **g** aux  **h** aux
**i** au  **j** au

**IV  a** Je vais au Havre.  **b** Je vais au Mans.  **c** Je vais aux
Champs-Élysées.  **d** Je vais aux Deux-Alpes.  **e** Je vais au
Lavandou.  **f** Je vais au Louvre.  **g** Je vais aux Menuires.
**h** Je vais à la Cité des Sciences et de l'Industrie.

## 6.1.3

**I  a** à la vanille  **b** au citron  **c** à la pistache  **d** au cassis
**e** à l'abricot  **f** au chocolat  **g** à la banane  **h** à la fraise
**i** à l'orange  **j** à la mangue

**II  a** au jambon  **b** au poulet  **c** au saucisson  **d** au
fromage  **e** à la sardine  **f** au thon  **g** aux rillettes  **h** au
camembert

## 6.1.6

**I  a** J'ai mal à la tête.  **b** Avez-vous mal aux dents?/As-tu
mal aux dents?  **c** Elle a mal au pied.  **d** J'ai mal aux bras.
**e** Il a mal au genou.  **f** Avez-vous mal à la tête?/As-tu mal à
la tête?  **g** Elle a mal aux oreilles.  **h** Avez-vous mal au
cœur?/As-tu mal au cœur?  **i** Avez-vous mal au dos?/As-tu
mal au dos?  **j** Il a mal au dos.

## 6.2.1

**I  a** du Japon  **b** du train  **c** des monuments  **d** du
Louvre  **e** de la Concorde  **f** de Bir-Hakeim  **g** de la Tour
Eiffel  **h** de la Place du Trocadéro

## 6.2.2

**I  a** du  **b** de l'  **c** de la  **d** du  **e** des  **f** du  **g** de l'
**h** des  **i** des  **j** de la

**II  a** de la  **b** du  **c** de la  **d** du  **e** du  **f** du  **g** du
**h** du  **i** de l'  **j** du

**III  a** des  **b** du  **c** du  **d** du  **e** du  **f** de la  **g** des
**h** du  **i** du  **j** du

## 6.2.3

**I  a** Il n'y a pas de ketchup.  **b** Il n'y a pas de confiture.
**c** Il n'y a pas de mayonnaise.  **d** Il n'y a pas de sucre.
**e** Il n'y a pas de lait.  **f** Il n'y a pas de beurre.  **g** Il n'y a
pas de fromage.  **h** Il n'y a pas de soupe.  **i** Il n'y a pas de
jus d'orange.  **j** Il n'y a pas de yaourt.

**II** **a** Je ne mange pas de noix. **b** Je ne mange pas de cacahuètes. **c** Je ne mange pas de sucreries. **d** Je ne mange pas de viande. **e** Je ne mange pas de poisson. **f** Je ne mange pas de laitue. **g** Je ne mange pas de tomates. **h** Je ne mange pas de légumes. **i** Je ne mange pas de pain. **j** Je ne mange pas d'escargots.

## 6.2.4

**I** **a** J'ai beaucoup de livres. **b** J'ai beaucoup de cartes postales. **c** J'ai beaucoup de CD. **d** J'ai beaucoup de photos.

**II** **a** J'ai assez d'essence. **b** J'ai assez d'argent. **c** J'ai assez d'informations. **d** J'ai assez de temps. **e** J'ai assez de catalogues.

**III** **a** J'ai trop de travail. **b** J'ai trop d'invitations. **c** J'ai trop de déplacements. **d** J'ai trop de bagages. **e** J'ai trop de papiers.

## 6.3

**I** **a** 3 **b** 6 **c** 1 **d** 2 **e** 4 **f** 5

**II** **a** sur la table **b** sur l'étagère **c** sous le placard **d** dans le tiroir **e** derrière le rideau

## 6.6

**I** **a** Il prend des cours d'espagnol depuis deux ans. **b** Il habite à Paris depuis cinq ans. **c** M. Proudhon habite à Paris depuis deux mois. **d** Il joue de la guitare depuis un an. **e** Il travaille dans cette boulangerie depuis six mois. **f** Il joue aux échecs depuis son enfance. **g** Constance est végétarienne depuis l'âge de treize ans. **h** Elle fait du ski depuis cinq ans. **i** Ils font de la planche depuis l'été dernier. **j** Ils sortent ensemble depuis six mois.